LEGENDARY VOICES

LEGENDARY VOICES

VOICES

Nigel Douglas

ANDRE DEUTSCH

First published in 1992 by
André Deutsch Limited
105-106 Great Russell Street
London WC1B 3LJ
Second impression 1993

C.I.P. data for this book available
from the British Library

ISBN 0 233 98790 8

Design by Jeffrey Sains
Phototypeset by Falcon Graphic Art Ltd
Printed in Great Britain by
St Edmundsbury Press, Bury St Edmunds

To the memory of my parents, who knew nothing about singing except how much it meant to me.

CONTENTS

LIST OF ILLUSTRATIONS

Courtesy of the Metropolitan Opera Archives.

ACKNOWLEDGEMENTS

There are several people whom I would like to thank for their help in the preparation of this book. At the head of the list come Ilsa Yardley, 'Opernnärrin' par excellence, whose enthusiastic support has been unflagging, and Michael Dealtry, who has provided greatly appreciated assistance of several very practical kinds. Then Robert Tuggle and John Pennino of the Metropolitan Opera, Francesca Franchi of the Royal Opera, Covent Garden, Professor Jürgen Schmidt in Vienna, Dottore Francesco Ricci in Milan, and Frau Eva Wunderlich in Munich, all of whom have gone to great trouble at one time or another to help me with my researches. I would also like to express my thanks to the Bank of England, for the provision of the various financial statistics.

FOREWORD

Until recently the enjoyment of old operatic recordings was something for the specialist. To hear through the hiss and crackle; to combat the fact that so-called 78s had in fact been made at speeds of anything between 70 and 85 revolutions per minute, with the result that fabled sopranos, played at the speed on the label, could sound like indisposed baritones or hysterical hens; or to comb through the second-hand shops in search of a rare Caruso which did not appear to have been played by its last owner with a screwdriver rather than a needle – this was strictly for the dedicated collector, the 'acoustic record nut'. When LPs came along quite a number of historic recordings were reissued, but the transfers were not often of sufficiently arresting quality to persuade the uninitiated that this was an area worth exploring. Now, however, thanks to the advent of CD, the picture has changed dramatically. Many of the great voices of the past are being brought back to us with astonishing impact and immediacy; problems of speed and recording level are being seriously addressed, so that it is possible to listen to twenty arias or more, all at the right pitch, without having to twiddle a single knob; and every recording ever made by a Caruso, a Tetrazzini or a Gigli is there for the asking.

Were they all such giants, these legends from the past, or is that merely the familiar human habit of turning every yesteryear into a Golden Age? Well, I am not one of those people who feel that to count as 'great' a singer must have been dead for fifty years – I have heard, known and shared the stage with too many marvellous artists to subscribe to so sterile a belief. The main point, to my mind, is that every generation produces its towering talents. Fashions change, styles change, the repertoire changes, but a great voice remains a great voice, and as the invention of the gramophone arrived in time to preserve the greatest of this century, it is a pity not to listen to them.

In fact, the singers whom I write about in this book range over two or three generations – some of them I heard in the flesh, one or two of them were known to me personally, but most of them were before my time. The recordings which I discuss extend from the infancy of the gramophone to the glories of stereophonic sound, and the techniques of the various CD companies vary too, some 'doctoring' the quality of the original discs much more than others. My selection of singers is a purely personal one. None of them was perfect – singing is too complex and too human an activity to countenance perfection – but all of them, for a variety of reasons, are favourites of mine. If reading about them, and I hope listening to them, may infect a few people with the bug of enthusiasm that bit me many years ago, I shall be happy.

JUSSI
BJÖRLING

SWEDISH TENOR

b. Stora Tuna, 5 February 1911
d. Stockholm, 9 September 1960

In the galaxy of twentieth century tenors Jussi Björling is something of an odd man out. In terms of his recorded legacy he occupies a proud position in the 'Italian' royal lineage; a line that can really be drawn from Caruso, via Gigli, Björling and, I suppose, di Stefano at his best, to the crowned heads of today, Domingo and Pavarotti. Björling, though, was a very different animal from the rest of them, and the clue lies in his nationality. His voice possessed all the sweep, the ease and the power of the finest Latin singers, and the beauty too – but it was another beauty than theirs, not the uncomplicated beauty of the golden Mediterranean sunshine, but the haunting beauty of the more melancholy and introspective North. The most telling description I have heard of the actual quality of Björling's sound was in a letter written to me by a lady listener after one of my *Singer's Choice* programmes for the BBC. 'To me,' she wrote, 'it is a voice heavy with unshed tears', and when an instrument like that is harnessed to a style and technique ideal for the extrovert outpourings of the Italian composers it can produce a magic all of its own.

I doubt if anyone has been more inevitably predestined to a singing career than Björling. His father had been a good enough tenor to have reached the Metropolitan Opera, and Jussi was gifted with an exceptional boy's voice, as were both his brothers. The four of them formed what was billed as the Björling Male Quartet, and toured first Sweden and then the many Swedish communities in the United States while Jussi was between the ages of eight and eleven. The boys even made a couple of acoustic records, and Jussi Björling must surely be the only singer whose professional recording career spanned four-fifths of his life.

The Björling Male Quartet, however, did not sing for high fees; it was often a matter of a collection at the end of the performance. By the time Jussi was sixteen both his parents were dead, and his life became a struggle for survival. Survive he did thanks to a variety of labouring jobs, and then, while still only seventeen, he applied for an audition with the leading Swedish tenor of the day, Carl Martin Oehmann. This resulted in an immediate recommendation to the Director of the Royal Opera, Stockholm, and on 17 September 1928 an interesting item appeared in the minutes of the Opera's Board of Management, namely that Mr Josse [sic] Björling should be granted a stipendium of 320 krone per month (then a very generous sum), to pay not only for his tuition in the Conservatorium but also for his board and lodging and a new suit of clothes. The arrangement was made dependent on young Mr Björling lodging with Rector Svedelius of the Conservatorium to ensure that he behaved himself, which at that stage of his life it seems that he did. It is true that under the pseudonym Erik Odde he earned some useful money on the side by singing and recording with a local dance band, but that either failed to come to the Rector's attention, or was not regarded as an infringement of the contract.

It was a stroke of luck for Björling that the Director of the Opera was a man who really understood young voices – John Forsell, himself a baritone of distinction. He personally undertook Björling's vocal training, and also drilled him strictly in matters of style, musicianship and theatrical discipline. By 1930, while he was still in his twentieth year, Björling was considered ready for the stage of the Royal Opera. After sniffing the operatic air in a couple of walk-on parts he was granted an official debut in the taxing role of Don Ottavio in DON GIOVANNI, shortly to be followed by the terrifying one of Arnold in Rossini's GUILLAUME TELL. By 1935 he had clocked up no less than forty-four different roles with the Royal Opera, and it was time for him to be launched onto the international circuit. And what a launch it was – his first operatic appearance outside his native land was in no less a house than the

Vienna State Opera; the role was one never normally attempted by a tenor in his twenties, Radamès in AIDA; his partner was one of Italy's foremost dramatic sopranos, Gina Cigna; the conductor was the mighty Victor de Sabata; and Björling only knew the part in Swedish! Thereafter, though, the offers came pouring in, with Salzburg, Paris, London, New York and numerous other musical capitals taking their places in the queue.

During his formative years in Sweden Björling made quite a number of recordings, apart from his offerings as Erik Odde, but they were strictly aimed at the domestic market and almost all in his native tongue. It was in December 1936 that he made his first recordings for the international public, and three of them, together with fifteen more from the decade 1937–47, comprise a recital disc of outstanding quality in EMI's *Références* series (*CDH 7 61053 2*). The three 1936 arias are 'Celeste Aida', 'Che gelida manina' (LA BOHEME) and 'Recondita armonia' (TOSCA), and they bear striking witness to Björling's precocious talents. Anyone coming new to this voice will be struck most immediately, I think, by the brilliance of the tone. I have sometimes heard Björling's voice described as 'silver' to Gigli's 'gold'. I understand this imagery, if one disregards the fact that the one metal is worth only a fraction of the other. Björling's is a fabulous instrument, one of those heaven-sent voices which are basically lyrical in character, but which can be put under considerable dramatic pressure without losing one jot of their quality. A sensitive musical personality is also immediately detectable. In the AIDA aria Verdi has been liberal with his markings of 'sempre dolcissimo', 'ancora piano' and so on, to ensure that Radamès does not open the evening by merely raising the roof, and all of these injunctions Björling scrupulously observes. When Verdi asks for a 'forte con entusiasmo', Björling is equally willing and able to oblige, and his first high B flat, crowning the phrase 'Ergerti un trono', is a thrilling, marvellously focussed note, full of promise for the glories which were to follow when the voice had fully matured. The TOSCA aria is a full-throated effusion of tenorial passion, flawless in its legato, fastidious in its avoidance of sobs and gulps, and again topped by a climactic B flat on 'Tosca, sei tu!' which he could clearly have hung onto for a week, but prefers to relinquish when Puccini asks him to.

In the BOHEME aria, too, many of the same virtues are apparent, and it is a joy to hear a Rodolfo who really does sound young enough to be a penniless student. Here, though, there *is* something missing, and the main reason for this is that Björling was a sloppy linguist. This is not an aria in which you can get away with generalized emotion. Puccini gives Rodolfo endless opportunities for vocal characterization, and the singer who is not genuinely conversant with the language misses trick after trick. This is a young chap, after all, who has about four minutes in which to persuade a girl whom he has just met for the first time to stick around in his cheerless garret, and he tries everything he knows, from a teasing seductiveness to a jocular attempt at self-dramatization – 'Who am I? I'm a poet. What do I do? I write. And how do I live? (Shrug and grin) I live.' If all that this becomes is a flood of sound, however gorgeous, rather than a chain of subtle touches, it detracts from the effect when Rodolfo's flirtatiousness does build into a genuinely passionate outburst. Björling's Italian at this early stage of his career was inadequate for such a task; indeed, especially in the BOHEME aria, it is not merely that his pronunciation is unidiomatic – in certain phrases he is singing something pretty close to gibberish.* I have a feeling that he must have been hauled over the coals about this when he first went to the Met, which he did only two years after making this recording, and in the role of Rodolfo too. There were sections of the Met's auditorium in which Italian was scarcely a foreign language, and it is noticeable that thereafter Björling's Italian did certainly improve – though I remember being told by a distinguished accompanist in Rome around the time of Björling's

---

* It is interesting to contrast this aspect of Björling's work with that of his compatriot and successor Nicolai Gedda whose linguistic versatility made him entirely at home in an astonishingly wide spectrum of the tenor repertoire.

death that it was his defective Italian which had stopped him from achieving the recognition in Italy itself which his qualities as a singer surely merited.

I would not wish, however, with these strictures, to put anybody off this CD of the young Björling, because the virtues vastly outweigh the vices. It contains such treasures as his gorgeously poised 'O paradiso' (L'AFRICAINE), the mellifluous flow of his 'M'apparì' (MARTHA), the famous 'Cujus animam' from Rossini's 'Stabat Mater' with its effortless high D flat, a 'Lamento di Federico' from Cilea's L'ARLESIANA in which he allows his emotions an almost Mediterranean freedom of expression, two essential samples of his French repertoire in the FAUST cavatina and des Grieux's impassioned 'Ah fuyez, douce image' from Massenet's MANON, as well as the version of 'Nessun dorma' from TURANDOT, which put that splendid warhorse as firmly on the map for my generation of opera addicts as Pavarotti's was to do for the world's football public.

One other delightful memento of Björling in the springtime of his career is to be found in the Nimbus Prima Voce series as part of their compilation 'Great Singers Vol. 2' (*NI 7812*). This is Beethoven's song 'Adelaide'. Björling was not in general a very illuminating Lieder singer, largely once again because of his lack of interest in languages. It is true that he steals a march on his Latin peers, who find it notoriously difficult to wrap their vocal mechanism round all those daunting Teutonic consonants, but he can seldom be called truly idiomatic. The musicianship was certainly there – the speed with which he was able to learn operatic roles in those early years was astonishing, and I have been told by one of the staff conductors of the Stockholm Opera, Kurt Bendix, who conducted him on countless occasions, that he was apparently incapable of making a musical mistake, and that any role, once learnt, was there for good. The main thing which prevented Björling from achieving the same greatness in Lieder as he did in opera was laziness, of which more anon, but for seven precious minutes he did achieve it, happily while he was record-

ing 'Adelaide'. If ever his voice earned the soubriquet 'silvery' it
is here. The vocal line is a steady thread of wonderfully sustained
'piano' singing, swelling into the occasional full-voiced phrase, and
with a magical *mezza voce* high A on the phrase 'strahlt dein
Bildnis'. It is a performance which absolutely captures the spirit
and the enchantment of Matthisson's poem as well as Beethoven's
setting of it, and gives one a tantalizing glimpse of the Lieder singer
Björling might have become had he taken the trouble.

There used to be a saying: 'No man is a hero to his own
valet', and of singers I think one could safely say that very few
are heroes to their own accompanists. Fascinating insights into
famous performers' working methods are to be found in certain
accompanists' memoirs, and in the case of Jussi Björling the late
Ivor Newton provides a trenchant vignette. 'Björling,' he wrote,
'was a man of surprising contradictions; as an artist he was superb,
with a remarkable range and an impeccable style . . . As a man he
was obstinate, difficult, taciturn and unusually lazy. He hated to
rehearse and would find endless excuses – his health, the weather,
all varieties of ingenious reasons – to avoid doing so.' Something
which Newton tactfully omitted to mention, but which was very
much part and parcel of Björling's uncomfortable temperament,
was his drinking – a problem which grew worse and worse as
he felt increasingly burdened by the public's expectations of
him. Elisabeth Söderström once told me that when she sang
her first season at the Met she was partnered by Björling in
her second role, which was Marguerite in FAUST. She was given
minimal rehearsal, and as she had never sung the role before she
was understandably nervous. She said as much to Björling, the
Met's favourite Faust over many a season, to which he replied
'What have you got to worry about, my girl? They won't be
expecting anything from you – I'm the one who should worry!'
I remember another soprano telling me of a gala performance of
TOSCA in the Stockholm Opera late in Björling's career. He
was very much the star attraction, but ten minutes before the
performance was due to start he had not shown up. The Director

was on the verge of announcing to the packed auditorium that there would be no show, when the great man tottered through the stage door, apparently only just able to stand. My informant, never having encountered the Björling phenomenon before, found it inconceivable that he could get through Cavaradossi in that state, but in the event not only did he sing the whole role without a hint of a mistake – when the performance was over he called the rest of the cast round him and told all of them where they had gone wrong! This may not add up to an appealing portrait of Björling as a colleague but not for nothing did Ivor Newton call him 'a man of surprising contradictions'. The young lady who told me the TOSCA story also told me with a twinkle in her eye that 'Jussi was a very easy man to forgive', and in certain of his closest associates he inspired a deep devotion. When he died, the American baritone Robert Merrill wrote of him 'If we have one great friend in our lifetime, we are truly blessed. In Jussi, I had that'; and Victoria de los Angeles has told me that for years after his death she was quite unable to listen to the recordings that they made together, so much did she feel his loss.

I myself first became acquainted with the Björling voice through the few 78s which were in the HMV catalogue during the Second World War. I had no knowledge of who he was or what his age might be, but rather assumed that like many of the other singers listed there he had had his day. It was an excitement, then, to discover after the war that not only was he still around, but that he had scarcely reached what most singers consider to be their best years. He had stayed in America until the autumn of 1941, when he made the rather bold decision to return to Sweden, and serve his obligatory six months as an artilleryman in the Swedish army. In 1942 he managed to fit in some performances in Budapest and Florence, but he was banned by the Nazis from appearing again in the Vienna State Opera, because he refused to learn RIGOLETTO and LA BOHEME in German. Thereafter he stayed put in Sweden until 1945, when he became the first major European artist to return to the United States; and by a fortunate piece of timing, when the introduction of the long-playing record revolutionized the scene, making it so much simpler than it had previously been to record operas in their entirety, Björling was at the absolute peak of his powers. Most of the Björling full sets have been reissued on CD, others (one hopes) are still to come. The first of them – and I well remember what a stir it caused – was IL TROVATORE, recorded in New York in March 1952 and conducted by Renato Cellini. There had been a certain sameness about some of Björling's more recent 78s, a tendency to sing everything flat out as if rather bored by the whole business. His Manrico, however, was a totally different story, and on RCA Victor *GD86643(2)* (*two discs*) it comes up again with newly burnished brilliance. He sets about 'Di quella pira' and the other riproaring set pieces with heroic splendour, but this is only half the story. While Manrico and Leonora enjoy their short-lived dream of the 'gioie di casto amor' he becomes the lightest of lyrical tenors – even Schipa could hardly express himself with greater delicacy – and in his various scenes with Azucena he is the very model of filial concern. In their final duet he takes the full eight bars of that gorgeous phrase 'Riposa, o madre' in one easy breath, the words flowing from his lips as if at their own bidding, (by this stage of his career *sounding* like Italian too), and in his tragic lament from the prison window there is a true nobility. Manrico is one of those roles which, like Don José in CARMEN, almost needs two tenors to sing it, one lyric and one dramatic, and it was an outstanding virtue of Björling's that he could so convincingly encompass both. The Leonora of the great Yugoslav soprano Zinka Milanov is also a performance to be treasured, and I can think of few others who could rival the ravishing soft high notes with which she swoons her way through the two big arias. Throw in for good luck an Azucena as formidable as Fedora Barbieri, a di Luna with the tireless top notes of Leonard Warren (whether or not you are particularly enamoured of his rather cavernous tone), and a conductor who keeps this melodious old pot boiling as vigorously as Cellini, and you have got yourself a rather special TROVATORE.

The following year, 1953, found the same team of soprano, tenor and conductor at work on Mascagni's CAVALLERIA
RUSTICANA, and though it is not a piece which calls for the
same wide spectrum of vocal skills as TROVATORE, what it
does call for, namely a full-throated wallop, it most assuredly
gets. It is no great surprise that a Yugoslav can make the leap
in temperament over the water to Sicily, but that a Swedish
tenor should transport himself so far South is remarkable indeed.
Especially in the quarrel scene, which is really the heart of the
role, Björling operates at a white heat, of which few people had
considered him capable before the release of this recording. The
intensity of anger in his 'Bada, Santuzza, schiavo non sono di
questa vana tua gelosia' ('Watch out, Santuzza, I'm no slave to
this empty jealousy of yours') is terrifying, and it is achieved
without a trace of vulgarity, the voice never for a moment sounding forced or harsh. It is difficult to identify this blaze of sound
with the lack of involvement of which people often complained in
Björling's acting, and here again Ivor Newton's 'strange contradictions' come to mind. An American friend of mine who heard
Björling countless times at the Met said to me recently 'It was a
shame that he had no stage personality', but I also recall another
remark from Kurt Bendix – 'People say Jussi couldn't act, but I've
conducted him in performances of PAGLIACCI when I thought
the walls were going to fall down – what more do people want?'
That outstanding Swedish director, Lars Runsten, once said to
me 'Björling basically just stood on stage, but he did so with
colossal authority', and Elisabeth Söderström put it this way –
'When you were on stage with him he didn't seem to be acting,
but when you looked into his eyes you saw that he had ceased
to be Jussi, and had become des Grieux, Rodolfo, or whatever
role he was playing.' She added that the sound he produced was
so beautiful, and so utterly free, that you could not help losing
your own tensions and singing better than you ever had before.

This I find easy to believe when listening to our next full set,

Puccini's MANON LESCAUT on RCA Victor *GD60573* (*two discs*). I think that I would have to rate Björling's des Grieux as my favourite of all his complete recordings, indeed I would go so far as to say that I cannot imagine the role being vocally, musically or dramatically better performed. From the first note the voice is exactly as Söderström described it – 'so beautiful, and so utterly free'. Björling at this time was forty-three years old and had been singing (as an adult) for twenty-four years, but the tone quality still has the freshness and the brilliance of youth, which gives it the appeal and vulnerability so essential for des Grieux. His first conversation with Manon has exactly the right touch of naivety – his 'Oh, come siete bella', 'Oh, how beautiful you are!', is not the opening gambit of a practised seducer, it is something which, in his youthful enthusiasm, he just could not help blurting out. Every note of Björling's throbs with ardour and sincerity – he has indeed *become* des Grieux. As for his singing of 'Donna non vidi mai' – the first and surely one of the most ecstatic of Puccini's great tenor arias – it is enough to make other tenors despair. In this role once again it is an extended duet which lies at the psychological centre, but the 'Tu, tu, amore, tu' is a much more complex scene than the bare-knuckled confrontation in CAVALLERIA RUSTICANA, and for every shifting mood Björling finds exactly the colour which Puccini seems to be begging for. Through the desperation of 'O tentatrice, o tentatrice!', 'Oh temptress, oh temptress!', and the foreknowledge of catastrophe in 'È questo l'antico fascino che m'accieca!', 'This is the old fascination that is blinding me!', to the final resignation of 'Nell' oscuro futuro, di', che farai di me?', 'In the dark future, tell me, what will you be making out of me?', Björling unerringly plots the downfall of a young man who loves not wisely but too well. His appeal to the Captain in Le Havre is a perfect example of how to open the floodgates of emotion without letting them overflow into the realms of exaggeration, and even if Puccini's creative powers flag somewhat on the dusty plains of Louisiana, the quality of this des Grieux holds up tirelessly to the end. I wish I could be quite so enthusiastic about the Manon of Licia Albanese, but although she was in fact a couple of years younger than Björling, she sounds somewhat beyond the age for being whisked into a convent. There is still some lustre in the top notes, but the middle register, so important in the conversational passages, sounds a trifle dry. The rest of the cast are admirable, and the Romanian conductor Jonel Perlea achieves luxuriantly Puccinian sonority from the Rome Opera Orchestra and Chorus.

The same combination of conductor, orchestra and chorus does Verdi proud as well, with the 1955 recording of AIDA (RCA Victor *GD86652(3)* – *three discs*), in which Björling was joined by a suitably heavyweight cast (vocally speaking, of course), consisting of Milanov, Barbieri, Warren and, as Ramfis, the Bulgarian bass Boris Christoff. Here again it is Björling's ability to combine the heroic with the lyric which scores so heavily throughout the role. To sample the former one only has to hear his cry of 'Sacerdote, io resto a te' at the end of the Nile Scene, and for the latter the final phrase of all, as he and Milanov embrace their 'Liebestod' with two seraphic 'piano' high B flats. In expressing certain reservations about Björling's next full set I am assailed by feelings of disloyalty, because I was given the LP version as a present when it first came out, and it brings back many happy memories. I know, too, that by being modified in my rapture I am voicing a minority opinion, but there we are. I refer to the famous version of LA BOHEME, now on EMI *CDS 7 47235 8* (*two discs*), which came about more or less by chance, when Sir Thomas Beecham's manager spotted that Victoria de los Angeles, Björling, Robert Merrill and Sir Thomas himself were all going to be in New York at the same moment, and with just enough time on their hands to make a recording. Björling took a bit of persuasion, complaining that he was troubled by a low back ache (shades of Ivor Newton!), which allegedly gave rise to a waspish comment from Sir Thomas about the parts of tenors' anatomies usually employed for the projection of their tones. To be fair to Björling, this time he was not making a fuss about nothing – indeed, at the Met that season his death fall in TOSCA became such a problem that someone hit on the bright idea of having him face the firing squad tied to a stake. Be that as it may, I do not get the feeling that with this Rodolfo his full heart was in the job, particularly not in Act I. The give and take of the dialogue from the moment of Mimi's first appearance finds him in stodgy, humourless mood, and although I know that back in 1920 Sir Thomas had had detailed discussions with Puccini about the tempi in this piece, I cannot see that his unusually stately handling of the last twenty minutes of Act I does much to help. In Act II Björling perks up (so does the tempo), and from then on he treats us to some very beautiful singing. As Victoria de los Angeles is a Mimi in a thousand, Lucine Amara a splendid spitfire of a Musetta, Robert Merrill a fine full-voiced Marcello, and the rest of the cast uniformly excellent, perhaps all I am really missing is a taste of Italy somewhere in the mixture.

For RIGOLETTO (RCA Victor *GD60172 – two discs*), recorded a couple of months later, Björling found himself back with Perlea and the Roman team, and this time there is no hanging about. The Duke's opening dialogue and the 'Addio, addio' after his duet with Gilda both whizz along as fast as the singers' tongues can carry them, if not a little faster. This may be the reason why Björling settles into an uncharacteristically violent performance, going at almost everything full tilt, and riding roughshod over Verdi's numerous requests for a 'piano' or a 'dolce'. Robert Merrill's interpretation of the title-role, too, though vocally stupendous, is low on subtlety, and of the principals it is the suitably girlish Roberta Peters who fares the best. Unless my ears deceive me there is also something odd about the sound quality – weird extraneous noises keep intruding, as if someone not too far from a microphone were suffering from digestive problems. Happily Björling's next visit to Rome produced altogether more satisfactory results. For TOSCA on RCA Victor *GD84514(2)* (*two discs*) the conductor is the Austrian-born Erich Leinsdorf, in his early days an assistant to Walter and Toscanini. He extracts both clarity and lushness from the orchestra, greatly enhanced by the fact that we have now reached the age of stereo. Milanov, the Tosca, had made her belated Covent Garden debut in the role the year before, when the general 'on dit' had been that she was still magnificent, but, at fifty, slightly past it. On the strength of this recording I would confirm the first part of that verdict and reject the second. Leonard Warren's Scarpia is one of his finest recorded performances, and Björling as Cavaradossi is right back at the top of his form. In the first act he is passionate and mellifluous, in the second he hurls at his tormentor a 'Vittoria' to stun the senses, and in the third, both in 'E lucevan le stelle' and in 'O dolci mani', he floats a gossamer *mezza voce* to quite breathtaking effect.

Six weeks after completing his Cavaradossi, Björling betook himself to Florence for a stereo remake of CAVALLERIA RUSTI-CANA. I do not think it would be possible to overpraise this disc (DECCA *425 985-2*). Everything which I wrote about Björling's scorching performance in the earlier recording still applies, but it comes even more electrifyingly to life in stereo, and mighty sparks are struck off him by his partners (or perhaps in this piece one should call them opponents). Renata Tebaldi's Santuzza finds her in her sumptuous prime, and the basically rather unrewarding role of Alfio is brought right into the foreground by the dark satanic tones of Ettore Bastianini. With such a starry cast it is to be assumed that all the set pieces will hit the bull's-eye, but it is a special virtue of this performance that the tension never drops in the various subsidiary but vital links that lie between them. In the brief scene, for instance, of Alfio's issuing of the challenge and Turiddu's remorse at the probable fate of Santuzza, Bastianini's chilling immutability and Björling's tragic desperation positively leap from the disc. In passages such as this, Björling, however phlegmatic his stage persona may have been, treats us to vocal acting of riveting immediacy, and he is backed to the hilt by that doughty champion of *verismo*, the conductor Alberto Erede.

It was in the summer of 1959 that Björling sang his last complete operatic role in a recording studio – Lieutenant B. F. Pinkerton in MADAMA BUTTERFLY (EMI *CMS 7 63634 2 – two discs*), with his beloved Victoria de los Angeles and the forces of the Rome Opera, under the baton of Gabriele Santini. Björling's Pinkerton is predictably not the cheery extrovert that di Stefano's was, and perhaps one could do with a bit more of a chuckle behind the Act I banter about taking wife and house on a 999-year basis. The vocal quality, though, is so glorious, the attack on high-lying phrases such as 'Vinto si tuffa' so effortless, the security of 'È notte serena' so triumphantly assertive, and the flow of 'Addio fiorito asil' so immaculately smooth, that again and again, what may be lacking in subtlety of characterization is amply repaid in the coinage of sheer sound.

And so to Björling's very last full set, Verdi's REQUIEM, on DECCA *421 608-2 (two discs)*. This was recorded in Vienna in June 1960, with the Singverein der Gesellschaft der Musikfreunde, and the Vienna Philharmonic Orchestra, conducted by Fritz Reiner; the other soloists were Leontyne Price, Rosalind Elias, and Giorgio Tozzi, who had first swum into my ken eleven years before under the name George Tozzey, entertaining London audiences as a glamorous boxer in the musical TOUGH AT THE TOP. In terms of sound quality this ranks alongside the second CAVALLERIA RUSTICANA and the MADAMA BUTTERFLY as the finest of the Björling sets, with a mass of orchestral detail revealed in full stereophonic glory. Although I find Reiner's tempi often excessively broad, his forces were miraculously able to sustain them, and there is not a complaint to be made about a single bar of the solo or choral singing. This is, in any case, a recording which has a special place in my affections because I was studying in Vienna at the time, and I was smuggled into one of the sessions. As luck would have it I caught Björling's performance of the tenor solo 'Ingemisco', and for a student tenor it was a fascinating experience. I can see Björling now, short, tubby, seeming older than his forty-nine years, wearing a formal brown suit, and looking more like some sort of salesman than an opera star. His attitude to the job in hand was entirely business-like. Reiner said he would like to take the passage through, just for the orchestra. While he did so, Björling sang along, marking the whole piece in rehearsal voice, which in his case meant a sustained *mezza voce* of such beauty and technical perfection that it seemed almost a crime to let it disappear on the morning air. Then came the take, for which he simply did the same thing again, but opening his mouth a bit wider and bringing in his effortless chest voice. The result, 'in the can' for all to hear, is an 'Ingemisco' of supreme vocal and musical quality, and it appeared to have cost him nothing.

All of this becomes even more surprising if one reads in the autobiography of John Culshaw, Decca's recording manager, what strange things were going on behind the scenes. Three months before these sessions Björling had returned to Covent Garden for the first time since 1939, to sing Rodolfo, and rumours were rife that the drink problem was getting out of hand. Those members of the public lucky enough to win the battle for tickets were enchanted by the undiminished lyricism of Björling's singing, but he virtually opted out of acting the role, (one newspaper aptly summed things up with the headline: **BUT OH HOW JUSSI CAN SING!**), and when one performance, attended by the Queen Mother, started over half an hour late, not everybody was convinced by the official announcement that Björling was suffering from a strained heart. The Decca team took heed of all this, and were delighted when Björling turned up in Vienna in the best of physical and mental health. Shortly afterwards, however, he came crashing into Culshaw's bedroom late one night, uncontrollably drunk and apparently spoiling for a fight, which was averted by the appearance of Culshaw's colleagues. This was as nothing, however, to events the following month when a recording of UN BALLO IN MASCHERA in Rome collapsed entirely, because Björling, around whom it had been planned, was incapable, day after day, of getting to the studio, thus leaving such busy people as Birgit Nilsson and Georg Solti, not to mention the rest of the cast and the orchestra, hanging around with nothing to do.

The picture which Culshaw paints of this great artist lying in his hotel room incapable of anything but semi-coherent abuse is a tragic one; yet the astonishing thing is that even during this period of his life neither his voice nor his phenomenal memory showed the slightest sign of wear or tear. When I heard him sing that 'Ingemisco' he struck me as being physically the perfect singing instrument. His podginess was deceptive, because he was a man of exceptional strength. He loved getting people to play the arm-wrestling game 'braccio di ferro', which he was never known to lose, and this muscular power was applied to his voice production with absolute technical efficiency. The voice itself, I believe, had been one of those seamless boy sopranos which do not so much break as simply settle down into being an equally seamless tenor. Of course he had had plenty of work to do in his early years on breath control, placing of the tones and so forth, but nature had not implanted into him that awkward gear-change between head and chest registers which so bedevils most of us. It is also remarkable how little his voice changed as he grew older. Usually with the passage of time what a singer gains in technical know-how he loses in vocal quality – singing is very much a case for the old Italian proverb 'Se il giovane sapesse, se il vecchio potesse', 'If the young man had the knowledge, if the old man had the power' – but Björling's voice, while gaining in substance and security, never seems to me to have lost anything in brilliance and beauty. And that despite thirty years of singing, not to mention the whisky!

Anyway, besides these full sets there are three more Björling 'singles' available, one of which, RCA Victor *GD60520*, was taken live at a Carnegie Hall recital in March 1958. If it does not find him at his most compelling throughout the programme, there are plenty of compensations. Least interesting to me are the Lieder, which are not helped by the prominence given to some rather ham-fisted accompaniments – Schubert's quicksilver trout emerges more like an overweight halibut. 'Adelaide' is beefier and less magical than of yore, and although things brighten up with a humorous account of Brahms's 'Ständchen', it is not until Björling reaches a group of his favourite Swedish songs that he really gets into his stride. (I often feel that he becomes most marvellously himself when he is singing in his native tongue, and it is very much to be hoped that EMI will one day reissue the many Swedish studio recordings which they presumably have somewhere up their sleeve.) Rachmaninov, sung in Björling's clear and very charming English, brings his audience further towards the boil, and Grieg's 'A Dream', sung in Norwegian, completes the process. Then comes a shout from the back of the hall of 'Nessun dorma!', and we are happily launched into overtime. Whatever the technical disadvantages of live recording it is fascinating to have moments like this preserved, when you can hear a great artist's audience being turned into his friends. I remember this feeling at a recital of Björling's in London. He needed longer than the more charismatic Beniamino Gigli to build a rapport with the public, and it was the last half hour which really got off the ground. In the Carnegie Hall Björling put 'Nessun dorma' down a semitone, but lifted the temperature by several degrees nonetheless. Then came a Tosti 'Ideale' of gorgeous expansiveness, a far better tempered 'La donna è mobile' than the version in the complete RIGOLETTO, an 'E lucevan le stelle' complete with ethereal soft high A, and finally a performance of Richard Strauss's 'Zueignung' which leaves the Lieder section earlier in the programme stone dead. Björling gave this recital during a Met season when he was no longer welcome there having fallen foul of Rudolf Bing. Perhaps he was making a point, I do not know. In any case, it turned out to be his vocal adieu to the New York public, and if there had to be so premature a parting, one can only say of this 'Zueignung' 'What a glorious way to go!'

Next we come to a disc which I think any lover of Björling's singing will want to possess, especially those whose pockets do not stretch to the acquisition of numerous full sets. It is RCA *Victor GD87799*, and it presents him in concerted numbers from nine different operas, including the great duets from the TOSCA and AIDA sets with Zinka Milanov, and from the MANON LESCAUT set with Licia Albanese. A most welcome addition to these is part of Act I of TURANDOT, another of Björling's last recordings, in which we are given Liù's 'Signore ascolta', exquisitely realized in the creamy tones of Renata Tebaldi, followed by 'Non piangere, Liù', and the Unknown Prince's formal challenge to the Ice-girt Princess – in all of which Björling once again proves himself a Puccini tenor par excellence. The rest of the disc consists of five scenes which he recorded in 1950–51 with Robert Merrill, under the baton of Renato Cellini. One is an extract from DON CARLOS, extending from the tenor aria 'Io l'ho perduta', to the 'Friendship' duet – a particularly valuable item, as Don Carlos was reckoned by many to be the finest of Björling's Verdi roles, and he never recorded it 'in toto'. Views on the musical quality of the duet vary from regarding it as one of Verdi's noblest inspirations to one of his most tawdry, but I hardly suppose that there could be such divergence of opinion on the quality of this performance. It calls to mind the opinion expressed by the American critic Irving Kolodin – 'As for Don Carlos, there has been – for me – only one, worldwide: Jussi Björling'. The next Verdi number is not one whose musical value has ever been called into question – 'Solenne in quest' ora' from LA FORZA DEL DESTINO. For those who might wish to compare the vocal styles of Björling and Gigli, the manner in which the two of them handle this great arching *cantilena* could be taken as a litmus test. Do you want the liquid Italian tones of the one, fragile with the approach of death, and with many a sob and sigh to remind you that his state is not an enviable one? Or do you want the brilliant Nordic outpourings of the other, remarkably robust after the loss of so much blood, and relying on the tragic element intrinsic in Verdi's melody (plus, of course, the text) to tell us that all is not well with him? (I know what I want – I want them both.)

We stay with Verdi for one more scene, and this time there is the danger of a comparison being drawn with Caruso, which is never fair on anyone. It is the oath duet from OTELLO, and if Caruso had never recorded it I would be doubting whether any other tenor could make it sound more thrilling than Björling. Perhaps his voice is too bright to be ideal for the role – had he lived to attempt it on stage I somehow doubt that he would have rivalled Domingo – but the focus of his tone in this performance does give it a searing dramatic impact. Heard in conjunction with the opening number on the disc, 'Au fond du temple saint' from LES PECHEURS DE PERLES, its high legato line floating with dreamy ease, and the gently attacked high B flats sounding somewhere in the middle of the voice, it gives us an idea of what a versatile instrument we are listening to, and with what a masterly technique it is employed. I should emphasize that by concentrating in this way on Björling I mean no offence to Merrill, possessor of one of the richest baritone voices of the post-war period; he comes perhaps most completely into his own in the one duet still to be mentioned, that from the last Act of LA BOHEME, in which both of these two good friends are shown to more vivid effect than on the Beecham set.

Which leaves me with just one Björling disc to discuss, DECCA *421 316-2*, and it is very much a case of 'last but not least'. It opens with a recital of six Italian arias, recorded in 1959 with the Orchestra del Maggio Musicale Fiorentino under Alberto Erede, all of which, in their different ways, are stunningly performed. We met four of them – 'Ch'ella mi creda', 'Amor ti vieta', the 'Lamento di Federico' and 'Di tu, se fedele' from UN BALLO IN MASCHERA – on the EMI disc of early recordings, but in every instance the later versions strike me as even more impressive. For one thing they are in impeccably balanced stereo and for another, as I have mentioned above, the voice seems to have gained so much more than it has lost. The group is completed by a jaunty rendering of des Grieux's mini-aria 'Tra voi belle' from MANON LESCAUT, always a favourite titbit of Björling's, and a 'Cielo e mar' from LA GIOCONDA which sweeps all before it as it builds from its rapt, atmospheric opening phrase to the passionate urgency of its conclusion. For good measure we have that memorable 'Ingemisco' from the Reiner set, and three sizzling excerpts from the stereo CAVALLERIA – the quarrel duet with the gorgeous Tebaldi, the Brindisi and the whole of the final scene. The last track of all is something of a curiosity. When the Decca

Company decided to include a gala party scene in their recording of DIE FLEDERMAUS, they asked each of their most prominent contracted artists to chip in with something outside their normal repertoire. Björling contributed 'Dein ist mein ganzes Herz' from Lehár's DAS LAND DES LÄCHELNS, and this is it. The first half is sung in Swedish, the second in extremely wayward German, and to be honest it is not vintage Björling – a pity, because in his youth he had made some enchanting operetta recordings – but it is fun to have it nonetheless. Indeed, it was a source of lasting disappointment to me that I was not at home when one of the Decca crew rang me in my Vienna flat, on the day this recording was made, to ask if I could spend the evening with him, his colleagues and Jussi Björling at a *Heuriger* – one of the wine-gardens on the outskirts of Vienna, where local wine is drunk, sentimental songs are sung, and a good time is had by all. By general request Björling regaled the company with 'Dein ist mein ganzes Herz', accompanied by fiddle and squeeze-box – and I missed it.

There is, of course, a bitter irony to these late recordings of Björling's. He sounds like a man with at least another decade of glorious singing to come, but that was not to be. At the beginning of March he had been terribly shocked by the news that Leonard Warren had died of a heart attack in mid-performance on the stage of the Metropolitan Opera. Björling became obsessed by worries about his own heart, and it is reasonable to suppose that this fear may have intensified his drinking. As late as 5 August he was still able to give a masterly account of himself in an orchestral concert at Gothenburg – there is a recording to prove the point – but a few weeks later, at his summer home in Sweden, he suffered the heart attack he had been dreading, and on 9 September 1960 he died in Stockholm, aged only forty-nine.

His last role in Stockholm had been Manrico in IL TROVA-TORE, and in the Royal Opera House there hangs a dramatic portrait of him in Act III, standing on the castle steps, sword in hand, and just about to let fly with 'Di quella pira'. It is a worthy memorial to a great artist. He was a man who caused many headaches for managements, impresarios, agents and even colleagues, and it is a sad thought that he himself apparently never found the happiness that his singing brought to countless others. But, to quote Kurt Bendix one last time, 'Jussi was the kind of vocal and musical genius whom one is lucky to meet once in a lifetime – and such people should be easy to have around?'

ENRICO CARUSO

ITALIAN TENOR

b. Naples, 25 or 27 February* 1873, d. Naples, 2 August 1921

* There is some doubt as to whether the actual birth date was 25 or 27 February.

Opera, by its very nature, arouses intense reactions. Likes and dislikes tend to be extreme and partisan, and when opera lovers discuss the relative merits of their favourite singers unanimity is rare. In the first two decades of this century, however, there was one issue over which few people disagreed. Amongst those who heard him, amongst those who wrote about him and (to my mind the most significant indication of all) amongst those who sang with him, Enrico Caruso was regarded as being quite simply incomparable. To many people living in the present era of sophisticated recording techniques it may seem fanciful to take this assertion one stage further and say that he still is incomparable – how, after all, can someone like myself, born several years after he died, maintain on the evidence of recordings made in the infancy of the gramophone, that this was the greatest of the great? There is, I think, only one answer to that. Every tenor since Caruso's day has listened to those recordings, and not one of them has claimed to be his equal.

Caruso did not tread an easy path to success. To a great extent it was through his own determination that he became the phenomenon he did, and the emergence of the golden voice was inextricably mingled with the warm humanity of his personality. To his parents the very fact of his existence must have seemed almost miraculous, as he was his mother's eighteenth baby and the first to survive infancy – an exceptionally gloomy statistic, even for the crowded backstreets of Naples.* Though poor, the

---

* Caruso's various biographers have always regarded these facts as correct, but according to a new publication, *My Father and My Family* by Enrico Caruso Jr and Andrew Farkas, Amadeus Press 1990, Caruso was the third of seven children, two of whom died at an early age.

Caruso family was not destitute as Enrico's father was never out of work, but a disproportionate amount of his earnings went on drink and he could not afford to send the boy to school, which in those days had to be paid for. Enrico's mother, who was clearly an exceptional woman, taught him to read and write, and from the age of ten he earned his own living, working first as a mechanic in a factory, and then, after being refused a rise in salary, for a manufacturer of public drinking fountains. As if a full day's work were not enough for a child of ten, in the evenings he attended a school run by a certain Father Bronzetti, who trained the choristers for various of the Neapolitan churches, and it was here that he learnt to read music. As he was blessed with an unusually beautiful alto voice he was able to pick up occasional small sums of money by performing at church services, and sometimes even by lurking under young ladies' balconies, to serenade them, Cyrano-like, on behalf of their less vocally gifted admirers. When he was fifteen his mother died, which was a grievous blow. He did not enjoy a comfortable relationship with his father, but it became less comfortable still when he made the dramatic decision to give up his job and try to live off his singing. This he succeeded in doing in a very small way, and after his voice had broken he extended his repertoire from religious music at church festivals to Neapolitan songs in street cafés.

It was in the latter milieu that he was 'discovered' by a baritone student of comparative affluence named Eduardo Missiano, who insisted that Caruso should audition for his voice teacher, a prominent maestro named Guglielmo Vergine. Vergine's initial verdict has gone down in operatic history. 'Your voice,' he told Caruso, 'is like the whistling of the wind through a window.' Missiano, however, was not to be discouraged. He made it his business to teach Caruso two operatic arias, then took him back to Vergine who this time reluctantly agreed to accept him – though to begin with Caruso was allowed to do little more than sit and listen while other pupils received their instruction.* Gradually Vergine began to recognize what had fallen into his lap, and he made a contract with Caruso which stipulated that as the young man was unable to pay for his lessons he would receive four years' free tuition, in return for twenty-five per cent of his earnings during his first five years of professional singing – a contract which, as we shall see, was open to various interpretations. In any case, it appeared likely that the four years' tuition would be subject to a three-year interruption, as Caruso was conscripted into the army for his compulsory national service, but in this respect luck was very much on his side. When he had only been serving for a few months his habit of singing in the barracks brought him to the attention of an operatically-minded officer named Major Nagliati, who first arranged for a voice teacher to train Caruso during the remainder of his service and then announced that as it really wasn't tolerable to have a soldier around the place making so much noise, it would be better for all concerned if Caruso would bring his national service to a premature conclusion – which he was free to do, if he could persuade his younger brother Giovanni to take his place. To any aspiring vocalists who have served their time in the British army this episode may sound too Utopian to be true; but Italians have different priorities, and it is a fact that within a short time Giovanni was in uniform and Caruso was back with Maestro Vergine.

Vergine did not believe in bringing young singers on too fast, and in any case Caruso's voice was not a simple one to train – the quality of his middle and lower registers was exceptionally rich, but the top of the tenor range presented him with agonizing problems. By the time Caruso was twenty-one, however, Vergine felt that the time had come for a professional debut, and after much cajoling he persuaded his friend Nicola Daspuro, the manager of Naples's Teatro Mercadante, to give the lad a hearing. Daspuro was impressed and offered Caruso an ideal role for a voice of his type, Wilhelm Meister in Ambroise Thomas's MIGNON, but

---

* It was typical of Caruso that when he was established as the supreme star of the Metropolitan Opera, and Missiano had fallen on hard times, he engineered his old benefactor's engagement there as a singer of small roles.

when Caruso arrived for rehearsals disaster struck. Despite his years of vocal study he had had no general musical education such as he would have received in any Conservatoire, and when he found himself surrounded by experienced performers, all of whom seemed to know exactly what they were supposed to be doing, he went to pieces. His voice cracked, he missed cue after cue, he forgot his words. It was the realization of every beginner's nightmare, and Daspuro had no alternative but to cancel the contract.

For any singer the balance between the necessary degrees of self-confidence and self-criticism is a delicate one, and for someone as unsophisticated and vulnerable as the young Caruso the fiasco at the Mercadante must have been a vicious set-back. It is easy now to say that with his prodigious gifts success was bound to come sooner, or later, but at the time it cannot have seemed that way to him. He did manage to get a foot back on the ladder though, and it was one of his church solos which did the trick. Shortly before his twenty-second birthday he sang in the Cathedral at Caserta, and one of the participating instrumentalists was so impressed that he recommended Caruso to a wealthy dilettante composer of his acquaintance named Domenico Morelli, who was looking for a tenor to take the leading role in a new opera of his entitled L'AMICO FRANCESCO. It was billed for four performances in the Teatro Nuovo, Naples and, as only two of these performances took place, it seems safe to assume that the piece was not favourably regarded. From the fact, though, that the composer not only paid Caruso his full fee of eighty lire as if he had sung all four performances, but even added a bonus of fifty lire, it seems equally safe to assume that Caruso *was* favourably regarded.* More important still, there were two gentlemen in

---

* As frequent mention is made in this chapter of Caruso's fees, it may be helpful to indicate approximately what they would represent in today's values. During most of Caruso's career one pound was the equivalent of $4.80 or twenty-seven lire, and one pound in 1910 had the purchasing power of forty pounds at the time of writing. This means that Caruso's fee per performance at the Metropolitan Opera was roughly equivalent to £20,500 today, and the fee which he declined from Oscar Hammerstein to £41,000.

the audience who made their rather precarious livings as agents-cum-impresarios around the harum-scarum circuit of provincial theatres which proliferated all over southern Italy, and they were onto the new tenor in a flash. In Caserta he appeared as Gounod's Faust, winning his first complimentary press notice, shortly followed by Turiddu in CAVALLERIA RUSTICANA, which he had learnt during his military service with the teacher whom Major Nagliati had detailed to instruct him. Then came a chance to step in for a sick tenor in the Teatro Bellini in Naples, starting again with Faust, and subsequently adding to his repertoire the Duke in RIGOLETTO and Alfredo in LA TRAVIATA. The fees were minuscule but he was learning his trade, and as soon as the season at the Bellini was finished he was off to Cairo where he appeared in four different roles with a scratched-up touring company typical of the times. One of the productions was Puccini's MANON LESCAUT, and although it was the Egyptian premiere of this sensational new work, Caruso was given precisely three days in which to memorize the long and demanding role of des Grieux. Naturally he failed to do so, and his Manon found herself obliged to play her death scene with Caruso's vocal score propped against her posterior. There were one or two other little lapses as well, such as a performance of CAVALLERIA for which Caruso had not left himself time to recover from a bibulous lunch. He paid for his youthful indiscretion by cracking twice on his high notes – not something to be recommended in front of audiences noted for their excitability.

In general, however, Caruso's brief season in Cairo had so clearly revealed his potential that he did not even have time to disembark on his return to Naples before an agent had boarded his ship and offered him the role of Alfredo in the Teatro Mercadante – the very theatre in which scarcely a year earlier he had proved himself incapable of rehearsing, let alone performing. Of course he still had a great deal to learn, and for several years the insecurity of his upper register was to bring him painful periods of self-doubt. The fear of cracking on a high note is a frightening thing to live with, and there are certain operas in which one single tone can loom larger to a young and inexperienced singer than the whole of the rest of the role. Gradually, though, as he climbed the ladder of the Italian provincial theatres Caruso began to gain a fuller understanding of the extraordinary instrument with which he had been blessed – or burdened, according to his mood. He was greatly assisted during an early engagement in Salerno by a certain Maestro Vincenzo Lombardi, one of those theatrical all-rounders who used to exist in much greater numbers than they do today. Lombardi fulfilled the function of voice teacher as well as those of conductor and coach, and it was to him, as well as to his own determined application, that Caruso owed much of his growing confidence with his top notes – notes which were so soon to electrify opera lovers throughout the world.

The beginning of Caruso's career coincided with a time of profound change in the nature of Italian opera. Verdi in certain of his middle-period works had already blazed a trail away from the artificiality of the Rossini-Bellini-Donizetti repertoire and into an era of greater vocal and theatrical realism. Now his pioneering work was being carried to its logical conclusion by composers such as Puccini, Leoncavallo, Mascagni and Giordano, the leading lights of the so-called *verismo* school, and Lombardi was quick to realize that Caruso's voice, with its thrilling virility of timbre, was perfectly suited to this new style of writing. The leading contemporary composers, too, were being alerted to the young tenor's existence. During a season in Leghorn in 1897 Caruso, having just sung Rodolfo in Puccini's new opera LA BOHEME for the first time, paid a visit to the great composer at his home some forty kilometres away. He had only sung a couple of pages when Puccini leapt up from the keyboard and asked 'Who sent you to me – God?' Shortly afterwards Caruso was entrusted with the role of Federico in the world premiere of Cilea's L'ARLESIANA in the Teatro Lirico, Milan, and a year later with that of Loris in Giordano's FEDORA. Music was being written which has formed part of every Italianate tenor's staple diet ever since, and Caruso's was the perfect voice to send it winging on its way – indeed, at the premiere of FEDORA his personal success was far greater than that of the composer. In 1898 his reputation began to spread abroad when he was engaged for a season in St Petersburg – the honour of launching his true international career can hardly be accorded to those ramshackle events in Cairo – and one of his partners there was Luisa Tetrazzini, who left a detailed account of the impression which he made. She had come across him a couple of years before on the Italian provincial circuit and had vivid memories of his frustration as his voice kept cracking even on 'such ordinary notes as G or A'. Of his Rodolfo in St Petersburg, however, she was to write 'I can hear that velvet voice now, and the "impertinenza" with which he lavishly poured forth those rich, round notes.'

For Caruso at this stage of his life 'impertinenza' is the *mot juste*. With his newly found technical security he began to revel in his singing, and as his performance fees of fifteen or twenty lire gradually had an increasing number of noughts added to them he could afford to give his natural propensity for bonhomie ever freer rein. In his early years he was a slender, even handsome young man, one of his salient features being the dark intensity of his eyes, and, as is to be expected from a youthful tenor who is regularly on the move, he slipped easily in and out of numerous romantic attachments. He carried good humour with him wherever he went, and his extrovert personality tended to find riotous expression in the loudness of his clothes. The American soprano Geraldine Farrar wrote in her memoirs that she would never forget the apparition in screaming checks which confronted her at their first rehearsal together – but then went on to recall that when this ebullient extrovert opened his mouth to sing full voice in the performance she was so mesmerized that she missed her next few cues. Another colleague who wrote most revealingly about Caruso the man was Percy Pitt, head conductor at Covent Garden. 'He was not only a very reliable artist,' Pitt recalled, 'but a delightful creature to have about the place, larking around and playing practical jokes.' It was the tradition at that time that the principal singers should meet for gargantuan lunches at a restaurant called Guffanti's, where Pitt presided over heaped-up dishes of spaghetti and generous supplies of Chianti. 'Caruso,' Pitt goes on, 'was always the life and soul of these gatherings, and when he ceased to come to Covent Garden with such regularity the meetings were gradually dropped; without him there seemed no reason for their existence.'

Something which could scarcely have been carried off without at least a dash of 'impertinenza' was the famous episode of Caruso's first recordings. In the early spring of 1902 the Gramophone and Typewriter Company of London sent their representative, Mr Fred Gaisberg, to Milan, hoping that some famous artist might be persuaded to lend their machine a little much-needed respectability. Caruso was at that moment in his second season at La Scala, creating yet another new *verismo* role, this time in an opera called GERMANIA by a composer named Franchetti. So overwhelmed was Gaisberg by Caruso's performance and by the public's ecstatic reception of it that he forgot all about the established stars whom he was supposed to be chasing and went instead straight for the young comet. When Caruso asked for one hundred pounds to record ten arias the London office wired: FEE EXORBITANT. FORBID YOU TO RECORD, but luckily Gaisberg felt too embarrassed to retract. Thus it came about that on the sunny afternoon of 11 April, a snappily dressed young man presented himself at the Grand Hotel Spatz, where Mr Gaisberg had converted his room into a studio and set up his primitive apparatus. Within two hours the ten arias had been recorded, to the piano accompaniment of Maestro Salvatore Cottone and at a turntable speed which has now been authoritatively established as 71.29 revolutions per minute. The young man then took his hat and his stick and breezed out with his hundred pounds in his pocket, leaving Mr Gaisberg feeling faintly shocked that anyone should be able to earn so much money for so little work. Mr Gaisberg, however, though he did not know it at the time, had not only earned his company around £15,000 but had also set in motion the most far-reaching innovation in the history of music. In his book of memoirs there is a photograph of Caruso with the simple caption 'His records made the gramophone'.

These ten pioneering arias together with thirteen other tracks recorded in Milan between 1902 and 1904 are now available on CD in the EMI *Références* series (*CDH 7610462*). They also, of course, form part of the Pearl and RCA Victor complete sets, to which I shall be referring anon, but to any serious student of the art of Caruso whose pocket may not stretch to twelve CDs, this EMI disc is a valuable reissue. Compared with Caruso's later recordings these cannot be called easy listening, and the layman coming to them with the sound of the latest stereo release in his ear could be forgiven for wondering what all the fuss was about. Compared with the same recordings in their original form, however, a disc like this is manna from heaven. Three of the tracks were recorded on cylinders, which very few people in recent years have been able to play at all, and the rest, recorded at speeds varying between 68 and 75 rpm, used to need very careful handling on specialist equipment if the great tenor were not to sound like a rather frantic male alto. Now, to those who are willing to hear beyond the surface noise, the Caruso who stood in Mr Gaisberg's hotel room, his face inches from that funny old horn, will emerge as having already been a tenor *sans pareil*. It may also be of interest to know that for an excerpt from Cilea's ADRIANA LECOUVREUR and for Leoncavallo's familiar song 'La Mattinata', written expressly for the gramophone, the composers themselves took Maestro Cottone's place at the piano.

For a more detailed appreciation of Caruso's extraordinary qualities I would like to move on, though, to a disc in the Nimbus Company's Prima Voce series (*NI 7803*), which takes us, via twenty carefully chosen tracks, from his first recording session in New York on 1 February 1904 through to the end of his career in 1920. The earliest of these is the aria 'Una furtiva lagrima' from L'ELISIR D'AMORE, and to my mind it is a performance which, for the sheer beauty of the sound which Caruso makes, for the technical skill with which he weaves his way along one of the most expressive of all Donizetti's melodic lines, and for the depth of feeling with which he invests every word he sings, has not been even remotely approached by any other tenor since. The quality of the voice is lyrical, but it is a lyricism of extraordinary richness, and the ease of its flow carries within itself a permanent hint of power in reserve. Part of the instrument's secret lies in the harmony of its contrasts, its *recondita armonia*. With such depth of tonal quality it would normally be rated as a heavy voice, and yet the various little embellishments with which Caruso decorates the melody are of a featherweight lightness, and the speed and precision of his concluding cadenza would shame many a *tenore di grazia*. The basic vocal colour is dark, but it is a brilliant, gleaming darkness, susceptible to endless subtleties of shading, all of which are employed as an apparently instinctive response to the words which Caruso is singing. The opening phrase, as Nemorino, the archetypal country bumpkin, notices 'one furtive tear' in the eye of the capricious Adina, is uttered as a kind of sigh, all sadness and regret. Then comes a marvellous expansion of the tone on the phrase 'che più cercando io vo?' as the penny drops. 'M'ama, sì m'ama, lo vedo, lo vedo', he sings, ('She loves me, yes she loves me, I can see it, I can see it!'); and the crescendo with which Caruso moves into the glorious F natural of that first 'm'ama' is one of the great moments of recorded opera.

Nemorino was one of the roles which Caruso kept in his repertoire throughout his career. His youthful slenderness did not last for long, and in roles which called for an aristocratic bearing – those in which his predecessor, the refined and elegant Jean de Reszke, had excelled – he knew himself to be, in a dramatic sense, at a disadvantage; whereas with earthier characterizations such as Nemorino he needed to have no inhibitions and always felt most at home. His first encounter with the role, however, was not a relaxed affair. In December 1900 he had made a bitterly disappointing debut at La Scala, Milan, when he opened the season as Rodolfo in LA BOHEME while still suffering from the aftermath of a feverish cold – not to mention the strain of endless harassment from Toscanini during the rehearsals. Puccini, feeling personally let down, left before the last act, and the critics were negative or even hostile. Caruso's next role was in a new comic opera by Mascagni which flopped, and the manager of La Scala, Giulio Gatti-Casazza, together with Toscanini in his capacity as musical director, decided to put on L'ELISIR as a stop-gap. It had not been seen for as long as anyone could remember, and the notoriously haughty subscribers of La Scala felt that they were being shortchanged by such a piece of frippery. At the first night they expressed their disapproval by resolutely declining either to laugh or to clap, and by the interval things were looking black. Early in the second half comes a big duet for Adina and Nemorino. As Gatti-Casazza was to recall in his memoirs, the Adina opened it in fine style but the public remained cool:

> Now it is Caruso's turn. Who that heard him would not remember? Calm, and conscious that at this point the fate of the performance will be decided, he delivered the reply 'Chiedi, al rio perchè gemente' with a voice, a feeling and an art which no word could ever adequately describe. He melted the cuirass of ice with which the public had invested itself, little by little capturing his audience, subjugating it, conquering it, leading it captive. Caruso had not yet finished the last note of the cadenza when an explosion, a tempest of cheers, of applause and of enthusiasm on the part of the entire public saluted the youthful conqueror.

And that from a hard-boiled manager who was deeply unimpressed by 'stars'!

Again and again, when reading accounts of Caruso's career, one comes across these reports of his ability to sweep an audience off its feet. He regularly suffered from nerves before going on stage, but it was a positive, not a destructive nervousness, and it created a vibrancy which communicated itself to the public the moment he came on stage. John McCormack relates in his autobiography how, on hearing Caruso's opening phrase in LA BOHEME, 'my jaw dropped, as though hung on a hinge'; and another typical instance of the Caruso magic was described by the great Italian conductor Vittorio Gui, recalling in his old age an incident from his student days in Rome. He attended a rehearsal of Puccini's MANON LESCAUT which Caruso was coasting through, using no voice, and carrying his bowler hat and cane. Suddenly, at the end of Act III, something astonishing happened.

> Caruso has thrown his hat and cane behind the wings; he is no longer there, in his place the living character of des Grieux, who explodes with his cry of desperate supplication. A great wave of emotion has overcome all of us – musicians, chorus, conductor. We, the students, dry our tears in the dark. Finally the rehearsal had to be interrupted, the poor old supporting singer who was supposed to ask "Do you want to go and populate the Americas, young man?" could not get beyond the word "populate" before he burst into tears. The conductor Vitale took a large white handkerchief from his pocket and, pretending to mop his brow, dried his eyes.

Sometimes it would be the sheer lyrical beauty of Caruso's voice which had this effect on people, sometimes it would be the overwhelming impact of his dramatic singing, and on the Nimbus disc we are treated to a feast of both. There is the volcanic 'Di quella pira' from IL TROVATORE, with its heart-wrenching switch of colour on the key change, and the noble, devastating 'Vesti la giubba' from PAGLIACCI, perhaps the most celebrated of all Caruso's recordings. From the same role there is the masterly 'No! Pagliaccio non son', recorded nearly four years later when the voice had acquired even more tragic overtones, and there is the 'O Paradiso' from L'AFRICAINE, in which Caruso catches the wonderment of the explorer Vasco da Gama in a matchless sweep of velvety legato crowned by an astonishing crescendo on the first high B flat. Verdi is well represented, with the 1911 version of 'Celeste Aida' – from 1903 until 1919 not a single season at the Met went by without Caruso appearing as Radamès – as well as

'O tu che in seno agli angeli' from LA FORZA DEL DESTINO, and two arias apiece from UN BALLO IN MASCHERA and RIGOLETTO. It was as the Duke in RIGOLETTO that Caruso liked to make his important international debuts – Covent Garden, the Met, Vienna, to name but a few – and it is easy to see why. His 'Quest' o quella' is bursting at the seams with 'impertinenza', and his 'Ella mi fu rapita' is a vocal tour de force, flung at the listener with a marvellous blend of anger and wounded pride. As examples of his classical smoothness of emission in music of the earlier school, huge in its scope, and carried on a rock-like support, we have the arias from Donizetti's DON SEBASTIANO and IL DUCA D'ALBA (the latter, in fact, generally reckoned to be an insertion by a composer named Salvi), and although the final pianissimo high C in 'Magiche note' from Goldmark's LA REINE DE SABA has never seemed to me a convincing tone, the rest of it provides another gorgeous display of legato singing. In des Grieux's 'Dream' from Massenet's MANON it is fascinating to hear how Caruso lightens his voice to achieve the *mezza voce*, which was one of his great glories throughout his career, but in which, presumably because of the limitations of contemporary recording techniques, he did not often indulge in the studio. Seven years after this recording of 'The Dream', in 1911, it was the turn of des Grieux's second great solo, 'Ah! fuyez, douce image' from the scene in St Sulpice, and here he produces surely some of the most exciting sounds ever to have emerged from a human throat. It is a particularly taxing aria, for ever climbing upwards, and calling for two full-voiced attacks on high B flats; but by this stage in his career Caruso was able to carry the full quality of his almost baritonal middle register right up to the top of his range, and the effect is overwhelming. This is the kind of singing which makes me feel that however great certain other singers may be, or may have been, Caruso somehow went beyond them.

On the Nimbus disc we also meet Caruso as the other des Grieux, hero of Puccini's version of the Manon story. 'Donna non vidi mai' is possibly my favourite amongst Puccini's tenor arias – into the mouth of the impressionable young lover the young composer poured such a spontaneity of passion. It is true to say that the Caruso of 1913 no longer sounds like a lovelorn youth – the tone is simply too magnificent for that – but how he rolls out the melody! It flows from him in an ardent flood, a stream of irresistible, irrepressible sound, glowing, vital, and resplendent. The disc only includes one other Puccini track, and this, funnily enough, I find much less convincing. It is the 1904 version of 'E lucevan le stelle', and it does not seem to me to have its source in that deep well of sincerity which usually binds Caruso and his listeners. In almost all of his recordings, partly through the exceptional cogency of his diction, and partly through the sheer amount of himself that he puts into his singing, Caruso the man leaps from the disc as few singers ever have; but in this instance something seems to be missing.

Chronologically the last of the tracks on the Nimbus disc is 'Rachel, quand du Seigneur' from Halévy's LA JUIVE. It was recorded in September 1920, twelve weeks before illness brought Caruso's career to its premature end, and it provides a supreme example of the extent to which he used to immerse himself in the music which he sang. The anguished figure of the old Jewish goldsmith Eléazar was the last new role that Caruso undertook, and he won unstinting praise from the New York critics, not only for the intensity of his singing, but also for the powerful authority which he now brought to the acting of such tragic roles as this and Saint-Saëns' Samson. As the recording shows, his voice had darkened even further than by the time of the 1913 'Donna non vidi mai', and though it never lost its flexibility, its earlier lyricism was yielding to these newly developed dramatic accents. This is a compelling and deeply moving account of the old Jew's agony of mind, and had Caruso lived, Otello would surely not have been far away.

There is one more track in Nimbus's admirable selection, and this will probably be the least familiar to many listeners – 'Quando nascesti tu' from an opera called LO SCHIAVO by the Brazilian composer Carlos Gomes. It is a straightforward outburst of lyrical ardour and stands high on the list of my favourite Caruso recordings. 'When you were born,' a young officer sings to the girl he loves (his father's native Brazilian maid-servant – a risky choice), 'so were the flowers, so was the sun.' It finds Caruso's voice brilliantly burnished as it swoops and soars through its flights of unbridled passion, knocking down high notes like so many skittles, but – and this is so much the essence of Caruso – every time he returns to repeat that simple opening phrase, 'quando nascesti tu', there is a tenderness to it, and a human warmth, which startlingly remind you that you are listening to a person, not just a tenor. This is singing of heroic power and pride, but sung by a hero with his heart on his sleeve.

The Nimbus Prima Voce series also includes a disc entitled 'Caruso in Song' (*NI 7809*), which offers nineteen of his non-operatic recordings. As is so often the case when a major artist tackles the lighter end of the repertoire, this selection gives us many delightful glimpses of the great man letting his hair down. In de Crescenzo's 'Tarantella sincera' we hear him simply having fun with that fabulous voice, and in another tarantella, Rossini's familiar 'La Danza', he flicks at the top notes with astonishing nonchalance, bringing the full robustness of the instrument to bear on them in the merest fraction of a second. That dear old evergreen 'For You Alone' is invested with an extra appeal by Caruso's very special use of the English language, d'Hardelot's 'Because' is titanically rendered in the original French, and in 'Campane a Sera', to a text by Caruso himself, we hear him not only competing with a battery of evening bells but imitating them too. As an interpreter of Neapolitan songs Caruso was naturally in a class apart, and the Nimbus selection includes several classic examples. My personal favourite will always be his incomparable 'O Sole Mio', permeated from the very first note with unplumbable depths of nostalgia. What must the thoughts of the erstwhile waterfront urchin have been, I wonder, as he stood in the recording studio, one of the most famous and highly paid men in the world, on a February day on the cold, damp eastern coast of America, evoking the sights and sounds of his sun-drenched Neapolitan childhood? His feelings towards his native city were certainly ambivalent in the extreme, because one of the few real set-backs of his career had been his reception as Nemorino at the Teatro San Carlo in 1901, shortly after he had so memorably conquered La Scala in the very same role. This was to be his triumphal journey home, no longer the faltering beginner with the insecure top notes, but the blazing young star, fêted from Buenos Aires to St Petersburg and now back to share his fame with his family and friends. Alas, that was not how it worked out. Confident that his vocal artistry was enough in itself to ensure success, he omitted to grease the right palms and flatter the right egos. He did not bother to court the critics or bribe the claque, and they made him pay for his hubris. After his first aria, 'Quant' è bella', there was a spontaneous burst of applause but it was stifled by hissing. Caruso was dumbfounded, and though he recovered himself well enough to give what most of the public regarded as a superb performance his high hopes had been shattered. However well he sang during the rest of his brief San Carlo season one critic in particular persisted in trying to cut him down to size, and he swore never to sing in Naples again. 'I shall only come back' he declared, 'to visit my dear stepmother and to eat vermicelli alle vongole.' He kept his word too, until, twenty years later, he came back there to die.

The Nimbus disc of 'Caruso in Song' also includes several items of a more solemn nature, such as Niedermeyer's 'Pietà, Signore', Handel's 'Largo', and the 'Domine Deus' from Rossini's 'Messe Solenelle' (recorded at his very last session), all of which bear witness to the massive breadth and amplitude of his voice in his later years. It also includes one inimitable item of a very different nature, a jingoistic ditty called 'Over There', written by Caruso's good friend Mr George M. Cohan to whip up enthusiasm for America's participation in the First World War. Caruso hurls his defiance at the Kaiser in such immortal couplets as 'The boys arre coming, the boys arre coming, the drums rum-tumming

ev'rywherre', and to understand why on earth the world's greatest
tenor should have recorded such a song as this, one has to form a
picture of what his life consisted of at the time. Since his first season at the Metropolitan Opera in 1903/4 New York had become
his base. Until the outbreak of war he used to return to Europe
every year, giving regular guest performances at Covent Garden,
in Vienna and in several of the leading houses in Germany as well
as taking occasional opportunities to relax in a palatial country
residence which he had acquired near Florence, but home was
a fourteen-room suite in New York's Knickerbocker Hotel. It
would scarcely be possible to exaggerate the extent of his fame
or his popularity in that city. In an age of great stars his drawing
power far exceeded that of any other contemporary singer,* and
even to that section of the population who would either not wish
to go to the opera or could not afford to do so, Caruso was
as familiar a personality as the Mayor or the leading baseball
players. In particular he was perhaps the most prominent single
individual in New York's vast Italian community, and when the
United States finally entered the war on the same side as his native
land it was a source of intense relief to Caruso. He was tireless in
his appearances for wartime benefit funds, once raising $47,000 by
conducting an auction of oranges at which he himself paid $4000
for a single box. In September 1918 he sang 'Over There' in the
Century Theatre in aid of the Tank Corps, leading a cast which
included Al Jolson and Sophie Tucker. A few days later he sang
it again to what was reported as being 'the largest audience ever
gathered in Central Park', and when one copy of his record of
the song was sold at an auction in aid of the New York Sun's
Tobacco Fund for Soldiers it fetched $125,000 – which must, I
imagine, still stand as the highest price ever paid for a gramophone
record. When the armistice was announced vast crowds gathered

---

* One indication of this is that when the company of the Metropolitan Opera
appeared for a brief season at the Théâtre du Chatelet in Paris in 1910, anyone
wanting to book for a Caruso evening was obliged to do so for a non-Caruso
evening as well.

outside his hotel. The mood of the moment seemed to require Caruso, and he obliged by singing 'The Star-Spangled Banner' from his balcony, nine floors up.

Earlier in this chapter I mentioned that two companies have brought out full sets of Caruso's recordings, and for people really wishing to explore the great tenor's output this is of course the answer to their prayers. RCA Victor's version is a twelve disc set entitled 'The Complete Caruso' (*GD 60495*), and Pearl's, entitled 'The Caruso Edition', also on twelve discs, is sub-divided into four volumes of three discs each, numbered *EVC 1 – EVC IV*. The two companies have aimed in their re-mastering at rather different sounds, with RCA Victor using a computerized technique, and going further than Pearl in the direction of eliminating surface hiss and other extraneous noise. This will be a recommendation to some listeners, though it carries with it the risk that the vocal tone may lose its shine, and my personal preference is for Pearl's less doctored quality of sound. (The same observation applies to a well chosen selection of favourite arias on a single RCA Victor disc, *RD 85911*, which, to my ear at least, does not bring the voice as far forward as the Nimbus disc.) In any case, for the collector of yesteryear who used to go in search of single-sided Caruso 78s as and when they appeared in the specialist shops, the idea of having over 230 titles dropped into his lap at once will be dizzying; and in comparison with single CDs of solo numbers only, the great glory of these full sets is that they open the door to Caruso's remarkable treasury of concerted numbers. To chart the development of voice and style from the golden lyricism of the earlier years to the triumphant magnificence of Caruso in his forties we have, for instance, four versions of the RIGOLETTO Quartet, recorded at intervals between 1907 and 1917. We have the one recording which he made with Nellie Melba, the Act I duet from LA BOHEME, magically recreating so many diamond-encrusted evenings at Covent Garden. As Sir Osbert Sitwell expressed it in his autobiography, these two singers summed up the age 'when, fat as two elderly thrushes, they trilled at each other over the hedges of tiaras', and it is extraordinary how much of this atmosphere their singing still evokes. With the words 'Dammi il braccio mia piccina' ('Give me your arm, my little one') the cheeky smile in Caruso's voice becomes almost visible, and we are reminded that he was the only tenor with the temerity to pull the leg of the formidable Nellie, Covent Garden's uncrowned queen. Then there is the magical performance of the PECHEURS DE PERLES duet with the baritone Mario Ancona, in which Caruso leans into his high B flat entry in a mood of dreamy ecstasy; and at the other end of the spectrum the Oath Duet from OTELLO which finds the two giants of the time, Caruso and Titta Ruffo, competing with one another to produce a level of sheer animal excitement such as has seldom, if ever, been attained since in any recording studio. There is the other-worldly 'O terra addio' from AIDA with Johanna Gadski, there are the excerpts from MARTA with Frances Alda, from BUTTERFLY with Scotti and with Geraldine Farrar, and from FAUST with Farrar and Journet; the FORZA duets with Amato, with de Luca and with Scotti, the resplendent trio from I LOMBARDI, and three different versions of the LUCIA Sextet – the list rolls on in mouth-watering profusion.

So abundant is the harvest of vocal splendour on these full sets that individual comment on every track would clearly be *de trop*. There are, however, just one or two more of my personal favourites which I would like to mention. Caruso twice recorded the aria 'M'apparì' from MARTA, first in 1906, then again in 1917. The earlier of these explains in the first eight bars why everybody hearing him for the first time at that stage of his career capitulated to the sheer beauty and ease of the sound which he produced – several critics became noticeably desperate in their attempts to avoid repeating the phrase 'a flow of liquid gold'. The later version, though, goes further than this. The gold is still there and so is the flow but they have been intensified by such a degree of magnificence, that expressions such as 'superhuman' cross the mind. It was indeed occasionally stated in print that Caruso was gifted with vocal cords of abnormal size, but according to his wife this was not so and the secret of his supremacy lay elsewhere. 'The cavities within Enrico's face' she was to write, 'were extraordinary. The depth, width and height of the roof of his mouth, the broad cheekbones and flat even teeth, the wide forehead above wide-set eyes – this spacious architecture gave him his deep resonance of tone.' She adds that he could expand his chest by nine inches, and relates how he could put an egg in his mouth, close his lips, and have no one guess that the egg was there. Caruso's own summing up of the requisites of a great singer were 'A big chest, a big mouth, ninety per cent memory, ten per cent intelligence, lots of hard work and something in the heart'. He was certainly adamant that without the hard work none of the rest would get you anywhere – 'When people think I sing freely,' he used to say, 'and think I take the life easy on the stage, they mistake. At such time I am working at the top of my strength.' One or two of Caruso's biographers have implied that he had no conscious understanding of his own technique, but this is directly contradicted by several people better qualified to know. An Englishman named Kenneth Downey took lessons with Caruso, and although a German gas attack dashed Downey's hopes of a career, I remember him telling me many years later that Caruso knew exactly how he sang, and how to explain it – though he was wise enough to warn young singers 'I am not an artist to imitate.' One of his Metropolitan colleagues, Cecile Ghilly, who later became a distinguished teacher in Paris, used to say that Caruso 'knew all there was to be known about the human voice', and recalled that he was always to be seen standing in the wings listening and learning while other singers sang.

Apropos Caruso's technical mastery there are two other recordings from his later period which I would like to mention in conjunction. One is 'L'alba separa dalla luce l'ombra', a positively epic setting by Tosti of a piece of high-flying romanticism from the pen of Gabriele d'Annunzio, and the other is a canzonetta entitled 'Mia piccirella', from an opera called SALVATOR ROSA, once again by Carlos Gomes. Caruso's performance of the Tosti song is the kind of thing that only he could have attempted. The middle of the voice is so sumptuous that the chance of anyone being able to carry that wealth of tone into the upper regions seems remote – until Caruso approaches an extended line of high A flats, whereupon the voice, like some gigantic oak tree which spreads its branches ever wider as it climbs, actually succeeds in expanding both in volume and in quality. 'Now surely,' the listener could be forgiven for assuming, 'he has shot his bolt', but he has not; for the final climactic high B flat he can, and does, pile on still more. 'All right,' the same sceptical listener might say, 'the man had an astonishingly powerful and beautiful voice, but is it not muscle-bound singing, a mere display of strength?' The answer to this is to play 'Mia piccirella', recorded two and a half years later when the voice had grown even darker and more huge. At the end of the aria (which was in fact written for the soprano voice) there is a brief cadenza, consisting of twelve semi-quavers, leading to a high B flat. The composer has marked this run with the word 'rapido', and I do not believe that the lightest of sopranos could rival either the rapidity or the precision with which Caruso scampers through it on his way to another of those Herculean climactic tones. The cadenza at the end of the Duke's 'La donna è mobile' from RIGOLETTO is another case in point. This has been recorded by every tenor imaginable, from the *robusto* to the *leggiero*, but I cannot think of one, with the possible exception of Alfred Piccaver, who dispatches it with the agility and accuracy of Caruso. Indeed the distinguished British soprano Agnes Nicholls, who appeared with him in DON GIOVANNI at Covent Garden, used to say that it was the greatest tragedy that he never recorded Don Ottavio's aria 'Il mio tesoro', 'because Caruso's "coloratura" would have been the envy of Luisa Tetrazzini'.

There is just one more individual number which I cannot leave unmentioned. It is of the variety which I think could best be classified as 'an Edwardian drawing-room ballad', it is in English (or at least in Caruso's English), and it is called 'Dreams of Long Ago'. The poem stakes no claim to literary distinction and the melody is a sentimental slow waltz, but the performance is ineffable. It is sung not only with infinite beauty and charm, but also with dedication and with pride, for Caruso himself was its composer. Doubtless for this reason it seems to bring one very close to Caruso the man, in all his glory and in all his simplicity, and, as I wrote at the beginning of this chapter, there has seldom been a singer whose singing and whose self were so closely interdependent. The exuberance and generosity of his nature seems to pour out through his voice, and yet at the same time for all his jocularity and love of fun he was an artist of dedicated professionalism. It is not often that star tenors are lauded by star conductors, but even that Olympian figure Otto Klemperer once wrote of Caruso 'In 1910 he visited Hamburg as a guest artist, where I had the honour of conducting his three performances. It was a very real pleasure, for Caruso was an exceedingly musical singer, who adapted himself perfectly to the ensemble, without showing a trace of soloist's temperament.'

One of Caruso's many attractive qualities was his willingness to laugh at himself, and nothing demonstrates this more delightfully than his own self-portraits. He was a caricaturist of more than amateur ability, always dashing off drawings for his friends and colleagues, and sometimes even scribbling them on bits of scenery backstage. He was a regular contributor to the humorous publication *La Follia*, and though he never accepted payment for them, his self-portraits are now collectors' pieces, fetching as much as $8000 each. They were always hilariously unflattering. As Don José in CARMEN, for instance, he depicts himself as consisting largely of two huge boots which rise straight into a generous contour of stomach, while his head has vanished into his helmet leaving nothing visible but an enormous mouth like a banana. While being fully aware of his own vocal stature he clearly had no illusions about the unsuitability of his appearance to certain of his roles, and in a letter to his wife, who was American, he once expressed the hope that their infant daughter would grow up to resemble her rather than him because 'I am offly ogly'.

Caruso's rapport with the public was legendary, and he devised all sorts of ingenious methods for bringing the applause to an end when he felt that he had done enough. After a TOSCA at Covent Garden in 1914 – his last season there, though no one knew it at the time – he took his final curtain with his wig in his hand; after a concert in Blackpool he eventually reappeared wearing an overcoat, carrying his hat and his stick, and smoking a large cigar; and after a CARMEN in Havana he was obliged to deliver a speech to the public in Spanish which he translated to his wife as follows: 'Excuse me, I feel so hungry, and your applause which is so kindly you are giving to me doesn't fool up my stomach, for consequence I beg you to go to bed.'

Caruso's marriage, which took place in 1918 when he only had three years to live, came as a surprise to everyone. It was a most unlikely union, as his wife was considerably younger than himself, they had only known one another for a very short time, and her father, the stuffiest kind of New York society figure, was so outraged that he cut her out of his will. Until then Caruso's private life had been a strange one. Early in his career he and an Italian soprano named Ada Giachetti started to live as man and wife; Giachetti was already married and apparently unable to obtain a divorce. She bore him two sons of whom he was extremely proud, and he was distraught when in 1908 she not only left him but did so in a particularly humiliating manner by eloping with his chauffeur. Thereafter his name was linked in the papers with a variety of young ladies, often on the flimsiest of grounds, one or two of them being comparatively obscure sopranos, who may well have felt that their careers would profit from an injection of free publicity. On one occasion, though, he both asked for trouble and got it, by discussing marriage with a nineteen-year-old shopgirl in Milan, then naively supposing that she (and her father) would go away when he changed his mind. She sued him for breach of promise, and although she lost the case Caruso was subjected to further humiliation by the publication of his love letters, all of which were read out in court.

This was not, in fact, Caruso's first experience of law courts. That had come as a result of Maestro Vergine's contract, referred to earlier in this chapter, whereby Caruso was to pay his old teacher twenty-five per cent of his earnings 'in his first five years of singing'. Once Caruso's career began to bring in serious money Vergine claimed that the contract had not merely referred to his earnings during a five year period, but his earnings from the equivalent of five years of solid singing – in other words the number of performances which he would have given had he sung every evening for five years. The case dragged on and on, and eventually Caruso settled the matter by paying Vergine the sum of 20,000 lire. His next, and most painful, brush with the law was the notorious 'Monkey House' incident, when he was arrested for molesting a woman in New York's Central Park Zoo. In what appears to have been an astonishing travesty of justice he was found guilty and fined ten dollars, although the policeman who arrested him was unable to produce the lady to bear witness claiming that she had given him a false name and address. It subsequently emerged that the policeman, an Irishman named Kane, was well acquainted with the lady, having been best man at her wedding, and the whole affair appeared in retrospect to have been a set-up, typical of the ill will which existed between New York's two largest groups of immigrants, the Irish and the Italians. In any case, Caruso eventually developed a particularly genial relationship with the New York Police. Towards the end of his life he was made an Honorary Captain in that noble body, a distinction which, according to his wife, gave him greater pleasure than any of the many other decorations which had been bestowed upon him. When the badge was pinned to his coat he asked the Commissioner if it gave him the power of arrest, and when told that it did replied 'I go straight to the Metropolitan and do a funny on Mr Gatti!'

The letters which Caruso wrote to his wife during those last years of his life comprise a very touching human document. The picture which emerges is one of a man who is beginning to find the burden of his own success almost more than he can sustain. He was on an exposed and lonely pinnacle of fame. When he went for a walk his car had to creep along behind him, ready to whisk him away when the crowds began to gather. Newspapers and rival impresarios were for ever stirring up controversy by saying that he had lost his voice. Certain small-time critics found that they could attract more attention to themselves by claiming to detect signs of deterioration in his singing than by joining in the usual paeans of praise. Cranks, hangers-on and threatening letters were always bothering him, and twice he was subjected to blackmail attempts by a Mafia-like organization known as The Black Hand. At every performance he had to satisfy the public's demand for something superlative, and the inflated price of tickets which accompanied his every appearance added to his responsibilities. Although he continued to sing at the Met for the comparatively modest fee of $2500 a night,* his earnings elsewhere were colossal. In Mexico City in 1919 he was paid $7000 a performance, but he was still a cheap artist to employ. With Caruso in the cast the impresario was able to transfer the performances from the theatre to the bullring, and sell 25,000 tickets – at $6.00 in the shade and $2.50 in the sun. The size of Caruso's earnings can be judged by the fact that in 1918 he paid $154,000 in US taxes, but he had developed a style of life commensurate with this level of income. Where he went a substantial entourage went with him – accompanist, secretary, valet, chauffeur, dressers and so on. On his Tuscan country estate an unspecified number of relatives and hangers-on lived at his expense. When he died it was found that over 120 people were on his list for regular financial assistance, and his bill for Christmas presents to employees of the Met alone came to many thousands of dollars. He had become a serious collector of

---

* When Oscar Hammerstein tried to lure him away with a promise of $5000 the Met felt obliged to match the offer, but Caruso insisted on staying on at his usual salary.

objets d'art, with a strong predilection for gold watches and gold snuff-boxes. His coin collection consisted of nearly two thousand items, dating back to the fifth century BC, again all gold. (King Victor Emmanuel III, a fellow numismatist, once remarked 'If I were Caruso I too would only bother with gold.')

The strain of it all, however, was beginning to tell. In photographs taken of Caruso in his mid-forties he looks at least ten years older. From his letters to his wife, written in inimitable English, it becomes increasingly evident that every performance was beginning to assume the aspect of a contest with his own reputation – every performance had to be sensational, or he had failed. In 1920 he wrote from Havana, where he was paid $10,000 a night, 'I win another battle with my second performance of MARTA. I took the public by the – what you call the lower part of the mouth, il mento [chin], and shake terribly until he came down at my feet.' A few nights later there was a little light relief, when the stage management failed to fire the off-stage pistol in LA FORZA DEL DESTINO, an incident which Caruso described as follows: 'At the moment which I throw down the pistol, the people inside of the stage dont shot and I make a big noise with my mouth like this, BUUUUM!!!!! and I kill the father of Leonora! You can immagine the public how laughing!' The general tone of his letters, though, can best be summed up by one sentence which he wrote later the same year from a hotel in Houston, Texas: 'I think I am a little tired of everything, and I need to live a little outside of the world, to let me forget and let people forget me.'

Caruso never lived to enjoy this longed-for solitude. On Christmas Eve 1920 he sang his last performance, as Eléazar in LA JUIVE at the Metropolitan Opera. He had been ill for some time, complaining of pain in his side and, although he sang superbly, several people in the audience that night who knew him well, including Toscanini, noticed that he was suffering. It turned out that he had the severest imaginable pleurisy, and the story of the last months of his life is little more than a horrifying list of unsuccessful operations, several of them without anaesthetic, and a chronicle of hideous pain. In the early Summer of 1921 he and his family travelled to Naples, and there, on 2 August, he died, aged forty-eight. The King of Italy gave orders that the Basilica di San Francesco di Paola, normally reserved for royal occasions, should be used for the funeral service, and the coffin was drawn by six black horses through the streets of Naples with vast crowds standing in silent homage as it passed.

The tributes written, both then and since, to Caruso as man and as singer, are innumerable. As Gatti-Casazza put it, 'He was a unique artist, with whom none other compared. I do not see how we can ever have such another.' The London *Times* declared with sober British understatement 'It is quite safe to say that no tenor voice equal to his, in its combination of power and extreme beauty of quality, has been heard in this generation.' Compton Mackenzie, founder of the *Gramophone*, wrote in more poetical vein 'His immortality is secure, for every day, somewhere, somebody will hear his voice for the first time and say "This was a singer."' To me, however, the most telling words are those which Beniamino Gigli was to write in his memoirs. If anyone might have been excused for resenting Caruso it would surely have been he, spending his early career, as he did, very much in the great man's shadow. Referring though to his own good fortune in coming from a friendly rural community, Gigli wrote 'I wonder what would have become of me if, like Caruso, I had been born in a city slum; for I did not have the gifts of personality that enabled Caruso to create life and warmth around him wherever he went.' That so much majesty, so much magnificence should have had their beginnings in that Naples slum was not merely the triumph of a supreme artistic talent – it was also a triumph of the human spirit.

GIUSEPPE DE LUCA

ITALIAN BARITONE

b. Rome, 25 December 1876, d. New York, 26 August 1950

O h! the baritones of my generation,' de Luca used to sigh in his old age, 'Ruffo, Amato, Sammarco, Stracciari – what I wouldn't have given to have a voice as strong as theirs!' Then, with a happy chuckle – 'But of course, with them around I had to learn to sing.' The extent to which he succeeded in doing so was never more effectively underlined than on 7 November 1947, when he celebrated fifty years as a professional singer with a recital in New York's Town Hall and, in the words of one of the critics, 'reminded us all what used to be meant by *bel canto*'.

De Luca was born on Christmas Day 1876, and he was the eldest child of a blacksmith. There was not much money around, and in the normal course of events he would have found himself at an early age helping his father in the forge. His mother though was endowed with a pleasant singing voice, and recognized that her son had talent in the same direction. His father understandably reckoned that getting down to a proper job of work made better sense than messing around with music, but luckily the maternal will prevailed, and at the age of eight de Luca was enrolled in the Schola Cantorum dei Fratelli Carissimi, a school which trained young choristers for the many Roman churches. There he was given a thorough musical grounding, especially in the invaluable skill of sight-reading, and he evidently prospered to a high degree because he was sent to the top of the tree – the choir of St Peter's Cathedral. His voice broke early; by the time he was fifteen it had settled into being an attractive light baritone, and he was anxious to move on to the Accademia di Santa Cecilia. Thanks to a handy friendship with a doorman in one of Rome's opera houses, the

Teatro Costanzi, he was able to slip in there regularly without the formality of buying a ticket, and he was hopelessly bitten by the operatic bug. The only problem was that his parents could not afford the fees at the Santa Cecilia, and there was no scholarship available. He was offered one in Naples however, but hardly had he arrived in that city when he received a telegram telling him that a private patron had materialized who would pay for him at the Santa Cecilia. So back to Rome he went, where he presented himself to the auditioning panel armed with an impressive array of operatic arias. He felt slightly deflated when it turned out that all the panel wanted to hear was a few scales and one or two random operatic phrases, but that was enough to secure his admittance, and he had the good fortune to be assigned to Maestro Vinceslao Persichini, teacher of the legendary Mattia Battistini, and a great believer in the gradual development of young voices.

It is a natural law that every vocal student's regular diet is the repertoire of the previous generation. When de Luca joined the Santa Cecilia OTELLO was still a novelty, FALSTAFF had not been written, Puccini had not progressed beyond LE VILLI and EDGAR, and *verismo* was scarcely in its cradle. The style in which he was grounded was that of the earlier masters, Rossini, Bellini and Donizetti, with the emphasis on elegance, ease and flexibility, and though he was soon to become a sought-after exponent, and indeed creator, of many twentieth century roles, he never deserted the virtues of a nineteenth century technique. To use an expression which crops up frequently in the singing business, he sang on his income not his capital; or, in the plainest of words, even when tackling dramatic roles he always sang, and never shouted.

De Luca was still seven weeks short of his twenty-first birthday when Persichini judged him ready to make his debut. This took place in the provincial city of Piacenza, in the role of Valentin in FAUST, and though it was no earth-shattering event it was enough to secure his promotion to the far more important Teatro Carlo Felice in Genoa. There he met Caruso. They were cast together in the Leoncavallo version of LA BOHEME and in LES PECHEURS DE PERLES, and it was the beginning of a regular stage partnership and of a friendship which lasted until the very end of Caruso's life. Caruso was nearly four years older than de Luca, and already able to afford a lifestyle which amazed his younger colleague. He earned 5000 lire to de Luca's 750, and though they both lived in the same pensione Caruso could afford a two-room apartment, while de Luca had to make do with one cramped little bedroom. Caruso though was ever the soul of generosity. Neither he nor de Luca cared for the cooking in the pensione, and whenever he hired a carriage to go and eat in the Ristorante Righi up in the hills, Caruso would take de Luca along with him. After performances their preferred eating place was Peppo's in the fashionable Galleria, where patrons of the theatre would recognize them, and the owner would beg them to sing. Such treats as Caruso's 'Flower Song' from CARMEN, or Caruso and de Luca in the duet from LES PECHEURS DE PERLES would be served up free of charge, the sort of behaviour which, within a year or two, would have landed them in the deepest of water with agents and managements. I only hope that the other diners had some inkling of how privileged they were.

De Luca's was a career which developed smoothly. Unlike Caruso he had nothing about him which could be called spectacular, but he had the wit and the patience to keep working away at every aspect of his job. He was a very small man, but this did not stop him becoming one of the finest operatic actors of his generation – 'an artist of protean versatility', as the magazine *Musical America* was to describe him. Vocally, as we have seen, his natural gifts were far outshone by those of several competitors, but by being skilfully nurtured they grew while others' waned. By the time he was twenty-five he had achieved sufficient prominence to be engaged by Milan's Teatro Lirico for the world premiere of Cilea's ADRIANA LECOUVREUR, alongside Caruso once again and with Toscanini conducting. The following year de Luca crossed the Atlantic for the first time when he, Caruso and Toscanini were all engaged for a season in the Teatro Colón, Buenos Aires – a season in which he produced early evidence of his versatility, as one of his roles – Beckmesser in DIE MEISTERSINGER – was not usually associated with an Italian 'belcantist'. On board the liner Caruso taught de Luca to play poker, something he later regretted because on a subsequent Atlantic crossing de Luca won so consistently that neither Caruso nor anyone else would continue playing with him – a unique occurrence, I believe, of de Luca having a problem with his colleagues. Back in Europe he was chosen in 1904 to create the role of Sharpless in MADAMA BUTTERFLY at La Scala. When the premiere turned out to be one of opera's most notorious catastrophes he was as mystified as everyone else involved in it, and to the end of his life he continued to regard his selection for the role as one of the highest honours to come his way.

As early as 1903 de Luca followed his friend Caruso into the recording studio. This was not his first experience of the new-fangled process however, because many years later he revealed that at the age of eighteen, when his family was in dire straits following the death of his father, he had entered into a very dubious recording contract with the owner of a Bar Automatico in Rome. This was a kind of primeval juke box, which enabled the customer, after the insertion of a small coin, to listen to a musical cylinder over a pair of earphones. De Luca recorded no less than forty of these cylinders at two lire a time, and they were then attributed to a dazzling galaxy of the world's greatest baritones. I wonder whether this youthful subterfuge may have crossed his mind when, 23 years later at the Metropolitan Opera, he created the role of opera's number one confidence trickster, Puccini's Gianni Schicchi, who was happy to sweep any peccadillo under the convenient carpet of 'extenuating circumstances'.

To turn, though, to de Luca's legitimate recording career, the earliest offerings on CD date from 1907, when he was thirty years old, and a regular member of La Scala. They are to be found on Nimbus's Prima Voce *NI 7815*, and consist of three

Verdi arias, 'O! de' verd' anni miei' from ERNANI, 'Il balen' from IL TROVATORE and 'Di Provenza' from LA TRAVIATA. The accompaniment is piano only – for a recording company to afford an orchestra in those days the singer had to be a gilt-edged bestseller – but the voice comes over on this reissue in splendidly clear and 'forward' shape. The style, not surprisingly, is reminiscent of Battistini, the Verdian *cantilena* evenly and smoothly unfurled, and any vocal decorations lightly and elegantly incorporated into the musical line. As with many recordings of this period I sense a determination never to drop below at least mezzo forte, as if the machinery might not respond to anything less imposing, and in general there is a slight feeling of anonymity about the performances. Especially in the 'Di Provenza' (an abbreviated version) de Luca has not yet quite become de Luca, but this is particularly understandable in a young baritone; where tenors so often have the problem of having to sound twenty-five when they are twice that age, baritones are frequently faced with the reverse situation. They are called upon to portray the worldly-wise older man while themselves still young and inexperienced, and as the dignified figure of Germont *père* de Luca was probably at his best some twenty years after he made this recording. Indeed, it was no less than thirty-three years later that his Germont provided the audience of the Metropolitan Opera with one of those evenings which become part of a house's mythology. In 1935 Gatti-Casazza, the Met's General Manager, retired and went back to Italy, and de Luca, after twenty years as a favourite member of the company, decided to do the same. Four years later Gatti's successor, Edward Johnson, suggested that de Luca might return for a few performances. In Europe war had broken out and travel was difficult, but on 9 January 1940 Johnson received a telegram from de Luca saying that the Government had given him permission to leave Italy, and that he hoped to arrive on the liner *Conte di Savoia* at the end of the month. He did, and on 7 February he was billed to make his come-back in LA TRAVIATA. It was a perfectly chosen role, not only because Germont does not appear until well into Act II, thus giving ample time for a build-up of tension and expectancy in the audience, but also because, when he does appear, it is during a passage of recitative which can be conveniently interrupted by applause. When de Luca stepped out of the wings that evening though, short, rotund and dignified, it was more than mere applause that interrupted the proceedings, it was a spontaneous explosion of enthusiasm and affection. **BARITONE'S OVATION STOPS PROGRESS OF TRAVIATA** ran one of the newspaper headlines the following day, and it was not to be one of those occasions when, after a frenzied welcome, the audience finds itself wondering what all the fuss has been about – as the critic of the *New York Times* put it 'the first five notes made the pulses beat because of the art and beauty of the song.' Also in the audience was the young Robert Merrill, destined to make his own Met debut in the same role nearly six years later, and as he was subsequently to write of de Luca in his memoirs 'the quality of the legato, the nobility of the concept and the dignity of his presence were unforgettable.'

Another of de Luca's most significant roles is represented on the Nimbus CD, with Figaro's ebullient 'Largo al factotum' from IL BARBIERE DI SIVIGLIA, recorded in 1917. This had been the part selected for de Luca's Met debut two years previously, when press and public had immediately taken him to their hearts not only for the skill and polish of his singing but also for the wit and vivacity of his stagecraft and the general attractiveness of his personality. By emphasizing the seriousness of de Luca's approach to his art I may have given the impression of a very earnest sort of person, but this could not be further from the truth. He was a delightfully merry little man, his conversation always punctuated by chuckles and snatches of song and, whenever one spots him in old photographs – strolling down the street with a bunch of colleagues or relaxing with his family – while the rest of them assume that formal air which went with the stiff white collars and the walking sticks, de Luca invariably breaks the pattern with a wide and puckish grin. Like many singers of the day he was a keen smoker, and he is occasionally to be seen in pictures puffing away at a cigarette held vertically in the bowl of a funny little pipe. Lucky Strikes were his favourite brand, and he used to endorse them in advertisements with the slogan 'They satisfy my taste in flavour and never irritate my throat.' As a performer he was equally at home with drama or comedy. One of the New York critics wrote of de Luca's Gianni Schicchi: 'Among operatic baritones of the day he remains the *farceur par excellence*, and this is the quality that bubbles through his "Largo al factotum".' He has graduated by now to an orchestral accompaniment, the vocal personality is fully fledged, the machine-gun patter is not merely faultless but filled with subtle little inflexions as it scampers along, and the whole thing is characterized by a genial, bustling self-importance. De Luca coined a nice phrase to describe his conception of Figaro as a fellow who is always plotting and planning – 'His head,' he said, 'is always rubbing its hands.'

This role was one of his visiting cards all over the world, and late in his career it at last enabled him to win over the one house which strangely enough had always resisted his charms – Covent Garden. During several seasons there before the First World War he failed to make any inroads into the immense popularity with the London public of Scotti and Sammarco. He was usually cast in slightly secondary roles, often in the shadow of some great prima donna, though it is true to say that even his Rigoletto failed to turn the tide. As Covent Garden's post-war management was predominantly interested in all things German and Viennese it appeared unlikely that de Luca would be given another chance to break down this bastion of indifference, but in 1935 it was suddenly announced, with no prior warning, that he would appear for one performance only as the Barber of Seville. To judge from the number of opera-goers I met in my young days who were still talking about this performance twenty years later, it was clearly something very special. Musical London was there en masse, and at fifty-nine de Luca must have felt that the

Covent Garden public had at last made amends for its lack of interest in him when young.

There is another 1917 recording on this Nimbus disc, a jaunty little song entitled 'Pastorale', in which de Luca positively juggles with the beauty of his voice, revelling in the fun of being a singer. We have several examples too of the nobility of his style in his serious repertoire – a deeply moving account of the death of Rodrigo from DON CARLOS in which, interestingly, he totally abjures the changes of colouring on individual words and phrases which were to become a stylistic hallmark of Tito Gobbi's, and simply uses an unaffectedly mellifluous delivery of Verdi's poignant phrases to express the pathos of the scene; an account of Riccardo's 'Ah, per sempre' and its preceding recitative from I PURITANI which could stand as an object lesson in how to express emotion with restraint; and an aria entitled 'De l'art splendeur immortelle' from BENVENUTO CELLINI (not the Berlioz version, but one by an obscure composer named Diaz), which displays almost more convincingly than any other what a sumptuous instrument de Luca's voice had become by the time he reached middle age. We are also offered several of his many duet recordings – in the *buffo* vein 'Venti scudi' from L'ELISIR D'AMORE with Caruso, in melodramatic mood 'Enzo Grimaldo' from LA GIOCONDA and in beautifully characterized tragicomedy 'Ah, Mimi' from LA BOHEME, the last two both with Beniamino Gigli. In almost all of his tenor/baritone duets, and in ensembles such as the RIGOLETTO Quartet and the Sextet from LUCIA DI LAMMERMOOR (many of which are available on CD in the various Caruso and Gigli reissues) I find de Luca excessively self-effacing. Whether the recording producers relied on his famed good nature to get away with placing him slightly behind his superstar partners I do not know, but that is how the performances tend to sound, which is a pity as he was a worthy partner for anyone. From three tracks, all with chorus, recorded in 1930, we are given resounding proof of the extraordinarily robust condition of de Luca's voice in his mid-fifties. With the misplaced exultation of the wicked di Luna ('Per me ora fatale' from IL TROVATORE), the evil machinations of the spy Barnaba ('Ah! Pescator' from LA GIOCONDA), and the carefree abandon of the dashing Rafaele ('Aprila, bella, la fenestrella' from I GIOIELLI DELLA MADONNA) he leaves all memories of 'an attractive light baritone' far behind him – this has become one of the great Italian operatic voices, with an upper register of quite exceptional beauty and carrying power.

Beauty and carrying power are qualities without which no baritone can become a great Rigoletto, and of this, one of de Luca's most celebrated interpretations, we have three examples on the Nimbus disc – the duets 'Ah! veglia, o donna' and 'Piangi, fanciulla', both with Amelita Galli-Curci at her childlike best, and the great scena from Act II, 'Povero Rigoletto . . . Cortigiani, vil razza dannata'. In the duets de Luca, totally unconcerned by the punishing tessitura, lets his voice flow in an unbroken stream of legato tone, tender, paternal and grieving. In the solo scene, surely the greatest showpiece of all for an Italian baritone, he gives a masterly performance. Through all the shifting moods – sarcasm, fury, heart-break, servility – he never ceases to *sing* and to sing beautifully. Sometimes, as in 'Miei signori perdono, pietate' it is a pathetic beauty; at other times, as in 'D'una tal vittoria, che? . . . adesso non ridete?' ('At a victory like that, eh? . . . now you're not laughing?'), it is a terrible beauty; but always, even when expressing extremes of emotion, for de Luca the 'canto' had to remain 'bello'.

The last, but to me not the least of the delights on this Nimbus disc is a ditty called 'Marietta'. It is in English, and although de Luca's English is always intelligible, which could not be said of Caruso's, it is sufficiently idiosyncratic to have a charm all of its own. The opening couplet 'Marietta, won't you come and play with me? Marietta, you're as cute as you can be' gives an idea of the literary level of the poem, and the jaunty little melody with its town band accompaniment fits it like a glove. It was one of de Luca's favourite party pieces which he sang whenever remotely possible, and I have no doubt that by the time he reached the inevitable line 'Marietta, won' you say you'll *murry* me?' there were plenty of ladies in the audience who would have been only too happy to jump up and shout 'Yes please!'

Another outstandingly successful CD portrait of de Luca, exclusively in opera this time, is provided by *Lebendige Vergangenheit 89036*. (This is an excellent Viennese label, and the rather daunting name simply means 'Living Past'.) Four of the fourteen tracks are duplications with Nimbus ('Largo al factotum', 'Ah! per sempre', 'Il balen' and 'De l'art splendeur immortelle'), but the remainder, all recorded between 1917 and 1924, are without exception valuable additions. We have several more examples of de Luca's authoritative gravitas. As Rossini's Guillaume (or rather Guglielmo) Tell, bidding his son stand motionless for the fateful shooting of the apple (though I do think it is a trifle tactless to encourage him with the words 'Think of your mother who awaits you in Heaven'), as the goat-herd Hoël carrying the unconscious Dinorah in his arms, as King Alfonso of Castile renouncing his beloved in LA FAVORITA, and as the young soldier Valentin (his debut role) committing his sister to the care of the Almighty, de Luca is ever moving and ever dignified. We have his Rodrigo again from DON CARLOS, this time including the extended solo 'Per me giunto' immediately before the actual death scene, and a sensuously phrased account of the one really familiar passage from Massenet's HERODIADE, the aria 'Vision fugitive'. His 'Eri tu' from UN BALLO IN MASCHERA, though wonderfully vocalized, strikes me as too dispassionate and insufficiently venomous, though there is emotion aplenty in yet another RIGOLETTO duet with Galli-Curci. This is the final scene of the opera, and it finds both singers at the peak of their form though for some reason it was never published. Lucky Victor Company if it could afford to keep a recording of this quality gathering dust! We have one fascinating sample of de Luca as a Mozart singer, with a bitingly characterized rendering of Figaro's

'Se vuol ballare' – this was a role which he sang to great effect during his first two seasons at the Met, but which inexplicably never came his way there again – and finally he and that spirited soprano Lucrezia Bori romp through one of my favourite *buffo* duets, 'Pronta io son' from DON PASQUALE.

When de Luca returned to Italy after his Met appearances of 1940 he went on appearing in many of the leading Italian opera houses, but when the Germans occupied Rome he refused to budge from his own home. 'I was not,' he explained later, 'in a good humour'; and he took no trouble to disguise his gratification when an allied bomb flattened the house of his next-door neighbour, Mussolini's propaganda chief Virginio Gayda, with its owner inside it – miraculously without even breaking de Luca's windows. He told his wife that he had lost his appetite for singing, but to use his own words once again 'She tell me "You always in the garden, with the dog and read the book. What is the life?"' So when the war was over, after participating in one or two concerts for allied troops, he decided to return to New York, and he and his wife took ship. It was not the *Conte di Savoia* this time, but a US Liberty ship, with the elderly star sleeping like a GI in an upper bunk for eighteen nights with no change of sheets and (worst of all for him) basic army rations. Safely back in the States he tried out his voice by singing Rigoletto with the Connecticut Opera Company in Hartford, and followed it up with a recital in the New York Town Hall. It was his first for twenty-nine years, and the audience would have been an autograph hunter's paradise. Jeritza, Alda, Rethberg, Martinelli, all the old-timers were there, but the oldest of them all was the one on stage. Needless to say he was greeted yet again with a tremendous ovation, of which he said to a reporter afterwards 'They didn't even know can I still sing. They saying "How do you do, my dear friend?"' The answer to this question was that their dear friend was doing very nicely – as the critic of the *New York World-Telegram* put it 'De Luca is with us again, as spellbinding as ever, as sparkling and alive and sensitive an interpreter as he had ever been before.'

After such a welcome Mr and Mrs de Luca decided to settle once again in New York. He sang a final Barber in the Newark Opera Playhouse – he was sixty-nine, and was described in the press as being 'spry as a cricket' – and shortly before his seventieth birthday came the farewell recital to which I referred at the beginning of the chapter. He took a teaching post at the Juilliard School, made a few more recordings and occasionally contributed a song or two at charity concerts. In the autumn of 1950 he was due to become head of vocal studies at the Curtis Institute in Philadelphia, but during the summer he was taken ill. His first wife had died in the influenza outbreak of 1918 (his second wife was her sister), and he had had a mausoleum built for her with a place in it for himself. It was to this that he referred with almost his last words to his doctor, 'I think you send me to my little white house in Rome.' He died on 4 August 1950 and in accordance with his wishes he was indeed sent to his little white house.

For a brief sketch of de Luca in his old age I would like to turn again to the memoirs of Robert Merrill. 'Now over seventy,' Merrill wrote, 'resting on his laurels and counting his lire, de Luca was an adorable man with sparkling eyes and a gay and open face. With his fringe of white hair round his shiny pate, he looked like a sweet and jolly Benedictine monk.' Anyone, I think, who is familiar with de Luca's recordings is likely to share this feeling of affection. There is nothing flashy about them – they are characterized by human warmth and artistic sincerity. I feel that if I had been lucky enough to hear the great Italian baritones of that time I would have revered Battistini, and I would have been astounded by Titta Ruffo – but I would have loved Giuseppe de Luca.

KIRSTEN FLAGSTAD

NORWEGIAN DRAMATIC SOPRANO

b. Hamar, Norway, 12 July 1895, d. Oslo 7 December 1962

The hardest of all soprano roles to cast are the dramatic heroines in the operas of Richard Wagner, most notably Brünnhilde and Isolde. The demands which they make upon a singer's vocal stamina and sheer physical staying-power are staggering, and the world seldom contains more than one or two interpreters of these roles at any one time who achieve undisputed greatness. During what can be loosely described as the gramophone era various ladies have, for a period, held sway over this domain – the names of Olive Fremstad, Frida Leider and Birgit Nilsson spring to mind – but the most majestic of these uncrowned queens was surely the Norwegian soprano Kirsten Flagstad.

Flagstad's career was one of the century's strangest. Born and bred in a country which was outside the mainstream of operatic life, she performed in obscurity until she reached middle age. During her twenties and thirties she made a habit of announcing her decision to retire, but then in her fortieth year she rocketed, literally overnight, to the highest pinnacle of international acclaim. Of all the twentieth century's great singers she probably set the highest value on her personal privacy, and yet, having inured herself with difficulty to the pressures engendered by universal adulation, she was soon to become a subject of passionate controversy and an object of such violent dislike that crowds demonstrated against her in the streets and a police escort was required to conduct her unharmed into her own recitals.

The name Flagstad originally belonged not to a person, but to a farm. It was in the mid-eighteenth century that one of Kirsten's ancestors adopted the name for himself, because in

those days it carried a considerable social cachet in rural Norway
to own a farm and to be able to call yourself after it. In time the
family began to follow a different calling, and several generations
of Flagstads became gunsmiths, but gunsmiths with an ever more
prevalent streak of musicianship. Kirsten's grandfather combined
looking after the guns of the Oppland County Mounted Cavalry
Corps with playing the horn in their regimental band, and by the
time Kirsten's father came along music had won the day – turning
his back on the guns he became first a professional violinist, and
subsequently a conductor. He supplemented his income by working as a stenographer in the Storting, the Norwegian parliament,
but every evening he performed in Kristiania's Central Theatre,
(Kristiania being the old name for Oslo), and in due course he
married the young lady who trained the chorus, coached the
soloists, and accompanied at rehearsals. Kirsten, the eldest of
four children, grew up surrounded by music. Her mother held
coaching sessions in their house, her father played chamber music
there with a group of friends every Sunday, and Kirsten herself
showed unusual promise as a pianist. While still a schoolgirl she
used to pick up useful pocket money playing for local dances
and theatrical events, and when she was eventually enrolled in
the Conservatory it was with the aim of graduating as a piano
teacher. She had, however, always enjoyed singing. At an early
age she acquired an impressive repertoire of Schubert songs by
working her way through an album (in the contralto key) which
happened to be lying on the family piano; and when her parents
gave her a vocal score of LOHENGRIN for her tenth birthday,
it took her little time to memorize the role of Elsa. That was soon
followed by the title-role in AIDA, but her taste was admirably
eclectic, and when the universal MERRY WIDOW fever struck
Norway in 1907, she scored a considerable hit in family circles,
performing the role of Count Danilo to the Hanna of her cousin
Astrid.

It was a close friend of Flagstad's mother, a voice teacher
named Ellen Schytte Jacobsen, who first persuaded her parents

that it would make sense for the girl to have singing lessons –
although she was going to be a piano teacher, within the somewhat
limited scope of Norwegian musical life it was always helpful to be
an all-rounder, and she might as well learn to use what little voice
she had in a reasonably proficient manner. Thus it came about that
when the National Theatre was due to present d'Albert's *verismo*
opera TIEFLAND, and nobody was considered suitable for the
short but vital role of Nuri, who must be seen to be a very young
girl, Kirsten's mother put her name up for an audition and she was
given the part. On 12 December 1913, in the presence of the King
of Norway, Kirsten Flagstad made her professional debut, and
Oslo's leading critic commented that 'A very melodious voice and
a modest manner show great promise for the future of the young
singer.' The following winter found her back on the stage, this
time as Germaine in Planquette's then very fashionable operetta
LES CLOCHES DE CORNEVILLE, and although the role (as
operetta roles have a habit of doing) emphasized how much she
still had to learn as an actress, once again her voice, small as it
was, met with general approval. Assisted by a providential grant
from a Norwegian businessman who insisted on preserving his
anonymity outside the Flagstad family circle, she set off for two
years of vocal study under a gentleman in Stockholm named Dr
Gillis Bratt, who combined the twin functions of voice teacher
and throat doctor. Before she had completed her studies, however,
she became engaged to a Norwegian salesman named Sigurd Hall,
whereupon she decided that until they were married it would be
sensible to accept an engagement with a newly formed company
in Oslo, known as the Opéra Comique – thereafter, of course,
she would retire from the stage and devote herself exclusively to
looking after her husband and their very small flat.

Things did not turn out that way. For the next ten years Flagstad
was kept consistently busy on Oslo's various musical stages, and
a list of her repertoire makes unexpected reading – seductive
millionairesses in the operettas of Emmerich Kálmán and 'flappers'
in the latest musical comedies rub shoulders with Desdemona in

OTELLO and Amelia in UN BALLO IN MASCHERA. After the birth of her daughter in 1920, and another of her decisions to retire, it was the sensuous melodies of Lehár's ZIGEUNERLIEBE which lured her back to the bright lights, and in all she sang no less than thirty roles in operetta during that time, to only a dozen in opera. (To those of us who first saw and heard Flagstad in the 1940s, the idea of her dancing a csárdás may seem a trifle bizarre, but I do wish someone had been sufficiently imaginative to record her singing Mariza's Entrance Song or 'Komm mit nach Varasdin'.) In 1928 Flagstad received what amounted to giddy professional promotion when she was engaged as leading dramatic soprano by Stora Teatern in Göteborg, Sweden – still distinctly provincial, but a house in which she was able to concentrate for the most part on serious opera. There were still two roles to come which might seem incongruous to those who only know of Flagstad as the greatest Brünnhilde of the century – Lucie in Suppé's operetta DONNA JUANITA, and Mollie Farrell in Richard Rodgers's Broadway hit THE GIRL FRIEND. Several of her operatic roles, too, such as Mimi in LA BOHEME, or Magda in LA RONDINE, lay some distance from what was to become known as Flagstad territory, but it was precisely because she did not rush into the heavy Wagnerian repertoire that she was able in the fullness of time to master it with such sovereign ease. She herself used to compare the preparation required for singing Wagner with weight-lifting – it is essential to take the strain off the actual voice by developing the necessary muscularity elsewhere.

In 1929 Flagstad came back to the National Theatre in Oslo, and with the familiar role of Elsa in LOHENGRIN she dipped a toe for the first time into Wagnerian waters. This was followed by the title-role in TOSCA, and in the audience for her final performance as Puccini's temperamental diva sat a certain Mr Otto Kahn, Chairman of the Metropolitan Opera in New York, and thus one of the most influential figures in the entire operatic firmament. Convinced that Flagstad was destined for higher things, Mr Kahn sent her his card with a request that she should contact him – but she, equally convinced that a small-town soprano could not possibly be of interest to a being as far removed from her humdrum world as the Chairman of the Met, put the card on one side and forgot about it. In any case she had other things on her mind. Her marriage had ground to a halt, and she had fallen in love with a wealthy widower named Henry Johansen; now she was waiting for the completion of her divorce proceedings before marrying him and, of course, retiring from the stage. The piece scheduled for her farewell performance in Göteborg was a basically unsuitable one, Krenek's jazz opera JONNY SPIELT AUF, but it was an emotional occasion, and general regret was expressed that she should so prematurely desert the world of song. Within a year she was back, and in retrospect it seems extraordinary that a person so little given to self-deception as Flagstad should not have realized earlier how strong a compulsion is exercised by the desire to sing. In any case, in her new position as Fru Johansen she only needed to become involved in productions of special significance, and one of these, her first Isolde in June 1932, turned out to be more significant than most. It led to a visit from one of the great Wagnerian stars of the previous generation, the Swedish soprano Ellen Gulbranson, who urged Flagstad to set her sights on Bayreuth, where she could immerse herself in the true Wagnerian style. With characteristic directness Flagstad replied that there was no point in doing that, as Bayreuth would have no interest in her, and she had no interest in an international career, so Gulbranson took the matter into her own hands and wrote to Winifred Wagner. Frau Wagner could not ignore a recommendation from Ellen Gulbranson, and eventually, out of politeness to a respected senior colleague, Flagstad accepted Frau Wagner's invitation, went to Bayreuth and sang an audition. Frau Wagner and her artistic director, Heinz Tietjen, were both delighted with her, so she was engaged for the following summer in the roles of the Third Norn in GÖTTERDÄMMERUNG and Ortlinde in DIE WALKÜRE. They were small parts, naturally, but she was also entrusted with the task of covering two of the leads, and most importantly of all, she fell under the spell of Bayreuth. From then onwards, however much she might on one level yearn for the joys of family life, she recognized that on another level she had a different destiny to fulfil.

Back in Oslo the Norwegian Opera Association celebrated Flagstad's new status as a Bayreuth singer by mounting some more performances of TRISTAN UND ISOLDE, and for the role of King Mark they brought in the great Russian-born bass, Alexander Kipnis. Kipnis was bowled over by the quality of Flagstad's singing, and set about recommending her to various theatres on the international circuit. Suddenly she had a reputation outside the confines of Scandinavia – as Flagstad herself expressed it 'I was soon to discover what it meant to be recommended by Alexander Kipnis.' Her two small roles in Bayreuth went well, and she was offered Sieglinde in DIE WALKÜRE and Gutrune in GÖTTERDÄMMERUNG the following summer. Meanwhile she was to go to Brussels and sing her first Sieglinde there. Naively she asked the management of the Brussels Opera how on earth they had heard of her. 'You were recommended to us by Alexander Kipnis,' came the reply. Then out of the blue came an urgent summons from someone called Eric Semon, the Metropolitan Opera's European agent, to betake herself to Switzerland, and audition for the General Manager, Giulio Gatti-Casazza, in St Moritz. Once again she asked how this had come about – it was, after all, five years since Mr Kahn had contacted her, and that had come to nothing. 'Alexander Kipnis suggested it,' she was told. In any case, the audition was a success, and the list of roles which she was told to bring with her to New York in four months' time, all fully prepared, comprised the small matter of the three Brünnhildes, Isolde, Elsa, Sieglinde, Elisabeth in TANNHÄUSER, Leonore in FIDELIO and the Marschallin in DER ROSENKAVALIER.

Flagstad's Metropolitan debut took place on 2 February 1935 in the role of Sieglinde. The management had kept very quiet about their new acquisition in case she failed to come up to their expectations, and Gatti-Casazza chose a Saturday matinée, always the week's thinnest house, to introduce her to the New York public. He need not have worried. In the whole history of the Metropolitan Opera no debut had ever rivalled the sensation which Flagstad created that afternoon. Funnily enough, as her career developed, few people would have named Sieglinde as a true Flagstad role. To the Covent Garden public, especially, that was Lotte Lehmann's preserve, while Flagstad was regarded as supreme in the 'hochdramatisch' department, as Brünnhilde and Isolde. At her Metropolitan debut, however, Flagstad's Sieglinde was enough to establish her instantaneously as *the* Wagnerian soprano of the day. The critics devoted their entire reviews to unrestrained expressions of ecstatic enthusiasm about every aspect of her performance. 'The singing that we heard yesterday,' wrote Lawrence Gilman in the *New York Herald Tribune*, 'is that of a musician with taste and brains and sensibility, with poetic and dramatic insight. She is solacing to the eye – comely and slim, and sweet of countenance. The voice itself is both lovely and puissant. In its deeper register it is movingly warm and rich and expressive, and yesterday it recalled to wistful Wagnerites the irrecoverable magic of Olive (Fremstad) the immortal. The upper voice is powerful and true, and does not harden under stress.' Olin Downes of the *New York Times* found that 'No Sieglinde of the past ten years has made such an impression here, by her voice, stage business, her intelligence and dramatic sincerity, and by her evident knowledge of Wagner.' The performance was broadcast, and one of the great stars of the previous generation, Geraldine Farrar, acted as commentator. In the first intermission she announced 'Since I spoke to you an hour ago I have heard the greatest singer I have ever listened to in my life – Kirsten Flagstad.' The audience shared her view, and when the final curtain fell they stormed to the front of the stalls, demanding again and again that Flagstad should take a solo bow. As Flagstad herself was to write of the occasion 'What completely took my breath away was the tribute of the audience to me personally.

I was not unfamiliar with applause, but the way the Americans
showed their enthusiasm completely overwhelmed me.'

Quite suddenly Flagstad's life was transformed, and by no
means entirely to her gratification. Her hotel was besieged by
all manner of people, reporters, salesmen of everything under
the sun, deliverymen with armfuls of flowers, and a constant
stream of messenger boys with invitations to this, that and the
other. The publicity department of the Metropolitan Opera,
previously so cautious, went to town on their new star, and
she rapidly emerged as the company's most gilt-edged investment since Caruso. Every one of her appearances for the rest
of the season was instantly sold out, and a severe financial crisis
which had been threatening the future of the Met was solved as
if by magic. The pressure on Flagstad herself was, of course,
tremendous. The expectations aroused for her first Isolde, four
days later, would have been enough to terrify anyone, and she
was later to admit 'For once I was really nervous.' Her triumph,
though, was even greater than it had been as Sieglinde, and this
time the *Herald Tribune* informed its readers that 'Last night's
performance of TRISTAN was made unforgettable for its hear-
ers by a transcendently beautiful and moving impersonation of
Isolde – an embodiment so sensitively musical, so fine-grained
in its imaginative and intellectual texture, so lofty in its pathos
and simplicity, of so memorable a loveliness, that experienced
opera-goers sought among their memories of legendary days to
find its like.'

And so that extraordinary first engagement at the Met rolled
on. In two months Flagstad appeared in seven of the great
Wagnerian roles. Three of them, the WALKÜRE and GÖTTER-
DÄMMERUNG Brünnhildes and Kundry in PARSIFAL, she
was singing for the first time, and it was only a severe bout of
illness which prevented her from singing her first SIEGFRIED
Brünnhilde too. The Met in those days did not waste its resources
on stage rehearsals – the foreign singers were supposed to know
what was required of them – and in most of these roles Flagstad

was simply bundled on. To survive such a baptism of fire, let alone to emerge from it in triumph, a singer clearly needs to possess a most unusual combination of attributes – and Flagstad did. First she was musically rock-solid; secondly she shone across the vast spaces of the old Met as the epitome of youth and beauty, in sharp contrast to certain of the more venerable and less mobile warrior maidens of previous years; and thirdly her voice, by that stage of her career, was an instrument such as had not been heard in living memory, and has not, in my opinion, been heard since.

The earliest example of the Flagstad voice available on CD is the WALKÜRE Battle Cry, which she recorded on her return to the United States for an extended concert tour in October of that same eventful year, and which now comprises part of a Wagner recital on RCA Victor *GD87915*. It was with this passage that Flagstad won a gratifying little victory over the snooty accompanist who played for her at her audition in St Moritz – at their brief rehearsal he made it evident that he was not impressed by unknowns from the provinces, so she let fly at him with 'Ho-jo-to-ho!' and, as she later recalled, 'he nearly tumbled off the piano stool'. During the coming years thousands of opera-goers were to experience the thrill of that riveting vocal outburst, but it has to be regretfully admitted that the recording techniques of 1935 were simply not able to cope with so huge and resplendent an instrument in a passage of such extreme dynamic scope. Perhaps the engineers tumbled off their stools as well – they certainly played safe by putting their new superstar a nice long way away from the microphone. There are other tracks on the disc, however, which give a clearer impression of Flagstad's miraculous vocal quality, notably her 1939 recording of Isolde's 'Liebestod'. From the first note, a wonderfully warm, rich, soft but full-bodied low E flat, through all those endlessly expansive phrases, right up to the glorious high G sharp of the 'Welt-Atems wehendem All' and the final sigh of 'höchste Lust', the tone is of a creamy and effortless lustre. Something which sets this voice apart is that it was not really a dramatic one in the sense that that label is generally used, but rather a lyric one of heroic proportions. By that I mean that the quality is always velvety and smooth, it is never hard or in itself aggressive. Whereas the voice of Flagstad's pre-eminent successor in the Wagner roles, Birgit Nilsson, would be hurled into the auditorium like some gleaming spear, winging its way victoriously *through* the mighty sonorities of Wagner's orchestra, Flagstad's voice simply rolled *over* them, as tireless as the waves of the sea. It was a marvellous feeling, when hearing Flagstad in performance, to sit back in comfort, knowing that whatever storm of passion the orchestra might unleash, Flagstad's next entry would ride it, and without the faintest audible or visible effort. It is normal professional parlance to talk of a singer's 'attack' at the beginning of a phrase, especially a high one, but with Flagstad there was no sense of 'attack'. An entry such as 'Heller schallend' on a high G sharp, when the 'Liebestod' is really getting into its stride, provides a perfect example of what I mean – she seemed merely to open her mouth and the tone was there, waiting. Of course she was capable of electrifying dramatic accents when she needed them – one only has to listen to her monumental rendering of the GÖTTERDÄMMERUNG finale on the final track of this disc to recognize that – but she never had recourse to any harshness or shrillness in order to achieve them.

Other tracks which demonstrate this marvellous smoothness of emission are Elsa's Song to the Breezes, and Sieglinde's 'Du bist der Lenz' from Act I of DIE WALKÜRE. The latter I find particularly interesting, as it encapsulates in two minutes of song the diametrical difference of approach between Flagstad and Lotte Lehmann. In Lehmann's famous version of the whole of Act I under Bruno Walter this passage reaches a red-hot level of urgency and passion. When Lehmann sings a phrase such as 'Als mein Auge dich sah, warst du mein Eigen' ('From the moment I saw you, you were my own'), it seems likely that she may suit the action to the words before she has even had time to leave the stage. When Flagstad sings it, it is a statement of fact – an exciting fact, gloriously expressed, but in no way giving rise to the fear that anything indecorous would occur. This element of emotional reticence on Flagstad's part was something which often aroused negative comment when she appeared, trailing clouds of American glory, in European cities such as London, Vienna and Prague. The singing, everyone agreed, was of an unparalleled splendour, but the stage personality was phlegmatic – an opinion which ran entirely counter to those of the critics in New York who had been enraptured by the depth of Flagstad's insight into the dramatic and psychological content of her roles. In fact Flagstad herself did not admire unbridled passion in a performer. On one of the only three occasions on which she and Lehmann appeared together in DIE WALKÜRE (Flagstad, of course, as Brünnhilde), she greatly hurt Lehmann's feelings by sitting in the wings throughout Act I and not speaking a word to Lehmann afterwards. She went so far as to say some time later in a BBC interview that she was as embarrassed by such emotional abandon as if the singer were undressing in public. This remark would not have surprised anyone whose memory stretched as far back as Flagstad's first romance, at the age of twenty-one, when her fiancé broke off their engagement because he found her too prudish; or the incident when, at the ripe old age of twenty-three, she expressed misgivings about singing the role of Ganymed in Suppé's DIE SCHÖNE GALATHEE, because of the briefness of her costume.

It would, however, be quite wrong to suppose that Flagstad was a mere Nordic ice-maiden, unable or unwilling to generate excitement in her singing. In the Prologue to GÖTTERDÄMMERUNG this disc offers us one of the finest recorded examples of Flagstad really letting fly, both vocally and histrionically, and in the great Danish *Heldentenor* Lauritz Melchior she has the perfect partner. His voice is another that is always pleasing in quality while being heroic in size, and during those last pre-war years at the Met they formed a fabled partnership. On a personal level it had its ups and downs, and in July 1938 Flagstad even felt moved to send

Sir Thomas Beecham a telegram from Australia, followed by a very explicit letter, informing him that she would not be able to sing for him at Covent Garden if Melchior had been engaged as well. 'So many unpleasant incidents have occurred during the past months in my relationship with Mr Melchior,' she wrote, 'that for some time now I have determined not to accept any engagements where his services are also involved.'* I am not sure what the Great Dane did to make her feel better, but by the time they recorded the GÖTTERDÄMMERUNG Prologue, a little over a year later, they sounded like a convincingly adoring couple once again; and on the final track of this particular disc they combine to give an equally compelling account of that emotionally most demanding of scenes, the long Act II duet for Kundry and Parsifal. Two more samples of this celebrated partnership are to be found on another RCA Victor disc (*GD87914*), which is basically devoted to Melchior. They are a heavily cut version of the LOHENGRIN Bridal Chamber Scene, and a less heavily cut version of the TRISTAN Love Duet; and although there are plenty of shortcomings both in the quality of the recording and in the playing of the San Francisco Opera Orchestra under the inexperienced baton of Flagstad's faithful pianist, Edwin McArthur, the singing is thrilling in the extreme.

When the war broke out in Europe, Flagstad was in the United States, and so was her daughter, who married an American and settled down there, but Henry Johansen was at home in Norway. On 9 April 1940 the Germans invaded both Norway and Denmark. Flagstad was distraught, as was Melchior. For another year Flagstad remained in the States, and included in her activities many concerts for Norwegian relief funds. Early in 1941 she received a series of telegrams from her husband urging her to come home,

---

* The following year Sir Thomas was to have further trouble with Flagstad's contract following what he saw as a bit of sharp practice by Eric Semon's agency in New York. One of his telegrams ended with a splendid flourish – 'I resent deeply this double dealing and bad faith and shall expose the same in every newspaper in the United States and British Empire. Stop. Thomas Beecham.'

and in April of that year, against the advice of all her friends and colleagues, she did so. The journey, via Lisbon, Madrid, Barcelona and Berlin, was a hazardous one. Today people might look back on Flagstad's willingness to face the dangers of travel and the rigours of life under German occupation in order to be with her husband, as admirable, or even heroic. At the time, however, it was viewed differently. As the Norwegian Ambassador in the United States was later to express it, Norway was at war with Germany, and the heroes of the hour were the many young people who set out, some in open boats, to join the forces abroad and fight the common enemy.

The current was going *out* from Norway, and then suddenly the most famous Norwegian in America decides to go, for purely personal reasons, against that current and back to a land ruled by the enemy. The most damning aspect of it all was that Henry Johansen was a member of Quisling's Nasjonal Samling Party, and in certain people's eyes Flagstad was inevitably tarred with the same brush – whereas in fact she was instrumental in persuading Johansen to resign from the NS, and she never once sang for the Germans in Norway, restricting her wartime engagements to appearances in neutral Sweden and Switzerland. On 13 May 1945, five days after the German surrender, Johansen was arrested by the Norwegian authorities on a charge of profiteering through business deals with the enemy, and for Flagstad a nightmare period began. There was no charge of any kind against her, but the courts froze her assets along with her husband's and forbade her to leave the country. Johansen had been in prison for nine months when Flagstad received word that he was seriously ill, and six months later he died, with the case still unresolved.

At last in November 1946 Flagstad was given a new passport and allowed to leave the country. With her fortune impounded she desperately needed to start earning money again, and at her first few concerts, in Cannes and Paris, she found to her delight that her voice, at the age of fifty-one, was showing no sign whatever of deterioration. On 6 February 1947 she marked her return to London with a concert at the Albert Hall, and when she walked onto the stage the entire audience rose to its feet and cheered. Britain, which had only been separated from the German army by the width of the English Channel, had no quarrel with Kirsten Flagstad, but in the distant United States a hate campaign of unbelievable ferocity was being mounted against her in certain sections of the press. They claimed that she had given concerts for the German troops in Norway, and even that she had sung for Hitler in Berlin. She was reported to have declared that only in the Third Reich could an artist find true appreciation – there was no end to the rubbish that the papers wrote, and that many people consequently believed. On her first post-war concert tour of the States she needed every scrap of her native stubbornness to survive. Her audiences were friendly – it was only in Philadelphia that demonstrators actually found their way into the hall, making their presence felt with stink bombs, rotten vegetables and so on – but outside in the streets extraordinary scenes were enacted. Groups of ex-servicemen paraded up and down with banners saying such things as **LET FREEDOM SING, NOT FLAGSTAD** and **KIRSTEN ENTERTAINED NAZIS, WE FOUGHT THEM,** and in several cities they did their best to prevent ticket-holders from entering the hall. Flagstad herself, and the ever-loyal Edwin McArthur, had to be accompanied by armed police wherever they went, and (perhaps the unkindest cut of all for Flagstad) the doors of the Metropolitan Opera remained firmly closed. The Chicago Opera was the first American company to risk using Flagstad again, in November 1947. Two years later San Francisco followed suit, though there were countless threats of sabotage if she were allowed to sing, and TRISTAN had to be performed with the whole house, including the backstage area, teeming with police. Even as late as 1951, when the Met under its new manager Rudolf Bing at last showed the courage to ask her back, she was deluged with anonymous abuse, and Fritz Reiner had to conduct the opening bars of the TRISTAN Prelude with the house lights on so that the Chief of Police, seated in a central box, could survey the auditorium. Flagstad herself still had to be escorted on stage by her customary armed guards, but if she had harboured any doubts as to how the public might feel about her, they were very soon dispelled. When the curtain went up to reveal her lying on her couch there was such a tumultuous demonstration of enthusiasm that Reiner had to lay down his baton until normality was restored. After a welcome like that, Flagstad must have felt a particular irony in Isolde's opening utterance – 'Wer wagt mich zu höhnen?', 'Who dares to sneer at me?'.

One thing was immediately obvious to anybody hearing Flagstad at that time – her voice was still an instrument of quite astonishing beauty and power. I myself first heard her as Isolde at Covent Garden in 1948, and though I had to bow to the superior knowledge of those who declared that there was a mite less shine about the very top of the voice than there had been in pre-war seasons, it was hard to imagine how that could be possible. One thing had undeniably disappeared, and that was the impression of comeliness and youth which had so enraptured the New Yorkers in 1935. The Flagstad of my time was a matronly Irish maid, and Covent Garden's staging did not assist by raising the curtain to reveal her lying on her side with her back to the audience, so that the first thing one saw, swathed in dark red velvet, was a large and imposing posterior. There was a majestic dignity about her physical presence though, and a nobility in everything she did. Her stillness on stage could perhaps have been mistaken for placidity, but when she opened the floodgates of her regal temper in 'Fluch dir, Verruchter!' ('A curse on you, infamous one!') I would certainly not have wished to be the 'Verruchter' in question. The carpet of sound which she spread around her in the Love Duet, and the incredible reserves of richness with which she unfolded phrase after phrase of the 'Liebestod' were things which one is not often given to experience – and when I heard her repeat the role as her farewell to the Covent Garden public in 1951 I cannot pretend that my ear could detect any hint of deterioration.

The undiminished lyricism of the Flagstad voice during the

immediate post-war period is well captured by a recording which she made in London in 1948 of Elisabeth's Prayer from TANN-HÄUSER and which has now been reissued as part of a fascinating four-disc set entitled 'Wagner Singing on Record' (EMI *CMS 7 64008 2*). The brilliance of Flagstad's tone and the expansiveness of the phrasing would be the envy of most sopranos twenty years her junior, and indeed it is one of the numerous oddities of Flagstad's career that several of her most impressive recordings were made around the time of her final, irrevocable retirement from the stage, and others several years later.

One of the most valuable of these, as it gives us the only example of a famous Flagstad role in its entirety, is the complete TRISTAN, recorded in 1952 and now back with us on four CDs as EMI *CDS 7 47322 8*.* The Tristan, Ludwig Suthaus, though outsung by her (which *Heldentenor* in the period between Melchior and Vickers would not have been?) has many virtues to recommend him, not least his vivid use of text, and the choice of conductor fell on the man with whom, of all the world's great musicians, Flagstad had the greatest rapport – Wilhelm Furtwängler. She had sung the

---

* Since this chapter was written EMI have issued a TRISTAN set, (*CHS 7 64037 2* – three CDs) made up from two live performances at Covent Garden in 1936 and 1937, one conducted by Fritz Reiner and the other by Sir Thomas Beecham. It incorporates several of the cuts customarily made in stage performance and naturally the tone quality and balance cannot compare with a studio recording, but luckily TRISTAN is a piece in which the protagonists do spend a great deal of time downstage centre, and more or less stationary, so that several of the set pieces fare better than one might expect. In this imperfect world it does not often happen that the century's most phenomenal interpreters of two such roles as Isolde and Tristan are at their peak at the same time and in the same place, and to me the true value of this set lies in the fact that it has captured just such a miraculous occurrence, and captured it in the white heat of action. This is not the place to expand on the subject of Melchior's prowess, but as far as Flagstad is concerned it is fascinating to hear at how much higher a voltage she performed on stage than in a studio. This is the voice which extracted such superlatives from the New York critics – an instrument of unsurpassed loveliness, huge but supple, glowing and tireless, with the 'Liebestod' surely the most compelling of all Flagstad's recorded versions. Both conductors hold the performance at a high emotional level, and Herbert Janssen's fresh-voiced, deeply committed Kurwenal is fully worthy of the illustrious company in which he finds himself.

three Brünnhildes under him during the 1937 Coronation Season at Covent Garden, and the FIDELIO Leonore in the Salzburg Festival of 1949. They had worked together at La Scala, and in May 1950 they gave the first performance of Richard Strauss's 'Vier letze Lieder' in a concert at the Albert Hall.* Musically they were 'ein Herz und eine Seele', 'one heart and one soul', and on the recording it shows. The sweep and grandeur of Furtwängler's conception find in her their ideal interpreter, and though, score in hand and searching carefully, one can detect individual notes which would have been even more glorious fifteen years before, that is surely not what Isolde is about.

Unfortunately, however, there were two individual notes in the recording which were enough to cause an almighty rumpus. Twice, at the beginning of Act II, during the ecstatic reunion of the frantic lovers, Isolde has to flick up to a high C, and Flagstad felt that it was now beyond her to do this again and again, as is usually necessary in a recording session. Accordingly Elisabeth Schwarzkopf obliged by singing the high Cs for her and, as it was so cleverly done that nobody listening to the final result could possibly spot the subterfuge, EMI decided to keep quiet about it. Inevitably though, somebody let the cat out of the bag, and in no time this trivial affair was whipped up into such proportions that it even hit the front pages of the least artistically-minded London newspapers. Flagstad felt betrayed and humiliated, and from her home in Norway she bluntly announced that she would never make another recording as long as she lived.

Now one of Flagstad's most valued friends once said of her 'I have never met anyone else who could say "No" with such enormous and unarguable conviction', and on this occasion it seemed likely that she might hammer the point home by calling on the services of Loge, and surrounding her Nordic fastness with a protective barrier of magic fire. Thanks, however, in no small

---

* Strauss, who died in September 1949, had specifically requested that the unveiling of these songs, the final flowering of his creative genius, should be entrusted to Flagstad.

degree to the intercession of the British actor Bernard Miles, a man in whom she placed implicit trust, and to the persuasive charm of Decca's new recording manager, John Culshaw, the situation was saved – as long as nobody from EMI ever darkened her doors again, and as long as various other rather onerous conditions were met, she was prepared after all to rescind her draconian decree. Shortly before her sixty-first birthday she made a peerless recording of Wagner's 'Wesendonck Lieder', with the Vienna Philharmonic Orchestra under Hans Knappertsbusch, a conductor whose flair for theatrical magic in live performance was not always reproduced in the artificial environment of the recording studio, but who seems to have achieved the same kind of rapport with Flagstad in these five songs as Furtwängler did in TRISTAN. By this stage of her vocal career Flagstad's singing had acquired a kind of monumental authority, and such weighty phrases as 'Erkennt der Mensch des Ew'gen Spur, und löst dein Rätsel, heil'ge Natur' ('Man recognizes the mark of the Eternal, and solves thy riddle, holy Nature') emerge as if uttered by some latter-day Erda, imparting deathless truths to a benighted race. The recording, especially in its modern guise as DECCA *414 624-2*, provides much more ample space for the sheer size of the voice than had been technically possible in the days of Flagstad's prime, and its lustrous flow is still miraculously unimpaired by those ravages of time, to which mere mortals expect to find themselves exposed. In Mahler's 'Kindertotenlieder', on the same disc and with the same orchestra, this time under Sir Adrian Boult, the tonal majesty is used to express such a profundity of restrained and dignified grief that I find myself sharing Alma Mahler's view – why on earth did the composer wish to set these agonizing poems to music? The grief inherent in the 'Lieder eines fahrenden Gesellen', which complete the disc, is much more easily supportable.

Wonderful as the singing is on this 'Lieder' disc, I think one would have to hail Flagstad's Brünnhilde in Act III of DIE WALKÜRE, with Solti and the Vienna Philharmonic, as an even more astonishing memorial to her vocal and interpretative

powers. It is on DECCA *425 986–2*, and mercifully the glories of
stereophonic sound had burst on the world just in time to provide
the worthiest framework in which her recorded voice was ever set.
Though in the public's imagination she was probably most closely
identified with the figure of Isolde (she did sing it no less than
182 times), I cannot help thinking that Brünnhilde was truly her
greatest impersonation. The figure of the Nordic warrior maid,
helmet on head and spear in hand, must surely have struck louder
echoes of primeval kinship within such a fiercely patriotic breast
as Flagstad's, than that of the 'schmucke Irin', the 'fetching Irish
girl', who was Isolde. From Brünnhilde's first hectic entrance,
fiercely determined at whatever cost to herself that Sieglinde
should be protected; in the unshakeable conviction of rectitude
with which she defends her actions before Wotan; and with the
resolute pride of that final demand, that her place of banishment
should be made impenetrable to any but the world's most intrepid
hero, this is Wagner singing on the grandest of scales, with no
apologies needed for the fact that Flagstad's professional debut
now lay nearly forty-four years behind her.

For the role of Sieglinde, which Flagstad recorded a few months
later, the singing is undeniably too stately to be ideal. At the age
of sixty-two she was naturally even further from the uninhibited
torrents of spring than she had been at her New York debut,
but it was a role for which she always had a deep affection. She
specifically requested that it should feature in her farewell season
at Covent Garden in 1951, and six years later she was still positively keen to record it. On DECCA *425 963–2* the performance
(with Knappertsbusch in charge of the Vienna Philharmonic
again) sounds exactly what it was – Sieglinde, superbly sung by
Brünnhilde. Nobody who is willing to forget for the nonce that
Sieglinde is an impetuous young woman being swept off her feet
could fail to be bowled over by the glory of the Flagstad sound;
but, as far as characterization is concerned, Flagstad at this stage
of her life was definitely more at home when for the first time she
undertook the mezzo role of Wotan's formidable wife Fricka, in

Decca's celebrated three-disc set of DAS RHEINGOLD (DECCA *414 101–2*). I attended one or two of those sessions, held in Vienna, and well remember the sight of Flagstad, looking for all the world like anybody's favourite grandmother, as she sat at the back of the stage doing her knitting, while Culshaw and his staff busied themselves around her, preparing the whole vast apparatus for the next 'take'. To certain younger members of the cast she was merely a name from a previous age, and they did not feel at all happy about being called to piano rehearsals – necessitated, so they assumed, by the fact that the old girl did not know her role. The moment she opened her mouth, however, the story was rather different, and I remember Eberhard Wächter, the brilliant 29-year-old Donner, saying to me in astonishment 'She's the only one of us who really knows how to sing!' For many years, in Flagstad's usual soprano repertoire, the lower register of her voice had been of a resonance and sonority which would have put many a mezzo to shame, and although the RHEINGOLD Fricka is a comparatively minor role, Flagstad had no difficulty in dominating when she needed to. Indeed, her capability in this respect was not restricted to her work. At one point during the recording Decca gave a large party, attended not only by the RHEINGOLD cast but by many of the company's Italian stars as well, and, as John Culshaw was to put it in his book *Ring Resounding*, 'in a room full of strong and even overdeveloped personalities, her domination was absolute. I have never met anyone else who could exude, at one and the same time, such warmth *and* reserve.'

It was this same unlikely harmony of warmth and reserve which characterized Flagstad's persona as a recitalist. Standing totally still beside the piano she appeared to some people to be almost uninvolved, but that was her way – her voice was the instrument through which the words and music spoke to her listeners, and physical gesture was superfluous. Unfortunately her concert repertoire is lamentably under-represented on CD, and apart from the Mahler cycles mentioned above, all we have is five songs as part of a Grieg selection in the Decca *Weekend*

Classics series (DECCA *425 512-2*). They date from the very end of her recording career, and when one hears her, with her years of ceaseless travel behind her, singing the intensely evocative songs of her foremost national composer in her native tongue and with the orchestra conducted by her friend and compatriot Øivin Fjeldstad, one does not need to be fluent in Norwegian to sense the feeling of a great artist happily back home. The songs cover a wide emotional range, from the almost skittish exhilaration of 'Og jeg vil ha mig en hjaertenskjaer' ('And I will have me a sweetheart') to the drama of 'Efterårsstormen'('Autumn Storms'), and if anyone were to doubt whether Flagstad's voice in her mid-sixties could still be called genuinely beautiful, I would refer them to the opening bars of 'Til en' No. 1 ('To the one' No. 1).

Flagstad's official farewell recital in London took place during Coronation Week, 1953, when she and her accompanist, Ivor Newton, decided that the only way to stop the applause would be for her to sing the British National Anthem as her final encore. The first bar took the audience by surprise – by the third bar they were all on their feet, standing dutifully to attention. She was in fact to appear once again before her devoted London public. On 7 September 1957, at the special request of Sir Malcolm Sargent, she participated in a Promenade Concert at the Albert Hall wearing full Norwegian national costume to mark the fiftieth anniversary of the death of Edvard Grieg. She sang nine songs, and this time as her final encore she very purposefully chose 'Jeg elsker dig', 'I love you'. It was the last song that she ever sang outside Norway.

The last time that I heard Kirsten Flagstad (other than in a recording session) was as Dido in Purcell's DIDO AND AENEAS, which she sang in London no less than eighty-six times between 1951 and 1953. She did so as a labour of love to help her friend Bernard Miles with the launching of his Mermaid Theatre – she charged no fee, her contract merely stipulating that the management should provide her between performances (the opera, a short one, was given twice nightly) with a plentiful supply of stout. It was a remarkable experience to hear her scaling down that vast and majestic voice to suit an auditorium which seated precisely 176 people, but she did so with her usual sovereign ease, and when, in the third of these seasons, Miles was able to move to a larger venue, she chose it for her final farewell to the operatic stage. What could have been more apt, after all, than to close her career in the theatre with the final words of Dido's Lament, 'Remember me, remember me'?

Flagstad was much better than most superstars at handling retirement. Her home in Norway was run on meticulous lines, and she liked everything around her to be neat and tidy and of the highest quality. She herself had embroidered all her immaculate table linen, and the housekeeper knew the exact moment at which to appear every evening with a glass of her mistress's favourite champagne. Unlike most singers Flagstad was not gregarious, and although close friends were always welcome and treated with unfailing courtesy, she was not at her ease with strangers, and floundered badly if small talk was required. In any case, genuine retirement was not to last long. In 1958 plans were hatched to found a Norwegian National Opera Company, and to her genuine surprise, Flagstad was invited to become its general manager. She flung herself into her duties with tireless energy and in February of the following year the company was ready to open its doors – it can scarcely have been a coincidence that the work selected for its launch was d'Albert's TIEFLAND, in which a certain shy piano student had become unexpectedly involved all that time ago. It was Flagstad's hope to remain at the helm of the Norwegian Opera for its first five years, but within less than half that time she was obliged by failing health to resign her position. After a long and painful illness she died at the age of sixty-seven, and I suppose it is too much to hope that some of those people who had caused her such distress with the violence of their hostility in the immediate post-war years might have heard with some feeling of shame of the message on King Olav's wreath at her funeral – 'To a true daughter of Norway, who did much for her country.'

TITO
GOBBI

ITALIAN BARITONE

b. Bassano del Grappa, 24 October 1913, d. Rome 5 March 1984

To a certain extent Tito Gobbi, like his great predecessor Giuseppe de Luca, represents a triumph of mind over matter. Of course his voice was a very beautiful one, with a richly individual timbre, but I would not call it the most beautiful baritone voice of his generation nor the most powerful, and yet for over twenty years he dominated the Italian repertoire in a manner unrivalled by any of his competitors. He did so through his intelligence and the force of his personality, and though one might expect his recorded legacy to be impoverished by the loss of his physical presence and formidable impact as an actor, ironically almost the reverse is true. What he lacked as a singer on stage, notably the brilliant carrying upper register of a Robert Merrill or an Ettore Bastianini, he learnt to disguise with consummate skill in the recording studio, while the virtues of vocal characterization, which he possessed and cultivated to a rare degree, are preserved in their full array of imaginative detail.

Gobbi was not born into the same grinding poverty as so many other great Italian singers, but even so his early years were occasionally turbulent. His family were well-to-do shopkeepers in Bassano del Grappa, a country town in the Veneto, dealing in such things as agricultural equipment, bathroom fittings and general ironmongery. His father, Giovanni, however, who was an exceptionally handsome man, had a tendency, as Gobbi himself put it, 'to live up to his name', and from time to time found it expedient to escape the jealous husbands of Bassano by remembering urgent business in South America. During these periods the family finances became precarious, and when Gobbi decided to pursue his budding interest in singing, and headed south for

Rome in search of a teacher, he did so with very little money in his pocket.

Finding the right teacher is not a simple matter at the best of times, and it is certainly not the best of times when you only have enough cash to pay either for lessons or for food, but not for both. Some very potent guardian angel must have been smiling on the young Gobbi though, because he obtained an introduction to the once celebrated tenor Giulio Crimi, who not only took him on as a pupil, but also, when he noticed that Gobbi came to his lessons looking thinner and thinner, took him into his household free of charge and waived his fees until Gobbi should be earning enough to repay him. Moreover, on the day when Gobbi auditioned for Crimi, Crimi's daughter had a schoolfriend with her who was something of a pianist. This young lady played for Gobbi's audition, subsequently became his regular accompanist and in the fullness of time his wife – and as if that were not in itself a more remarkable slice of luck than anyone has the right to expect, who should her father be but Raffaello de Rensis, one of the most distinguished musicologists in Italy, whose house was frequented by the crème de la crème of Roman musical life.

All of this was naturally very good news for Gobbi, but in the opera business patronage and nepotism can only take you a very short distance – when you get out on stage either you can do it or you can't. Gobbi's early professional experiences were discouraging. He endured a dismally unsuccessful debut in a bass role in LA SONNAMBULA in a town called Gubbio; and shortly afterwards he stepped in at a moment's notice at La Scala Milan to sing the one line 'La Signoria del Doge e del Senato' in the world premiere of Pizzetti's opera ORSEOLO but unfortunately sang it at the wrong moment. Things improved when he picked up the first prize in a lucrative international singing competition in Vienna, but the operatic world still declined to recognize his prowess, and for a time he drifted into films. Then came another terrifying last minute takeover, this time of the long and taxing role of Germont in LA TRAVIATA, which of course he had never sung before, in Rome's number two opera house, the Teatro Adriano. A barely imaginable feat – it is alarming enough if one has to step in without rehearsal in a role that one has sung many times elsewhere. In any case, Gobbi survived the ordeal and it proved to be a milestone in his artistic development because it brought him to the attention of one of the greatest of all Italian opera conductors, Tullio Serafin, Musical Director of Rome's Teatro Reale.

There can be no greater good fortune for a young singer at the outset of his career than to get into the hands of one of those rare beings who understand how to nurture talent rather than merely exploit it, and on that list of honour the name of Serafin stands written in large letters. Gobbi spent the next six years as a company member at the Teatro Reale, and during that time he studied no less than sixty-six roles. Some of them he learnt merely as part of his operatic education, some he prepared as a 'cover' (the operatic term for an understudy), and others he was actually allowed to perform on stage. It was four years before Serafin judged him ready to undertake a part such as Posa in DON CARLOS, but once he began to sing these great roles in a framework worthy of his artistic talents Gobbi soon made it evident that he was very much a force to be reckoned with.

It was Gobbi's misfortune, however, to arrive on the scene in very troubled times. The year in which he joined the Teatro Reale was 1937. By the time he was beginning to make a name for himself the war was raging, and after the capitulation of Italy in the September of 1943 Rome was under German occupation. On the erstwhile allies who had ratted on them the Germans saw fit to impose an occupation of a particularly ferocious kind, and in common with everyone else in the city Gobbi lived through a number of hair-raising experiences. The immediate post-war period, too, was a confusing and uncongenial time. The recent political upheavals inevitably engendered an atmosphere of mistrust and retribution, and in a milieu as prone to intrigue as the world of opera certain people's careers rose or fell for reasons that had little to do with their artistic capabilities. For Gobbi, though, the international scene was beckoning. 1947 saw him guesting in Stockholm, in 1948 he gave his first concert at the Albert Hall and made his first trip to the States, and within a short time he was one of the most regular travellers on the international operatic circuit.

Gobbi's recording career began in July 1942, during his Rome Opera period, and four fascinating tracks from this particular session are included on an EMI CD entitled 'Tito Gobbi – Italian Opera Arias' (*CDM 7 63109 2*). This is in general a beautifully compiled disc, giving us twenty-one arias, several of them from comparatively unfamiliar operas, and taking us up to the year 1963 – in other words a comprehensive sample of Gobbi at his best. The recital begins with his very first recording, 'Come due tizzi accesi' from Cilea's L'ARLESIANA, and by the time we have heard one phrase we are aware of an arrestingly powerful artistic presence. This is Gobbi at twenty-eight, and it is interesting to note how many of his outstanding virtues are already on parade. It is a characteristic throughout the recital that the very first bar of each track makes you sit up and listen – every time you are made instantly aware that this is *somebody*. A striking dramatic imagination is always at work. This is a singer who does not go in for generalized emotion – every individual phrase, every single word of the aria is given its own colour and significance. At this early stage of his life the voice was more lush and sumptuous than it was later on when a certain dryness entered the upper register. He certainly crowns the L'ARLESIANA number with a juicier high A flat than I would ever have expected from him at the peak of his career, and in general the tone quality amply justifies the billing of 'Italy's most romantic baritone', which he was to receive a few years later when he filmed *The Glass Mountain* with Michael Denison and Dulcie Gray.

The fruits of that 1942 session continue with two mellifluous excerpts from Leoncavallo's ZAZÀ, the predictably irresistible

'Zazà, piccola zingara' as well as the less familiar 'Buona Zazà' from Act II, and conclude with Gobbi's first recorded sample of what was to become one of his most celebrated interpretations on the international stage, Posa in Verdi's DON CARLOS. Here we have the final pages of the death scene, and whether it was due to Gobbi's innate artistry or to the fact that he had recently made his first appearance in the role under the guidance of Maestro Serafin, it is already an arrestingly mature performance. Gobbi loved digging deeply into opera's more complex characters – baritones on the whole have a better chance of this than tenors, who are often one-dimensional purveyors of lyrical emotion – and Posa is a case in point. It is no coincidence that Verdi gives him one of his most affecting phrases when he sings the words 'Io morrò, ma lieto in core, chè potei così serbar' ('I am dying, but happy in heart that I should be able thus to be of service'). Now, what vocal colour do you choose for a man who is distraught to be taking his last farewell of his most devoted friend and of life itself, but is proud to be doing so in the service of his country? Conflicting emotions – the kind of challenge which always finds Gobbi at his best.

We certainly find him dabbing at a very different palette for the next item on this disc, Iago's 'Era la notte'. It is the scene in which he relates to Otello his lubricious account of Cassio talking in his sleep, and Gobbi uses a strongly characteristic and insidiously evil sound for the opening phrases. He himself, a more than mildly talented amateur painter, used to call this his 'yellow' tone, and he slithers like some odious reptile round Verdi's flesh-creeping chromatics. He pours his venom into the ear of Otello as sneakily as Claudius must have poured the liquid version into that of Hamlet's father, and though it does raise the question even more starkly than usual of how Otello could fail to realize that he was dealing with a 'demi-devil', that is Shakespeare and that is opera! A track or two further on Gobbi proves that he is equally at home as a delightfully puffed up Belcore in L'ELISIR D'AMORE. This was the first of the many roles in which I was lucky enough to see Gobbi in action, on the occasion of his Covent Garden debut with the company of La Scala in 1950, and a real ripe rendering it was too. The comic side of his repertoire is further represented by a delightful snippet from his celebrated Falstaff, and other samples of his mastery in the Verdian repertoire are provided by Iago's 'Credo', as well as arias from LA FORZA DEL DESTINO, NABUCCO, MACBETH, and SIMON BOCCANEGRA.

This remarkable disc also includes one other Verdi aria which I would like to discuss in some detail, as it makes unusually varied demands on the singer's interpretative powers, and thus demonstrates to the full those qualities which invested Gobbi with his particular greatness. In UN BALLO IN MASCHERA Renato can in a sense be considered the villain of the piece in that he assassinates the tenor, but in fact he is a good man wronged, a noble soul driven to an extreme act of vengeance because he has reason to believe that his ruler and dearest friend has seduced his wife Amelia; once again, conflicting emotions – rich territory for the mature Verdi and a perfect canvas for the vocal brush of Tito Gobbi. His great scene opens with a recitative of gripping dramatic expressiveness, and with the very first word, 'Alzati' ('Arise'), addressed to his prostrate wife, Gobbi sets the listener's spine tingling; outrage, revulsion, the appalling tension of an impending explosion – they are all packed into these three syllables. As the orchestra softens the mood, and Renato reflects that it is not really on his wife that the full force of his vengeance should fall, Gobbi manages with a sudden change of inflection on the three words 'suo fragile petto' to reveal to us the aching depth of his previous love for Amelia; which in turn gives way to a superbly implacable hatred as he faces the huge portrait of his betrayer hanging on the wall above him and hurls at it the words 'there is another whose blood will have to wipe away this offence – il sangue tuo!' The scene has now been grippingly set for the ensuing aria, the mighty 'Eri tu', with its majestic sweep of fury and grief, and Gobbi unfolds it as a masterly whole composed of ceaselessly telling parts.

For me, apart from the pure pleasure of listening to a great piece of operatic writing supremely realized, this track serves as a reminder of one particular red letter evening at Covent Garden in November 1953. The opera was BALLO, the singers were the regular company members who in those days sang the whole repertoire in English, and as the performance was about to begin the customary groan went up when a gentleman in a dinner jacket appeared before the curtain. Mr Jess Walters (the admirable house baritone), he informed us, was indisposed; but it was noticeable that he did not exude quite the air of apology which one has the right to expect on such occasions, and the reason soon became evident. The last minute replacement was to be – (nicely timed pause) – Signor Tito Gobbi! At which, of course, there was a roar of approval and the gentleman retreated behind the curtain having enjoyed his finest hour. This was, however, nothing compared to the roar that greeted Gobbi at the end of the 'Eri tu'. We were all starved of great Italian singing at that time, and this had been the real thing. It was also a performance which might easily have tumbled into catastrophe – a state of affairs which always adds piquancy to the proceedings – because we were not only presented with a star singer singing in a different language from the rest of the cast (a not infrequent phenomenon in opera), but with one who was not quite sure on which side of the Atlantic he was supposed to be performing. BALLO, as Verdi originally wrote it, was about the assassination of King Gustavus III of Sweden, but after interference by the censors he was obliged to reset it in Boston, with the King becoming the Governor, Riccardo, Conte di Warwick. The Royal Opera, however, had restored the piece to its original setting, so that Gobbi found himself being addressed not as Renato but as Anckarstroem, and while his fellow conspirators were plotting in English to kill the King, he was urging them in Italian to kill the Count. Moreover, when the moment arrived for Gobbi to obey Verdi's stage directions and plunge his dagger into the King/Count's chest, he found a chorus singer slipping a pistol into his hand and hissing 'In London we shoot him!' All in all a memorable evening.

But to return to the CD recital. There are two other tracks which I would like to single out for comment. The first is Jack Rance's solo 'Minnie, dalla mia casa' from Act I of Puccini's LA FANCIULLA DEL WEST. Rance, the sheriff who loves the heroine and hates the hero, is often portrayed as merely coarse and brutal, but Gobbi, as his singing of this passage indicates, made a far more interesting figure out of him, extracting every available ounce of sympathy from his expressively written vocal line. He made a handsome fellow of him too, no mere unshaven lout. The second track is a scene from Cilea's ADRIANA LECOUVREUR, which demonstrates perhaps more clearly than any other number on the disc what a rare gift Gobbi possessed for reproducing stage skills in the recording studio. Michonnet, stage director of the Comédie Française, is secretly in love with the actress Adriana Lecouvreur and is watching her from off-stage while she, invisible to the operatic audience, is giving one of her most inspired performances. He maintains a running commentary on her opening monologue. 'Bene . . . benissimo . . . così . . . così,' he sings, and then, as his enthusiasm mounts, 'stupenda! . . . mirabile! . . . sublime!' – a series of interjections superimposed by Cilea with considerable theatrical effect over the lush background of Adriana's principal theme, which wells up from the orchestra. Even in the theatre it is never easy to persuade an audience that you can genuinely see something which they cannot. To set the scene as vividly as Gobbi does in the prosaic surroundings of a recording studio is an even more remarkable achievement.

Luckily Gobbi, like Jussi Björling, was at the peak of his career when the record companies started to turn out a steady supply of operatic full sets, and several of his finest roles are available in their entirety. Between them they offer us splendid examples of Gobbi in his comic, romantic, dramatic and tragic veins – and, in his immortal Falstaff, one glorious combination of all four. On many of these sets he was teamed with Maria Callas – indeed, it is because of her rather than him that they have been reissued on CD. In certain operas she was, of course, the supreme star of the show. In the classic LUCIA DI LAMMERMOOR (EMI *CMS 7 69980 2 – two discs*) conducted by Serafin and recorded in 1953, Gobbi does everything that can be done with the somewhat uninteresting figure of Enrico, while inevitably remaining in the background compared to La Divina in perhaps her most totally successful role, and Giuseppe di Stefano on his best behaviour as Edgardo. The same is true of his Alfio in CAVALLERIA RUSTICANA, while Callas as Santuzza and di Stefano as Turiddu let rip with full-throated abandon; but in the twinned recording of PAGLIACCI his Tonio moves menacingly into the foreground (EMI *CDS 7 47981 8 – three discs*). This is another Serafin set, recorded eighteen months after the LUCIA, and it is vibrant with unbridled Latin passion. Gobbi encompasses the pathetic side of Tonio's nature as persuasively as the vicious – indeed, so touchingly does he lay bare his tender emotions to Nedda that the savagery of her response leaves us feeling that Miss Nedda deserves quite a bit of what she ultimately gets. In any case, the recording must have been a straightforward assignment for Gobbi compared to the occasion of his first Tonio on stage. That had been in Palermo in December 1941, when most of the audience stayed away because of the air raids. Gobbi's Prologue, nevertheless, was greeted with prolonged calls for an encore, to which he responded by explaining to the audience that with so few people out front the cast could not possibly start repeating numbers. This produced the retort from 'the gods' that surely the intrepid few who had braved the hazards of war deserved special consideration, and in the end the whole audience betook themselves to the front few rows of the stalls, and the opera started again from the beginning.

Gobbi was to record his Tonio again six years later, with Franco Corelli as Canio and Lucine Amara as Nedda, again with the orchestra and chorus of La Scala, but under the baton of Lovro von Matačić. This is now available as part of a 2-disc Corelli set (EMI *CMS 7 63967 2*), and it puts me in a bit of a quandary. It is coupled with a CAVALLERIA which does not include Gobbi, and I am not a very ardent admirer of Corelli, but on the other hand it is in stereo, and the subtlety of Gobbi's Tonio is brought into much sharper relief than on the mono set discussed above. If I were asked for an example, in a couple of bars, of what it was about the art of Tito Gobbi which distinguished him from other baritones, I think I would choose the words 'Non rider no! Non rider!' ('Don't laugh, no! Don't laugh!') after he has declared his love for Nedda. The first 'Non rider no!' is savage. It is more than angry; it is hostile and dangerous, the utterance of a man tortured by his own deformity and desperate to make someone pay. The second phrase opens with a 'Non' which is every bit as ugly, but on the word 'rider' the tone undergoes an extraordinary change, and in a flash Tonio is no longer threatening Nedda, he is at her feet, *beseeching* her not to laugh at him. It is a minuscule touch, it has passed in the twinkling of an eye, but it is what vocal acting is all about.

The opera which provided the most celebrated pairing of Gobbi the spurned lecher and Callas the resistant target of his passions was, however, not PAGLIACCI but TOSCA. This they recorded twice together, the first time in 1953 with the orchestra of La Scala, under the baton of Victor de Sabata and with di Stefano as Cavaradossi (EMI *CDS 7 47175 8 – two discs*); and the second time in 1964, shortly before Callas's vastly publicized come-back in London and Paris, with the Orchestre de la Société des Concerts du Conservatoire under Georges Prêtre, and with Carlo Bergonzi in the tenor role (EMI *CMS 7 69974 2 – two discs*). It is difficult to decide which of these two sets is the better. The later one has the great advantage of being in stereo, with all the improvement of sound quality and balance which that implies, and it offers a Cavaradossi of exceptional vocal elegance in Bergonzi. The earlier one, however, finds Callas in handsomer voice; and di Stefano's Cavaradossi, ardent and impulsive, is in its different way no less impressive than Bergonzi's. It is, however, Gobbi's Scarpia with which we are principally concerned at the moment, and to hear this superb characterization at its best I think one has to settle for 1964. The voice has in no way deteriorated since the earlier version; the interpretation has if anything gained in subtlety, and the sense of space imparted by the stereo recording lends greater authority throughout. One of the visual hallmarks of Gobbi's Scarpia was the aristocratic aloofness of his physical bearing – the cunning, the cruelty, the lust were expressed in the voice, and were all the more biting for the restraint of those passages in which he is passing himself off to Tosca as the perfect gentleman. Phrases such as 'O che v'offende, dolce signora?' ('Ah, what offends you, sweet lady?') in Act I, or 'Un sorso per rincorarvi' ('A drink to restore your spirits') just after confronting her with the sight of her tortured lover in Act II, are delivered with the suavity of a true man of breeding; and when Tosca hisses at him the question 'Quanto?' ('How much?'), his assurance that to a beautiful lady he does not sell himself 'a prezzo di moneta' has almost an air of detached amusement about it. It is the vocal equivalent to a favourite stage maxim of Gobbi's that 'terrifying power can usually be more fully conveyed by stillness than by a great show of action', so that when the mask falls and out he comes with the full rapacity of Scarpia's passion the effect is all the more shocking for the restraint that has preceded it.

To experience Gobbi at the opposite end of his theatrical range one can do no better than turn to his brilliantly effervescent Figaro in IL BARBIERE DI SIVÌGLIA (EMI *CDS 7 47634 8 – two discs*). It is hard to imagine this set ever being improved upon. It was a London-based recording, made in 1957 with the Philharmonia Orchestra in cracking form under the baton of Alceo Galliera, a bit of a 'rara avis' in the opera house. It is in stereo, the tenor is Luigi Alva, outstandingly the best Almaviva I have ever seen, the two crusty old comics are in the safest of hands, and Callas, though she did not enjoy stage success as Rosina, emerges on record as the perfect foil to the cornucopia of Gobbi's universal Mister Fixit. There have been other baritones, as I have hinted above, who could get more 'blade' into their high Gs, but there

have not been many who have made a more delicious meal of
the character as a whole. The 'Largo al factotum' is a number
which sometimes makes my heart sink – a sort of hurdle race,
with survival as the main objective. With Gobbi, though, you
only have to hear the jaunty swagger of phrases like 'Ah che bel
vivere, che bel piacere' to know that you can sit back with a smile
on your face and have fun. He scoots through the patter passages
with heedless aplomb, his recitatives explode like fireworks and
throughout every meteoric switch of mood and situation he is, as
every Figaro should be, supremely in charge of the proceedings.
Listening to this performance it is simply not possible to envisage
Gobbi in everyday clothes recording at the Kingsway Hall in the
depths of a London winter. He leaps off the disc, gorgeously
decked out and swathed in Spanish sunshine. 'Oh che vita, che
vita, oh che mestiere!'

Adept as he was with composers such as Rossini and Donizetti,
the core of Gobbi's repertoire lay in the great gallery of Verdian
drama. His Renato in UN BALLO IN MASCHERA is preserved
on another fine Callas set (EMI *CDS 7 47498 8 – two discs*) with
di Stefano as Riccardo, and with the Orchestra of La Scala,
this time conducted by Antonio Votto – Callas was reputedly
miffed at that moment with Tullio Serafin for having made a
TRAVIATA recording with one of her competitors, so out went
Serafin. Gobbi's noble performance is distinguished by all the
virtues which I mentioned in relation to his individual recording
of the 'Eri tu', and nobility is a characteristic with which he also
invests to an unusual degree his Amonasro in AIDA (EMI *CDS 7
49030 8 – three discs*). Though a prisoner of war he remains very
much the born leader of men. His opening solo, addressed to his
victor, is declaimed with a defiant dignity – a dignity which he in
no way lays aside when, with one of his typical switches of colour,
he begs for the lives of his fellow sufferers. The meat of the role
lies, though, in his Nile Scene duet with Callas's tensely theatrical
Aida. This finds Gobbi at his most commanding, in turn ferocious
and cajoling, at some points indulging in a touch of the 'yellow'

tone and at others unleashing a cascade of withering rhetoric. As Radamès we have the American tenor Richard Tucker, and this time Maestro Serafin is back in charge of the forces of La Scala.

It is a feature of this whole series of Callas reissues that her name appears on the box in letters twice as large as anyone else's. In the case of some of the operas this may be justified, but in the case of RIGOLETTO (EMI *CDS 7 47469 8 – two discs*) it is not. This is the hunchbacked jester's piece. Gobbi himself regarded it as the greatest of all Italian baritone roles, and it is not hard to see why. It is, in professional jargon, a very big sing. It calls for enormous stamina, it encompasses a wide emotional range, and dramatically it is as three-dimensional as nineteenth century opera ever becomes. It is a vehicle for a real star performance, and that is what Gobbi provides on record even more than he used to on stage. He digs a long way beneath the skin of the role. From his mockery of Monterone in the opening scene and the clipped conspiratorial utterances of the exchange with Sparafucile through to the recitative 'Pari siamo' which precedes his first duet with his daughter Gilda, this is vocal acting of the most imaginative order. Again and again one phrase is enough to present Gobbi's credentials. Take, for instance, his description of the Duke, 'Questo padrone mio, giovin, giocondo, si possente' ('This master of mine, young, gay, so powerful') – every syllable drips with resentment, but the ultimate venom is reserved for the last epithet of all, 'bello' ('handsome') which he spits out as if it were an emetic. In the duets with Gilda he floats a tender pianissimo, and in the Act II scena, which is really the heart of the role, and which I have already discussed in some detail in my chapter on de Luca, Gobbi uses far greater extremes of dramatic expression than that revered old master; now a snarl, now a biting Sprechgesang, now a heartrending legato. For some tastes it may stray too far from pure *bel canto*, and it is certainly a more modern, veristic approach than de Luca's. As I see it, Rigoletto, however desperately he may defy his social betters, is in essence a victim figure – a victim of his own deformity and of a malignant fate which has robbed him of his wife and is soon to rob him of his daughter. Now Gobbi was a compelling exponent of that other archetypal victim figure, Alban Berg's Wozzeck. I am not suggesting that he sings Verdi as he did Berg, but in any singer's repertoire the emotional experiences of certain powerfully conceived roles tend to rub off, however slightly, onto others; and I do not believe that any artist who immersed himself as deeply as Gobbi did in the persona of Wozzeck could fail to be touched by echoes of that haunting creature when portraying other of destiny's victims.

Destiny's victims. Does this classification include Verdi's last great baritone 'hero', Sir John Falstaff? Despite his ending up at every turn the loser, mocked, duped and ducked, I think not. The fat knight strides on in glory, and in this miraculous achievement of Verdi's declining years Gobbi found a role after his own heart, now to be savoured on EMI *CDS 7 49668* (2 discs). This is another London set, with the Philharmonia Orchestra again at the peak of its form, Karajan at the peak of his, and the sort of cast that makes you ask yourself if you will ever hear its like again. There's Schwarzkopf's gorgeously soaring Alice, Barbieri's Mistress Quickly, voluminous as a galleon in full sail, Moffo and Alva in dulcet voice as the embodiments of young love, Panerai virile and aggressive as Master Ford – and as Falstaff there is Tito Gobbi. Whether you pick out the famous numbers – the sheer musical and theatrical intelligence of the 'L'Onore' monologue, the wicked self-satisfaction of 'Va, vecchio John', the will o' the wisp 'Quand' ero paggio', the blossoming of his intimations of mortality into visions of blissful tipsiness under the influence of mulled wine – or whether you light on individual lines such as 'Vado a farmi bello' ('I'm off to make myself beautiful'), this is an interpretation packed to the brim with delights of every kind.

Gobbi was a sufficiently canny operator to retire from one role after another as he felt them becoming too much for him. As early as 1965 he had turned his hand to production, directing SIMON BOCCANEGRA in Chicago and at Covent Garden. The following year he made one of his few professional miscalculations when he agreed to direct di Stefano's first Otello, an undertaking rendered hazardous by the tenor's disinclination to learn the role, but thereafter Gobbi the director progressed to many more rewarding ventures, including a memorable GIANNI SCHICCHI at the Edinburgh Festival of 1969. It was Gobbi's view that most great opera composers were also great men of the theatre, and that they do not need to have their masterpieces rehashed in weird and eccentric ways, which may have stamped him to some tastes as a yesterday's man but which established him to others as a bulwark of operatic good sense. In his frequent Master Classes and in his Opera Workshop, which from 1971 until the time of his death, he directed for six weeks every summer in a country villa between Florence and Fiesole, he passed on the fruits of his experience to the younger generation. As his recorded legacy makes abundantly evident, this was the experience of one of the twentieth century's completest operatic performers.

ALEXANDER KIPNIS

RUSSIAN BASS

b. Shitomir, Ukraine, 1 February 1891
d. Westport, Connecticut, 14 May 1978

For a very specific reason, Alexander Kipnis holds a unique place in my affections. While I was still quite a junior schoolboy, one of my seniors, who prided himself on his deep and manly voice, sang Sarastro's aria 'In diesen heil'gen Hallen' from DIE ZAUBERFLÖTE in the annual singing competition. I assume that the performance must have been fairly inadequate, but the music itself bowled me over. After finding out what it was (I did not even know what opera was in those days, let alone that it had things called arias in it), I went along to the local music shop and asked if it existed on a gramophone record. It did. Kipnis's 'In diesen heil'gen Hallen' became the first record I ever bought, and it hooked me on opera. What I did not realize at the time was that in every sense except that of vocal register I had started at the top, with one of the most sublime passages in the whole of opera, sung by one of the greatest artists of his day.

Kipnis was born in the Ukrainian town of Shitomir, where his father scraped a living trading in materials for heavy winter coats. There was no music in the family, though Kipnis later recognized two tunes that his mother used to sing around the house as having been 'La donna è mobile' and Schubert's 'Serenade'; he could never imagine where she had picked them up. As a child his sole source of musical influence came from the peasants who lived in the neighbourhood, and by the time he was four or five he had imbibed most of the songs which he used to hear them sing. When he was twelve his father died and times were desperately hard, but in due course he somehow managed to win a place at the Warsaw Conservatory. His spur for this remarkable effort was a desire to avoid being conscripted as a private soldier in the Russian army – if you were a musician you could become a bandmaster, and thus go straight in as an officer. It was indeed as a bandmaster that he graduated from the Conservatory, but meanwhile his voice had started to make its presence felt, and he went to study singing with a teacher named Ernst Grenzebach in Berlin. After appearing during 1913 and 1914 in two of the many Berlin operetta houses, he managed to secure his first operatic engagement. This was in Hamburg, where he made his debut as the Hermit in DER FREISCHÜTZ, but when war broke out he was interned as an enemy alien. Through the good offices of an operatically-minded camp commandant he was soon released, but as Hamburg was a strategically sensitive city he was severely restricted in his movements, and had to report to the police every other day. Life became easier in this respect when he moved in 1917 to the Wiesbaden Opera, Wiesbaden being a city of military hospitals rather than naval installations. There he stayed for five years, accumulating a remarkably varied repertoire and building his reputation as an up-and-coming young bass – a reputation which, in 1922, brought him to the Städtische Oper, Berlin.

It was in Berlin that Kipnis made many of his finest recordings, and on one outstanding CD, Lebendige Vergangenheit *89019*, we have eighteen of them, all dating from 1930–31, when his voice was at its absolute best. There are sixteen operatic tracks and two Russian folk songs, all with the Berlin State Opera Orchestra; and as the operatic portion of the feast includes Sarastro's two arias from DIE ZAUBERFLÖTE, 'O Isis und Osiris' and my so highly prized 'In diesen heil'gen Hallen', I shall start now where I started all those years ago. I am happy to say that time cannot wither singing like this. There is an inherent majesty in the voice. It has the depth, the fullness, the power of the true dark bass, and yet there is a velvety gentleness on the edge of the tone, which suffuses both arias with that spirit of humanity and benignity so essential to the High Priest of the Temple of Wisdom. I do not always agree with the musical dicta of George Bernard Shaw, but when he describes this as being the only music which might fittingly proceed from the mouth of God I must concede that he has a point – which always makes it doubly disappointing if Sarastro is sung by a bass who cannot rise (or sink) to the occasion. Kipnis could, and it became one of his most regular visiting cards – in Wiesbaden, Berlin, Vienna, Chicago, Buenos Aires, at the Metropolitan Opera and at the Salzburg Festival. One thing which has been criticized about his recording of 'In diesen heil'gen Hallen' is that he ends on a low E, instead of taking it, as Mozart wrote it, in the higher octave. Pundits become very sensitive about that sort of thing nowadays, but when Kipnis sang the role under Toscanini in Salzburg in 1937 he asked if he could indulge in his customary variant, whereupon the Maestro consulted several ancient scores, announced that Mozart himself had sanctioned it, and granted his permission. In the previous year Kipnis had sung Sarastro at Glyndebourne, and Walter Legge, then a critic on the *Manchester Guardian*, had this to say about it:

> The great artist scaled down the volume of his noble voice to the requirements of the theatre without robbing the music or the character of any dignity. Only those, perhaps, who have heard this superb voice fill Covent Garden and the vast Continental opera houses could appreciate the skill and mastery of technique by which the singer adapted his vast resources to the acoustics of Glyndebourne.

This famous interpretation should have been preserved in its entirety, and we have Hitler to thank for the fact that it was not. When Legge undertook the management of the Beecham full recording of DIE ZAUBERFLÖTE in Berlin in 1937–8 he was obliged to look elsewhere for his Sarastro – Kipnis, being Jewish, could not be included. The same thing was true of Tauber, Legge's and Beecham's first choice for Tamino, so that the final cast list ended up looking less than ideal.

One thing which this disc convincingly establishes is Kipnis's extraordinary versatility. To indulge for a moment in a wide generalization, the bass voice tends to be used in opera for three main categories of character – in the first are kings, high priests

and various staid old gentlemen; in the second black-hearted villains, including the Devil himself; and in the third jovial fellows,
frequently given to excessive boozing. The first and second categories are undertaken by the serious or 'dark' basses, and the third
by their comic or *buffo* colleagues. Kipnis, though, as we shall see,
had feet in every imaginable camp, and to return to the Lebendige
Vergangenheit disc, we find him fairly scampering between the
categories. Besides Sarastro we meet him in two more of his
heavily serious roles, both from the pen of Giuseppe Verdi. In the
aria 'Il lacerato spirito' from SIMON BOCCANEGRA, and in its
preceding recitative, he displays a wide dynamic range from a wistful pianissimo, via a perfectly controlled crescendo, to the same
opulent sonority that we encountered in his ZAUBERFLÖTE
scenes. It is also a rare example of Kipnis in Italian, as his Berlin
recordings were basically aimed at the home market and recorded
in German translation. This is the case with his second Verdi aria,
King Philip's 'Ella giammai m'amò' from DON CARLOS, in which
he employs a totally different vocal quality, one which he used to
call on for certain of his Wagnerian roles. This ageing king is more
of an angry man than a sorrowing one – not a monarch whom I
would wish to cross. Of course, when he utters a sentiment such
as 'If the Prince sleeps, the traitor stays awake' and 'se dorme il
prence, veglia il traditore' becomes 'Wenn der Fürst schläft, wach
lauert der Verräter', the vocal delivery does inevitably arouse faint
echoes of Bayreuth, a place where Kipnis was a familiar name in
the late twenties and early thirties. There is only one item from
his wide Wagnerian repertoire on the Lebendige Vergangenheit
disc, Pogner's oration from DIE MEISTERSINGER. This was
the role in which, in 1923, he made his American debut with a
touring organization called the German Grand Opera Company.
It led later in the same year to his engagement by the Chicago Civic
Opera, with which he was to enjoy one of the longest and most
productive associations of his career, not to mention the effect that
it had on his private life – the Director of the Chicago Conservatory of Music had an attractive daughter named Mildred; Kipnis

married her, took American citizenship and thereafter, despite his many wanderings, regarded the United States as home. I digress, though, from Meister Pogner. It was a role which came up so often for Kipnis that when, surprisingly late in his career, he signed a contract with the Metropolitan Opera, he specifically requested its exclusion. When he made this recording, however, he was still tackling the part with gusto, but it does emphasize one curiously anomalous aspect of Kipnis's work. For a man of such fastidious musicianship, obviously gifted with a highly sensitive ear, it is remarkable how obtrusive a Russian accent he retained, and how little anyone seems to have objected to it. When Pogner enthuses about the 'deutscher Bürger' and his great work in preserving the 'deutsche Kunst', it is odd to hear him doing so in the tones of one who is clearly about as 'deutsch' as the Volga Boatman – but I suppose if the Wagner family did not mind, why should I?

One part for which one might suppose that Kipnis's Slavic vowels would have disqualified him is Ochs in DER ROSEN-KAVALIER, an 'echt'-Austrian dialect role, when all is said and done. But not a bit of it, he sang it all over the world, including in Vienna itself, and to judge from the final scene of Act II, another of the tracks on this CD, he did so with a fine rotund relish. The same geniality characterizes Kipnis's virtuoso assumption of that scion of Merrye Olde England, the farmer Plunkett in Flotow's MARTHA. In the aria 'Lasst mich euch fragen' he extols the virtues of porter beer, the dark brown elixir which enables John Bull to keep his pecker up despite the impenetrable fog in which we British are popularly supposed to spend three-quarters of our lives. This air of jollity pervades another classic example of a British soak as seen through German eyes – the Falstaff of DIE LUSTIGEN WEIBER VON WINDSOR; but when Kipnis turns to yet a third drinking man, that creepy fellow Kaspar in DER FREISCHÜTZ, the smile fades entirely from the voice, and it becomes a deeply sinister instrument. Kipnis remains with us as *basso diabolico* for Mephisto's 'Serenade' and 'Calf of Gold' from FAUST – two numbers to which I must confess that I am strongly allergic, however well they are sung – and the mock-sinister is represented by a beautifully judged rendering of Basilio's 'La calunnia', or rather 'Die Verleumdung', from THE BARBER OF SEVILLE. As the impecunious schoolmaster in Lortzing's DER WILDSCHÜTZ Kipnis gives a technical lesson in how to fine down a huge voice to meet the demands of a patter song, a trick which he repeats with Bartolo's 'Vengeance' aria from THE MARRIAGE OF FIGARO, and we are now firmly in the realm of the *buffo* repertoire. It was obviously the inherent nobility of Kipnis's voice and the dignity of his style which suited him to so many of opera's crowned heads, and yet both vocally and histrionically he was able to don these humbler hats as well. His two most regular Mozart roles, after all, were Sarastro and Leporello – chalk and cheese on a classic scale – and he appears to have felt equally at home in both. It is a pity that his version of Leporello's 'Catalogue Aria' is another of the numbers recorded in German, as that is bound to make it less interesting for the international public, and when he sang the role outside Germany he sang it, of course, in Italian. It was one of his roles at the Metropolitan Opera, and although he only sang it there twice, that was enough to cause a lasting coolness between him and the great Italian bass Ezio Pinza. Pinza, the outstanding Don Giovanni of the day, had a lighter timbre of voice than Kipnis, with a rapid vibrato in it, and during the scene in which Leporello has to impersonate his master, Kipnis raised a good laugh with his imitation of Pinza. Pinza was to be seen fretting in the wings, but when his turn came to mimic Kipnis he was not able to bring it off. In Kipnis's own words: 'From then on we were not friends.' Oddly enough, the Mozart role which, after Sarastro, would surely have been the most ideally suited to Kipnis, Osmin in DIE ENTFÜHRUNG AUS DEM SERAIL, a *buffo* but a dangerous one, never came his way – a misfortune which is emphasized by the sharpness of detail in the last of the operatic numbers on this CD, Osmin's 'Wer ein Liebchen hat gefunden'.

The disc is completed by the two Russian folk songs. The

first, dance-like and humorous, called 'Kalinka' or 'The Mulberry Tree', is one of Kipnis's happiest performances and a miniature vocal gem; in the second, entitled 'Soldier's Song', the voice becomes more voluminous, while the delivery remains every bit as effortless and free. Whether or not these are two of the songs which the young Kipnis absorbed from the neighbourhood peasants I am not able to say; but there is a sense of being brought several steps closer to Kipnis the man, when he puts his operatic make-up and costume aside, and simply breathes the air of Mother Russia.

In fact, having left Russia in his youth Kipnis never returned to it, but he retained other national characteristics besides his accent. American friends described him in such terms as 'a merry mystic' and 'an incorrigible dreamer', and Gerald Moore, his regular accompanist for London recitals and recordings, paints an interesting picture of Kipnis in his memoirs. When they rehearsed together for the first time Moore, then in the early stages of his career, felt that he had acquitted himself well but he received 'no answering glow from Kipnis who had a deep-seated prejudice against an Englishman playing Lieder'. Despite the formidable power of his voice, 'Sacha Kipnis was not easy, he was mortally afraid of the piano tone being too heavy for him' – a fear which, in Moore's experience, beset all deep-voiced singers, and cellists too. 'He liked the accompaniment to be a shadowy background,' Moore goes on, 'and in compliance to this foible of his my piano sounds as if I were playing in the next room in our album of Brahms Lieder, greatly to the detriment of the songs, in my opinion. Sacha would have preferred giving his recitals "a capella" if he possibly could.' Perhaps Gerald Moore had Kipnis in mind when he gave his book of memoirs the title *Am I Too Loud?* – in any case, despite all this, Moore considered Kipnis the finest recitalist and the most consummate musician of all the basses he played for. They became the best of friends, too, and by all accounts Kipnis was, in private life, a thoroughly congenial man. Opera singers have a certain reputation for healthy appetites

– I remember when I first married that my wife was constantly astonished at how much food would disappear whenever any of my colleagues came to a meal – but Kipnis was regarded as a gourmet par excellence. When not deploying his artistry on stage he enjoyed doing so in the kitchen, one of his specialities being shashlik of lamb, mushrooms and kidneys, broiled on a spit and quickly dunked in vodka.

This was a recipe clearly redolent of his origins, and another outstanding Kipnis CD, RCA Victor *GD60522*, is exclusively devoted to recordings in the Russian language, most of them made in the last two years of his active career, 1945–6. It starts with virtually the whole role of Boris Godunov – each of the monologues and the duet with Shuisky, complete with supporting cast and chorus. Though the voice has lost a little of its rock-like steadiness, and the high 'piano' passages have become a trifle dry, this remains a monumental performance – intense, tragic and sometimes downright terrifying. Gone is Sarastro's benignity as Kipnis threatens Shuisky with a death so ghastly that Ivan the Terrible himself will shudder in his grave. I fancy that his cry of 'Dovólno!' ('Enough!'), when Shuisky describes the seraphic smile on the face of the murdered child, will be enough to jolt any listener; but on the other hand I know of no other version in which Boris's final parting from his young son is so guaranteed to win sympathy for him, bloodstained despot though he is. Kipnis's first appearance in BORIS GODUNOV had been with the Chicago Opera in 1925, but on that occasion he had sung the role of Varlaam, to the Boris of Feodor Chaliapin. Considering what obvious casting Kipnis was for the title-role, he sang it surprisingly seldom and in comparatively out of the way places, such as Bordeaux, Vichy, and Pilsen. As BORIS GODUNOV is one of the comparatively few operas in which the bass is the absolute star of the show, Kipnis had hoped that it would fall to his lot for his debut at the Metropolitan Opera in 1940. Edward Johnson, though, the Manager of the Met, felt that the production was too old and shabby to be worthy of the occasion, and so Kipnis appeared in one of his other finest roles, Gurnemanz in PARSIFAL. This was greeted with unanimous enthusiasm by both press and public, who had to wait another three years to hear his Boris. It was the thirteenth and last of his new roles at the Met, and it was an outstanding personal triumph. One can take it, I think, as a strong indication of the standard which Kipnis demanded of himself, that three years later, while still able to perform as magnificently as he did in these recordings, he made the difficult decision to retire – and stuck to it.

The same disc also offers us Kipnis in his BORIS alter ego, the drunken Varlaam, as well as in four other favourite Russian arias and five songs. We have that rollicking roué Prince Galitsky's philosophy of life from PRINCE IGOR, the craggy, swirling narration of the Viking Guest from SADKO, the toe-tapping jauntiness of the Miller's song from the Dargomizhsky RUSALKA, and the restrained dignity of one of my favourite Russian arias, Gremin's account in the last act of EUGENE ONEGIN of how his marriage to Tatiana has beautified his life. (I must add that my affection for this aria even manages to survive the opening phrase of a translation used by Sadler's Wells back in the 1950s, which I seem to have ineradicably lodged in my memory – 'Onegin, I would not be human/If I did not adore this wooman'.) My appreciation of the finer points of Kipnis's various characterizations is inevitably limited by the fact that I do not speak Russian. Even so, I am left with a strong feeling that these are the sounds which this voice was really created to produce. It is impossible, too, to miss the subtlety with which his vocal colouring is adapted to fit the very different portraits in this particular gallery, and in the case of Gremin, the fact that we are clearly listening to a man of a certain age only adds to the authenticity of the performance.

The five songs which complete this disc further underline the rich variety of Kipnis's vocal and interpretative range – something which was almost invariably commented on in the press reviews of his many recitals all over the world. Mussorgsky's 'Song of the Flea' has him cackling manically at the idea of all those courtiers not being allowed to scratch because the king has dressed his pet flea in finest raiment and promoted it to the rank of Minister; in Grechaninov's 'Lullaby' he spins a high 'piano' line worthy of a *tenore leggiero* (this was recorded in 1939), then in the same composer's 'My Homeland' he pins you back in your seat with an opening phrase like a clap of thunder; in Rachmaninov's 'O Cease thy Singing, Maiden Fair' he sings one high-lying passage with an ease which explains how he came to be cast as Silvio in PAGLIACCI back in his Wiesbaden days; and the recital is rounded off with a high-octane romp through Stravinsky's setting of a nursery rhyme called 'Tilim-Bom' – a hectic depiction of events in the farmyard when Mr Goat's house catches fire, the alarm bell rings, and all the other animals flap around trying to help.

The Pearl Company have brought out a Kipnis CD (GEMM *CD 9451*) which opens interestingly with a group of his earliest acoustic recordings. The booklet dates them as 'c. 1916', but in interviews given late in his life Kipnis remembered his first recordings as having been made *after* World War One, during his Wiesbaden years, and it is hard to imagine that the Odeon Company would have engaged him as a raw beginner in his second season in Hamburg. Be that as it may, we have four samples of a marvellously rich and resonant young voice – Mephisto's 'Invocation' from FAUST, Figaro's 'Aprite un po' quegl'occhi', the first part of King Mark's monologue from TRISTAN UND ISOLDE, and Brahms's exquisite song 'Wie bist du, meine Königin'. In one of the interviews to which I referred above, Kipnis remarked on how inhibiting he found the acoustic recording process. It did not appeal to him to perform to a horn which protruded through the wall of a cramped little studio, having to lean forward or back according to whether he was singing 'piano' or 'forte', and it may be for this reason, or perhaps because he had not yet tackled Mephisto or Figaro on stage, that these two items are uncharacteristically monochrome. King Mark fares better; that unhappy monarch entered Kipnis's repertoire during his early Wiesbaden years, and in time he made the role very much his own. The Brahms song, mellifluous as it is, does not yet quite display the subtleties of nuance for which his Lieder singing later became renowned; but more of that in a moment. The operatic tracks continue with a searing account of King Philip's aria, recorded in 1922, and presenting the same vengeful, embittered figure whom we have already met on the electrical recording of eight years later. The next item, Marcel's outburst of religious fanaticism from Act I of Meyerbeer's LES HUGUENOTS, introduced Kipnis in 1927 to the Covent Garden public, and that was a debut which I do not suppose he forgot in a hurry. He was the one member of the cast who received unanimous praise from the critics; otherwise the performance was hailed as the most catastrophic evening at Covent Garden in living memory, the King and Queen left before the end, and the gallery erupted in a frenzy of booing. It proved enough of a disaster to keep LES HUGUENOTS out of the Covent Garden repertoire for sixty-five years,* but luckily it did not discourage Kipnis from regular return visits. During a period of eight years he was heard there in sixteen different roles, eight of them from his Wagnerian repertoire. He closed his account with Covent Garden in 1937 when he requested eighty pounds a performance for King Mark, and Beecham turned him down.

The last acoustic track on this disc is a fine memento of one of Kipnis's Berlin successes, Cardinal Brogni in Halévy's LA JUIVE. It must have been a strange feeling for him of all people to invoke God's help in bringing enlightenment to the Jewish infidels, but it is a grateful passage for any bass with a truly sonorous lower register, and Kipnis unfolds it with nobility. We then move on to two of the earliest of German electrical recordings, and here we are presented with a very different Kipnis. Kipnis the dark-hued *basso profondo* becomes Kipnis the heroic bass-baritone, in an infinitely moving performance of Wotan's final scene from DIE WALKÜRE. He sings in shorter phrases

---

* By an unhappy coincidence, the revival of 1990 was almost as big a fiasco.

than might be expected (in other words, he takes more breaths), but this is an astounding achievement none the less. There is the thrilling ring of the true *Heldenbariton* in 'Wer meines Speeres Spitze fürchtet, durchschreite das Feuer nie!' ('Let him who fears the point of my spear never step through the fire!'), and in the last farewell to his beloved daughter Kipnis finds with unerring aim that deeply touching quality of which he was such a master. With Hans Sachs's 'Verachtet mir die Meister nicht' from DIE MEISTERSINGER he is, to my mind, less successful. He has trouble with the awkwardly high 'Habt acht!' – there is a large proportion of consonant to vowel in that brief phrase – and in general he does not seem to be quite at the right address. The year before these recordings were made he enjoyed a resounding success as Wotan in Chicago, but he refused to play Hans Sachs on stage. In later years he gave this explanation: 'I did so solely on political grounds. I refused it at a time when Hitler's propaganda forces were nearing their zenith, and I wanted no part in any of it. I was not German by birth, and hence I did not feel myself possessed of Germanic blood or to be a member of some elite German race.'

I imagine it is possible that as early as 1926, when these two recordings were made, Kipnis may have begun to feel out of sorts with certain aspects of his environment; perhaps this was the real reason why he did not want to be the mouthpiece for Pogner's oration at the Met – I do not know. It is certainly a fact, though, that Kipnis, like so many leading artists of the time, began to find that his Jewish blood was dictating the shape of his career. During the Bayreuth season of 1933 Hitler was present at several performances, and to Kipnis's consternation Winifred Wagner invited him and his wife to her house one evening to meet the Führer. The thought of being introduced to Hitler caused Kipnis terrible distress, but it would have been difficult to refuse an invitation from Frau Wagner without a good reason. As luck would have it, he and his wife bumped into the distinguished British critic Ernest Newman who was out on a walk that afternoon with *his* wife; so Mr and Mrs Kipnis promptly asked Mr and Mrs Newman to dinner, and thus created a retroactive 'previous engagement'. It was to be Kipnis's last year at Bayreuth though, and two years later he was classified as an 'undesirable' in Berlin. The obvious place to move to was Vienna, and the State Opera was delighted to have him – only for the same thing to happen there a couple of years later. It was a time during which the operatic profession, like so much else, became a seething cauldron. At Covent Garden and in other international houses Jewish artists would find themselves engaged alongside Nazi supporters who had been delighted to see them driven from their homes; the atmosphere can be easily imagined.

But – to return to Kipnis and the Pearl CD. The two Wagner recordings were considered in their day to be miracles of modern science, and though we are scarcely likely now to endorse that view, it is certainly true that the accompaniment by the Berlin State Opera Orchestra under that renowned Wagnerian Leo Blech is of a vividness which would have been unthinkable before the invention of electrical recording. The disc continues with alternative versions of the two Mephisto solos from FAUST, sung in French this time, and generally preferable to the German-language recordings. Though I continue to be irritated by the music I cannot help being impressed by the malignant panache of the performance. An alternative version of 'In diesen heil'gen Hallen', however, recorded a year before my old favourite and for some peculiar reason only issued in Australia, leaves me true to my first love – the Australians, it seems to me, were fobbed off with rather an overblown rendering. Thereafter come four tracks with which we are already familiar, Bartolo's 'Vengeance Aria', the superb 'Il lacerato spirito', and the two folk numbers, 'Kalinka' and 'Soldier's Song'.

This brings me to the last three tracks of the Pearl disc, which introduce us at last to Kipnis the mature Lieder singer. He was recognized as a master of the art, something comparatively rare in the case of a 'dark' bass, and in the case of a Russian one, I think it is safe to say, unique. It was during his early days in Wiesbaden that he first took to the serious study of Lieder. His duties in the opera house left him with a certain amount of time on his hands, but wartime travel restrictions barred him from undertaking outside work, and he was not a man for wasting valuable time. In fact the Pearl Lieder tracks, beautiful though some of the singing may be, are only of marginal interest, consisting as they do of rejected test pressings of one Wolf song and two by Brahms, both much beset by clicks and crackles.

For a true feast of Kipnis's Lieder recordings we must move on to an invaluable American reissue on two CDs, Music & Arts *CD – 661*. Kipnis was one of the select band of singers chosen in the mid-1930s to record for the Hugo Wolf Society, an organization in which Ernest Newman, Walter Legge, Compton Mackenzie and others were heavily involved. Kipnis's contribution consisted of seventeen songs, and they are all included. They cover a considerable range of mood, from the skittish whimsy of 'Der Musikant' to the desolate pessimism of 'Alles endet, was entstehet', but despite Kipnis's versatility, and his deep involvement in every note he sings, it is the weightier and more sombre of the songs which, for my taste, emerge as being his natural territory. When he delivers an utterance such as 'Denn mit Göttern soll sich nicht messen irgendein Mensch' ('For no mere mortal should measure himself against the gods'), in Goethe's philosophical poem 'Grenzen der Menschheit', it is as if we were sitting at the feet of some Old Testament prophet, awe-inspiring and immutable. When, with the words 'Gelassen stieg die Nacht ans Land' ('Quietly night has settled on the land'), Kipnis unfolds the Mörike poem 'Um Mitternacht', his tone is as dark, as soft and as enveloping as night itself. When we come to Heyse's poems from the 'Italienisches Liederbuch', however, with their wry little insights into everyday human life, Kipnis, for all his skill, seems to me miscast. It was, I believe, on the insistence of the young Walter Legge that some perversely high keys were chosen, and this may well be the root of the problem. As I mentioned earlier, there are examples on record of Kipnis showing extraordinary skill in maintaining a soft high line, but several of these keys would be more appropriate for a lyric baritone, and two of them even for a tenor. Thanks to his exceptional technical control, Kipnis shows remarkably few signs of actual strain, but the voice simply does not sound at home, and the point is firmly underlined by the next group on the disc consisting of four Brahms songs recorded in New York in 1929. With the first phrase of 'Sapphische Ode' we are back with the true Kipnis quality, an unforced flow of dark and burnished sonority. In 'Immer leise wird mein Schlummer' we have the unlikely experience of hearing these hugely virile tones in what is basically a woman's song ('eine Andre wirst du küssen'), but so profound is Kipnis's identification with the text, and so restrained his style, that he fully justifies his assumption of it. For me, 'Feldeinsamkeit' is the least successful of the group; the sustained legato is exemplary but the voice is simply too massive to reflect the song's tranquillity, its enchanted mood of animation suspended in the shimmering summer air. 'Auf dem Kirchhofe', on the other hand, is one of those performances which makes one feel that no other singer has ever quite reached the heart of the song. From the drama of its opening to the serenity of its close, this is a memorable instance of the true art of Lieder singing.

The first disc closes with Schumann's 'Mondnacht' and 'Wanderlied', followed by Strauss's 'Traum durch die Dämmerung' and 'Zueignung', also recorded in New York in 1929, and each performance is, in its own different way, a revelation. 'Mondnacht', doubtless because of the scene it depicts, presupposes to me a silvery vocal colour, and Kipnis's was as far from that as one could imagine; and yet through the ease and deftness with which he spins the melodic line he transforms his voice from an instrument predestined to embody the darkness of night into one well able to conjure up the elusive sheen of a moonlit landscape. In 'Traum durch die Dämmerung' he achieves exactly the magic which I found missing in the Brahms 'Feldeinsamkeit' – it is a truly wonderful example of sustained soft singing. In 'Wanderlied' he unleashes the full splendour of the voice without missing any of the song's tenderer nuances, and with a measured, thoughtful 'Zueignung', he leaves me wondering if there was ever a richer, more purely *beautiful* bass voice than this.

The second of the Music & Arts CDs consists of the fourteen songs which Kipnis recorded in London in 1936 for the Brahms Society, and seven familiar favourites by Schubert. The Brahms songs are those to which Gerald Moore was referring when he complained so bitterly about being left out in the cold, and I have to say that I am on his side – listening to them one does rather gain the impression of a gigantic Mr Kipnis standing by the microphone, while a miniature Mr Moore has to make do on a tiny piano somewhere in the background. A song like the first of the 'Vier ernste Gesänge' needs to end with a good big bang, which we do not get, and when there is a contrapuntal relationship between voice and piano, as in 'Ein Sonett', there is definitely something missing if one partner so overshadows the other. Having said that, however, there is much marvellous singing to be enjoyed in these recordings. The biblical compassion of the 'Vier ernste Gesänge' predictably finds Kipnis in his element – how close to home the passage about the tears of those who suffer injustice must have seemed to him in 1936! – and the descending phrase 'Da lobte ich die Toten' in the second song reveals as neatly as any other four bars in his recorded repertoire what a musically imaginative singer Kipnis was. In 'Verrat' he switches flawlessly from the giddy twittering of the fickle young lady to the furious outburst of her cheated lover, and the same dramatic flair makes his 'Von ewiger Liebe' with its stupendously vocalized finale one of the finest achievements of the group. Once again I find the scale of some of the purely lyrical songs ('Erinnerung', 'An die Nachtigall', 'Die Mainacht'), for all the skill displayed in them, simply too massive. It seems harsh to consider a singer handicapped by the magnificence of his own voice but in this type of song I do find that to be the case. The 'einsame Träne' ('the lonely tear'), of 'Die Mainacht', for instance, becomes a pretty substantial object when described in Kipnis's heroic tones; though to set against this, when he aims for the light and playful colours of 'Ständchen', 'Vergebliches Ständchen' or 'Sonntag', he achieves them more successfully than I would have imagined possible. For me, however, the absolute pick of the bunch is 'O wüsst'ich doch den Weg zurück', the poet Klaus Groth's heartfelt plea to be readmitted to the enchanted world of childhood. However little enchantment Kipnis's own childhood may have contained, the sense of unfulfilled longing with which this song is imbued finds perfect expression in that blend of melancholy and nostalgia which seems to lurk within the undertones of so many of the great Slav voices.

The disc is completed by a Schubert group, starting with five songs recorded in 1927, and thus the earliest in the whole set. The sound is a trifle foggier than most of the later recordings – though the state of the actual masters from which the transfers were made seems to have been better than those of the Brahms songs, several of which are distinctly clicky – but this fades into insignificance compared to the quality of the performance. Each of the songs is ideal Kipnis country. 'Der Wegweiser' and 'Der Lindenbaum' are tense and introspective, the vocalization distinguished by countless subtle gradations of tone; 'Aufenthalt' is massive and embittered, with magnificent attacks on the high Es of 'Ewig derselbe'; 'Am Meer' is taken too dramatically for my personal taste, and thus loses some of its eeriness, but 'Der Doppelgänger' receives the most powerful and horror-struck rendering that I have ever heard. There is a flesh-creeping hatred in 'Da steht auch ein Mensch', leading to a fearful intensity in 'Der Mond zeigt mir meine eig'ne Gestalt', and throughout the song the voice becomes an instrument of terror. It never loses its beauty, but it is a beauty hauntingly different from that which we heard in 'Mondnacht' and 'Traum durch die Dämmerung'.

Finally we have two more Schubert songs which, in their guise as both sides of an old Columbia blue-label 78, must, I fancy, have featured on the shelves of most music lovers of my generation. On one side was that beaming effusion of youthful passion 'Ungeduld', and though I am sure that basses have every bit as much right to youthful passion as tenors or baritones, I cannot budge from the view that this is not a bass song. On the other side though was 'Der Erlkönig', and that is a very different story. The threatening darkness, the pounding hooves, the pleading child, the desperate father and the wheedling killer are all here – and Gerald Moore has crept far enough into the foreground to bring this immensely welcome set to a truly rousing conclusion.

There are two other CD reissues involving Kipnis which I would not like to leave unmentioned. One is a fascinating performance of the Mozart Requiem in D minor, recorded at a live performance in the Théâtre des Champs-Elysées in Paris in June 1937 with the Chorus of the Vienna State Opera and the Vienna Philharmonic Orchestra under Bruno Walter. Kipnis's fellow soloists are the seraphic Elisabeth Schumann, the outstanding Swedish mezzo Kerstin Thorborg, and the tenor Anton Dermota, then at the outset of his career. The recording inevitably suffers from some of the disadvantages of being taken live, but these are outweighed by the vital atmosphere of an exciting musical occasion; it forms part of an historic three-CD set (EMI *CHS 7 639122*), devoted to outstanding interpretations of Mozart by Bruno Walter. In another EMI compilation of special historical interest, a four-CD set entitled 'Wagner Singing on Record' (EMI *CMS 7 64008 2*) Kipnis is featured in what he himself thought to be possibly his finest role – Gurnemanz in PARSIFAL. The recording dates back to the Bayreuth Festival of 1927 and consists of a generous slice of the Good Friday scene between Gurnemanz and Parsifal himself. The tenor is Fritz Wolff, who emerges as a sensitive and interesting singer; and Kipnis is in glorious voice, fervent and rock-solid of tone, his phrasing expansive and effortless, with the old knight's delight at the return of Parsifal reflected in Kipnis's own self-evident joy in the act of singing.

As I mentioned earlier, Gurnemanz was the role in which Kipnis eventually made his belated debut with the Metropolitan Opera.

That was in 1940, shortly before his forty-ninth birthday, and six years later he made his decision to retire from the stage. Thereafter he turned much of his attention to teaching – at the New York College of Music, at the Juilliard School, at Tanglewood, and in his own studio in his home town of Westport. It was at Westport that he died, a revered old gentleman of eighty-seven. Only a month before his death he was still commuting to New York to give his pupils their weekly lessons.

I opened this chapter by expressing a debt of gratitude to Alexander Kipnis and I would like to close it by expressing one small regret. Though born a Russian, he spent the greater part of his life with an American passport in his pocket – what a wonderful recording he would have made of that great American classic 'Old Man River'!

LOTTE LEHMANN

GERMAN SOPRANO

b. Perleberg, N. Germany, 27 February 1888
d. Santa Barbara, California, 26 August 1976

Back in the early 1950s, when I was revelling in my first opportunity to go fairly regularly to opera, it so happened that one piece which I saw several times was DER ROSENKAVALIER. When talking to older connoisseurs I soon learnt that there was no point in enthusing about whichever soprano happened to be the Marschallin of the evening. The response was always the same – a wistful look, a mildly condescending smile and 'Ah yes, but of course I heard Lotte Lehmann.' It has always seemed to me, who alas never did hear her, that there can be no more irrefutable proof of her qualities as a stage performer than this universal acceptance of the fact that she *was* the Marschallin. There are, after all, three things that the Marschallin has to be: beautiful, aristocratic and Viennese. Off stage, Lotte Lehmann was none of them.

She was born in the respectable but unremarkable town of Perleberg, half way between Hamburg and Berlin, of respectable but unremarkable parents. Her father was an official employed by the Ritterschaft, a sort of cross between a trustee bank and a benevolent society; and it was assuredly not his ambition to see any child of his pursue a career on the wicked stage. When Lotte was fourteen the family moved to Berlin. At her new school she became increasingly interested in theatre and in due course she found her way to the opera, first to see LOHENGRIN and then Ambroise Thomas's MIGNON, with Emmy Destinn in the title-role. It was not, however, an instant love affair with the bright lights that prompted her to think about opera as a career, but the lady in the upstairs flat; she often heard Lehmann singing around the place and mentioned her to an uncle who ran the canteen in the Royal High School for Music. Through his good offices Lehmann secured an audition and was accepted as a pupil. Her father, despite the severe financial sacrifice involved, was brought round to the idea, and her foot was on the first rung of the slippery operatic ladder.

Some people make the mistake of supposing that the ladder only becomes slippery when you enter the competitive arena of your first professional engagement, but this is not so – surviving your time as a student can be just as traumatic. Lehmann's first teacher at the High School became ill, her second teacher did not suit her and she moved to a different school, run by Madame Etelka Gerster, who had herself studied with the legendary Mathilde Marchesi and had been one of the main rivals of Adelina Patti. She now presided over an establishment which appears to have been a sort of vocal Dotheboys Hall. Short wooden sticks were inserted between the pupils' jaws, to prevent them from changing the position of the mouth when altering the pitch or the vowel sound. Lehmann's personal teacher, a Fräulein Reinhold, insisted on Lehmann hammering away day after day at an aria which was patently too difficult for her – the 'Dove sono' from FIGARO – until every healthy natural instinct that the poor girl possessed had been crushed out of existence. She was then ushered into the fearful presence of Frau Gerster, made to struggle through the aria yet again and dismissed from the school for the most hideous crime known within those hallowed halls – failure to profit from instruction. As if all of this were not Dickensian enough, Lehmann's Christmas present to Fräulein Reinhold, a cushion which she had made with her own hands, was returned to her accompanied by a letter which reads as if it had been written by Mr Murdstone on an off day, and contains such gems as 'I believe that if you want to achieve anything in the future you should take up a practical career. Only then will you come to know the real meaning of hard work, and perhaps you will realize later on that you were not doing your duty with all your might.' The cushion was returned because 'the feeling that you had made any sacrifice for me would be painful to me'; and furthermore, Fräulein Lehmann having been taken on in view of her exceptional promise as a non-paying pupil, Fräulein Reinhold felt obliged to add 'Frau Gerster requests me to tell you . . . that even as a paying pupil you would have been expelled.'

It is probably best to go through an experience of this sort as early as possible in one's career – it does have a make or break quality to it. During the course of her life Lehmann had to survive many harsh knocks, and this toughening process may well have helped. With admirable resilience, but to her father's extreme displeasure, she decided to play one more card. Out of the blue she wrote to Frau Kammersängerin Mathilde Mallinger, Wagner's original Eva in MEISTERSINGER, asking if she could study with her; and this time she was in the right hands. Within two years, at the age of twenty-two, Lehmann signed a beginner's contract with the Hamburg Opera, and on 2 September 1910 she made her professional debut as Second Boy in DIE ZAUBERFLÖTE, the First Boy being her good friend Elisabeth Schumann. Her main diet for her first couple of seasons consisted of such things as pageboys in TANNHÄUSER and LOHENGRIN, and when she was entrusted with a more prominent task, Freia in RHEINGOLD, she fell figuratively flat on her face, one critic describing her as 'vocally and dramatically helpless', and another observing that amongst the deities of Valhalla Fräulein Lehmann appeared to be the chambermaid. Things looked up though when she was cast as Eurydice in Gluck's ORFEO. Unlikely as the coupling may seem to us today, this was presented as a double bill with PAGLIACCI, the star of which was no less a figure than Enrico Caruso. Caruso had a habit of standing in the wings, eternally listening and learning, and he was enchanted by Lehmann's singing. 'Che bella, magnifica voce!' he said to her in the presence of witnesses, followed by the greatest compliment an Italian can bestow – 'Una voce italiana!' He asked that she should be his next Micaëla in CARMEN, and his Musetta in Leoncavallo's LA BOHEME, and although in the end neither of his requests could be acceded to, no management could fail to take the point. Lehmann had already been allowed to tackle one Agathe in FREISCHÜTZ in an out-of-town performance, and now her repertoire gradually expanded from Second This and Third That to include more and more roles with names of their own. There were some ROSENKAVALIERS, intriguingly with Lehmann as Sophie and Schumann as Octavian, some Annas in DIE LUSTIGEN WEIBER VON WINDSOR, and then, most significantly of all, her first Elsa in LOHENGRIN under the baton of one of the Hamburg house conductors, Otto Klemperer. Klemperer had already formed the habit, which he maintained even towards the end of his long life, of pressing his sexual attentions on any reasonably attractive young soprano but, although he had previously indulged in chasing Lehmann round numerous pianos, during the short time available for the preparation of her Elsa he kept his hands on the keyboard. He gave her a rough time at her one rehearsal with the orchestra, but the final result was a triumph, the first of the countless evenings on which Lehmann was to find herself called in front of the curtain again and again by an ecstatically applauding public.

To judge from the reviews of this first Elsa, Lehmann had already tapped the source of those qualities which were in the fullness of time to add up to her particular brand of magic. The critics were charmed as much by the instinctive spontaneity of her embodiment of the role as they were by the lustrous freshness of her voice. Later on she was to be described again and again as 'eine singende Seele', 'une âme chantante', 'a soul that sings', an artist whose every performance was a creation of the moment, fetched as a new and living experience from somewhere deep within herself. These are not qualities which are easily projected onto a gramophone record, and in her recordings something of the spell which Lehmann used to cast upon live audiences is inevitably lost. It was also not a help that her early recording contracts, like those of her frequent tenor partners Alfred Piccaver and Richard Tauber, were with German companies which did not at that time aspire to the same technical level as those in London or New York. Despite all these caveats, however, several of the Lehmann CDs do succeed in bringing out a far more immediate and accessible timbre than I ever managed to extract from the old Parlophone 78s.

On EMI *CDH 7 610422* we have a selection of fourteen arias, several of them samples of her most celebrated stage roles, and with the exception of one acoustic record of 1924 they all date from the period 1927–1933. From Weber we have the monumental 'Ozean, du Ungeheuer' (OBERON), and Agathe's scene 'Wie nahte mir der Schlummer' from DER FREISCHÜTZ, which had not only been Lehmann's first starring part, but was also chosen for her official debut, when she moved in 1916 from Hamburg to the Vienna Court Opera. A dazzling debut it was too. She captured the Vienna public overnight, not an easy thing for a young singer from a North German opera house to achieve, and as one Viennese critic put it 'It is now understandable that she was the darling of Hamburg, and that they let her go with deep regrets.' In this 1929 recording she gives a vivid, compelling performance, pious and maidenly as she prays for God's protection, but a great deal less of both as she spots Max, her deadshot forester boyfriend, heading in her direction. When Lehmann sings 'All meine Pulse schlagen, und das Herz wallt ungestüm' ('All my pulses beat and my heart is furiously boiling'), it is there in the voice as it evidently used to be on stage. We also have on this disc what is surely the most heroic music ever written for the soprano voice, 'Komm, Hoffnung' from FIDELIO, and without this no portrait of Lotte Lehmann would be complete. In one of her books, *My Many Lives*, Lehmann was to write that in this role 'I found the most exalted moments of my opera career and was shaken by it to the depths of my being.' This recording was made within less than a year of her first appearance as Leonore, which had been in a gala performance at the Vienna State Opera on 26 March 1927 to mark the centenary of Beethoven's death, with a cast that included Piccaver as Florestan, Schumann as Marzelline

and Mayr as the jailer Rocco. By all accounts Lehmann's Leonore
reached its zenith with the performances which she sang under
Toscanini in the Salzburg Festival of 1935. The two of them had
for some time been involved in an on-off love affair, part physical
passion, part mutual artistic adoration, and when Lehmann wrote
of Toscanini's FIDELIO 'his glowing temperament, like a flow
of lava, tore everything with it in its surging flood', there were
doubtless many personal associations in her mind. Be that as it
may, those Salzburg performances inspired the American critic
Vincent Sheean to write 'Blaze is the word that comes to mind
most often in thinking of this collaboration between Lehmann
and Toscanini. They seemed to take fire from each other; the
resulting conflagration warmed all of us as long as memory can
last.' It would be idle to pretend that Lehmann's 1927 recording
scorches the mind as indelibly as that, but it is a resplendent and
exalted performance nonetheless, with great brilliance at the top
of the voice (a quality which she gradually lost as her career
progressed), and a startlingly virile quality to some of the chest
notes – highly suitable in this particular role.

The disc continues with three samples of Lehmann's Wagnerian
repertoire. Rapt and dedicated as is her singing of 'Elsa's Song to
the Breezes' from LOHENGRIN and Elisabeth's 'Prayer' from
TANNHÄUSER, I almost feel that she is wasted on such virgin-
ally virtuous fare, whereas with the third excerpt from the same
composer, Isolde's 'Liebestod', we are offered a right rich feast.
Lehmann never sang Isolde on stage. She longed to, and she almost
took the plunge. Two of her favourite conductors, Bruno Walter
and Franz Schalk, were prepared to help her with it, promising to
keep the orchestra down and to match her with one of the more
lyrical Tristans, but Richard Strauss was horrified at the idea, and
in a letter to the Viennese critic Ludwig Karpath he wrote 'What a
shame for that precious talent and that rare and beautiful voice!' In
the German operatic profession there is an exactly graded label for
every type (*Fach*) of voice, and Lehmann, as her good friends Leo
Slezak and Lauritz Melchior reminded her, belonged absolutely

to the *jugendlich-dramatisches Fach*, not the *hochdramatisches*. Luckily their counsel prevailed, and Lehmann contented herself with adding the 'Liebestod' to her concert repertoire, and to making this one incandescent recording of it. Anyone wanting to experience how differently two truly great singers can set about the same piece of music could scarcely do better than compare this recording with Flagstad's – no wonder the two of them did not see eye to eye! From the first note Lehmann is the epitome of femininity. Unlike Flagstad she allows us to detect a tinge of frailty, but it is a frailty which only adds to the unshakeable conviction of her love. Individual words and phrases are picked out and given entirely personal inflections. Isolde's question to Brangäne and King Mark, 'Seht ihr's, Freunde? Säht ihr's nicht?' is a perfect example. The words contain a grammatical subtlety, an intensification of emphasis, with the meaning stepped up from 'Do you see it friends?' to 'Is it possible that you do not?' Flagstad sings majestically through these two phrases; they form part of the arching architectural entity of her 'Liebestod'. Lehmann, on the other hand, delivers them as separate and vitally important appeals to her companions, the second even more urgent than the first. Her Isolde needs the assurance that they, too, understand the smile which illuminates her dead hero's face.

The other composer most generously represented on this disc is naturally Richard Strauss. There is a gloriously sung version of Arabella's Act I monologue 'Mein Elemer', recorded shortly after the first Vienna performance in 1933, and exactly echoing a description of the music which Lehmann wrote in a letter to a friend while she was studying the role: 'You'll like ARABELLA very much. I am delighted. It is an enchanting role, full of charm and high spirits. I am completely under the spell of this very graceful music.' Strauss had in fact asked Lehmann to create the role at its world premiere in Dresden three months earlier, but for the first time Nazi politics intervened. Fritz Busch was to have conducted, but he was hounded out of Dresden for his anti-Hitlerian views, and Clemens Krauss was brought in to conduct the new opera. Krauss insisted on having his wife, Viorica Ursuleac, for the title-role, and the shadow of things to come had fallen over the Austro-German operatic scene. Lehmann did sing the Vienna premiere three months later, but even that was not without its painful aspects as Lehmann's mother died on the day between the final dress rehearsal and the first night. She was eighty-three years old, but Lehmann's parents had followed wherever her main contracts took her – from Berlin to Hamburg, from Hamburg to Vienna – and her mother had always played an essential role in her life. When Lehmann went off on her first professional trip to America the old lady was touchingly convinced that her daughter would fall victim to Red Indians or Chicago gangsters, and even if the real perils of the international opera circuit are of a slightly different nature, it is always good to have that kind of support.

Richard Strauss is further represented in this selection by the Marschallin's monologue 'Da geht er hin', taken from the famous HMV recording of ROSENKAVALIER excerpts, of which more anon, and by Ariadne's 'Sie atmet leicht . . . Es gibt ein Reich'. Aspects of this particular scene were touched on in a hilarious interview, conducted in 1962 between Lehmann and her bitter rival Maria Jeritza for a Texaco-Metropolitan Opera intermission broadcast. Jeritza, who created the role, claimed to have mastered the singing of one endless climactic phrase in a single breath, as a result of working on it with Strauss himself for three weeks. Lehmann was obliged to admit that she used to have recourse to an extra breath, which produced a delighted cackle from Jeritza and the comment 'I'm sure you could do it, Lotte, but you didn't work three weeks!' Perhaps Lehmann was taking her revenge when she wrote some time later 'There is a lot I could tell about Jeritza, but so many years have passed that I'll place the mantle of oblivion over all that took place between her and myself. A Primadonna Assoluta allows no one near her who might bar her way, even if unintentionally . . . She was – and I mean this purely as a compliment – like one of the great courtesans of the past.' In any case, extra breath or no, there is nothing to apologize for in Lehmann's Ariadne recording.

Another contemporary composer whose music Lehmann adored to sing was Korngold, now totally out of fashion, and in the arias 'Der Erste, der Lieb' mich gelehrt' from DIE TOTE STADT and 'Ich ging zu ihm' from DAS WUNDER DER HELIANE she does positively wallow in his somewhat overripe and self-indulgent *cantilena*. DIE TOTE STADT was a famous Jeritza vehicle, but it is the kind of music in which their two styles absolutely overlap, and when Lehmann sang the double role of Marie/Marietta in Berlin, conducted, as was this recording, by the young Georg Széll, Korngold wrote her a letter of thanks which I feel sure he took good care not to mention to her rival. He even went so far as to express his gratitude to Lehmann for her 'unique achievement' – a veritable time bomb, should it have reached the wrong eyes or ears! In any case, beautifully as Marie/Marietta suits her, Lehmann finds even more ample opportunity in Heliane's soaring aria to display her gift for maintaining throughout an extended passage a quite extraordinary intensity of feeling. This was one of her own favourites among her recordings, and it is easy to see why. When she started stage rehearsals for the role she felt inhibited by the fact that Heliane had to appear on stage as naked as the conventions of the time would allow; the hero, unjustly condemned to die, expresses as his last wish the desire to see her beauty unadorned – pretty heady stuff. 'Ich ging zu ihm' is Heliane's own defence of her actions before the court, and Lehmann sustains it on a sizzling level of emotion.

After all this ecstasy it is rather a relief to turn to Lehmann in humorous mood, of which this disc gives us two delightful examples. 'Nun eilt herbei' from Nicolai's DIE LUSTIGEN WEIBER VON WINDSOR is the big number for Frau Fluth, (Shakespeare's Mistress Ford, and Verdi's Alice), in which she rehearses her reception of that ruthless destroyer of female hearts, Sir John Falstaff. Lehmann's recitative is a miracle of articulation, with every inflection right on the button, and the aria fairly crackles with malicious wit. Men in general, and 'jener dicke Schlemmer' ('that fat glutton') in particular, are not in for an easy time at the hands of this Merry Wife. Nor is she likely to give Eisenstein an easy time either, to judge from her FLEDERMAUS Csárdás. It is heavily cut, she does not bother with the phoney Hungarian accent, and she goes down rather than up on the final D, but in the Frischka there is paprika enough and to spare.

DIE FLEDERMAUS hardly counts as an operetta any more, so hallowed has it become as every opera house's gesture to the Lighter Muse. With the final item on this recital, however, we move to a style of operetta which Lotte Lehmann never sang on stage, but in which, to judge from this recording, she found great delight. It is the title-heroine's monologue 'So war meine Mutter' from EVA, Lehár's 1911 Operetta with a Social Conscience. It opens with a passage of 'Melodram' (speech over orchestral accompaniment), leads into a sung section of recitative-like descriptiveness as Eva recalls the vision of glamour that was her mother, and culminates in one of Lehár's most deeply felt waltz tunes, 'Wär' es auch nichts als ein Augenblick'. Perhaps it aroused echoes of Lehmann's own feelings towards her mother, perhaps it was merely her response to Lehár at his best, but in any case it receives from Lehmann a performance of touching simplicity and charm, as well as ending this outstanding recital on a note of intriguing contrast.

Lehmann was not, of course, only prominent in the German repertoire. She was a particular favourite of Puccini's in the roles of Manon Lescaut and Suor Angelica, and her Tosca was as highly praised in San Francisco and at the Met as it was in Vienna and Berlin. One of Pearl's Lehmann CDs offers several Puccini recordings (GEMM CD 9409), and although I imagine that they would only be of interest to the specialist listener, as they are almost all sung in German, they certainly confirm Caruso's verdict, both as to the quality of the 'voce italiana' and as to the smooth legato with which she deploys it. The fact that Tosca's 'Vissi d'arte, vissi d'amore' becomes 'Nur der Schönheit weiht' ich mein Leben' does not worry me too much, as I spent much of my own early career singing Puccini in German, but it may not be to everybody's taste. The two TOSCA duets are, in fact, sung in Italian, but Lehmann's partner, the Polish tenor Jan Kiepura, a man who had many admirers in his time, is not shown to vocal or stylistic advantage on these particular recordings. Apart from these three TOSCA numbers the disc gives us Lehmann's beautifully sung versions of Butterfly's Entrance and Act II aria, Mimi's Act I aria, and Turandot's 'Del primo pianto' ('Die ersten Tränen'). I myself would have thought that Lehmann was born to sing Liù, but at the Vienna premiere of TURANDOT it was the title-role that she undertook, and to great acclaim. After Puccini we move on to Johann Strauss – from DIE FLEDERMAUS a teasing 'Mein Herr, was dächten Sie von mir?' from Act I, the same Csárdás version as we had on the EMI reissue and an Act II Finale dominated by the irrepressible 'Schwung' of Richard Tauber, who flits between the roles of Falke and Eisenstein, according to which of them has the best tunes; then from DER ZIGEUNERBARON the Finales of Acts I and II, which again give Tauber more of a crack of the whip than Lehmann, and also establish how difficult the Odeon technicians found it in 1928 to cope with a full cast, chorus and orchestra. The disc continues with some lovely vocalization in the familiar Berceuse from Godard's JOCELYN, and ends with several rarities – songs by composers whose names, I imagine, will not ring many bells: Jensen, von Eulenberg and Werner.

If this disc takes us onto the byways of Lehmann's output, Pearl's *GEMM 9410*, with the exception of six of its tracks, heads back onto the highways of the two great Richards, Wagner and Strauss. The odd men out are Antonia's aria from LES CONTES D'HOFFMANN, with an uncomfortable high A at its climax, but with an ideal sense of tragedy-in-miniature colouring each of the repeated phrases 'Sie entfloh, die Taube so minnig'; a vivid rendering of Madeleine's Act III aria from ANDREA CHENIER, one of Lehmann's favourite excursions into the world of *verismo*; Lehár's EVA waltz song once again; a warm bath of a number called 'Das Zauberlied', a lushly orchestrated Palm Court hymn to the magic of love by a once popular composer called Erik Meyer-

Helmund; a collector's piece, with the diva soaring above heavenly choir, orchestra and organ in 'Andachtsstunde' ('Sanctuary of the Heart'), by Albert W. Ketèlby; and last, but a very long way from least, 'Amor und Psyche' from d'Albert's DIE TOTEN AUGEN, the piece in which Lehmann took her farewell from the Hamburg Opera in 1916. This particular aria was invariably demanded as an encore whenever she went back there for concerts, and it is surely one of the most exquisite of all her recordings.

But on to the two Richards. From Wagner's operas we have Lehmann's 1930 recording of 'Du bist der Lenz' (DIE WAL-KÜRE), a glowing performance, but obviously of less interest than the 1935 recording of the whole First Act, discussed in detail below; and the 'Liebestod', evidently not taken from quite such an immaculate original as the EMI version. Two of the Wesendonck Lieder, though, 'Träume' and 'Schmerzen', emerge with arresting immediacy, and as they are followed by two Strauss Lieder of equally vivid quality and recorded in the same session, it seems that on 13 June 1929 the Odeon technicians had one of their better days. Lehmann's account of 'Ständchen' is lucid and sensuous, making great use of swooning downward *portamenti*, which would doubtless get anyone into trouble with the critics nowadays, but which must clearly have been sanctioned by the composer; and in 'Traum durch die Dämmerung' she manages to combine her usual immaculate diction with an exemplary, seamless stream of tone. The group continues with an acoustic version of 'Cäcilie' (how she did love to pinch *men's* songs!), and this is of considerable stylistic interest as it was recorded back in 1921 before she had really begun to give much thought to Lieder singing as an art of its own. In those days she simply regarded Lieder as melodies which any other instrument could do at least as much justice to as the human voice, and it was her brother Fritz who first set her thinking that in fact each Lied has its own story, that it has been created out of some personal experience, and that its performer must try to recreate it in the same way. Her subsequent renown as a specialist Lieder singer was built up gradually, and she herself was the first to acknowledge her debt to Bruno Walter, her accompanist in the series of recitals which became annual events in the Salzburg Festival. In his memoirs Walter was to write of her

> It was admirable how Lotte Lehmann's dramatic feeling, to which she had formerly been inclined to yield almost to the point where she did violence to her voice, had gradually become restrained to fit the rendering of songs. Amazing, too, that her impetuous elemental personality should have found the way to the stylistic purity of the song by means of her own almost infallible instinct.

Well, in this 'Cäcilie' there is still plenty of the 'impetuous elemental personality' on hand, and it calls to mind a remark made to me by one of the great British connoisseurs of singing, Rupert Bruce-Lockhart. 'When Lehmann sang "Cäcilie",' he said, 'one began to worry that she might *fly* from the platform.' In the last two songs of the group, 'Morgen' and 'Mit deinen blauen Augen', both with violin accompaniment of the soupy variety, she naturally eschews such excessive elation – though in the former her well known disregard for note values crops up from time to time, and I think Jeritza might have rubbed her hands at the unexpected number of breaths that she takes.

This same disc also offers us five excerpts from Strauss operas – the Marschallin's ponderings on the ineluctability of time, a valuable snippet from a famous interpretation but, obviously, like the Sieglinde 'bleeding chunk', overtaken by the more extensive recording discussed below; the Ariadne and Arabella arias which we encountered chez EMI; and for good measure the rest of that same ARABELLA session, recorded three weeks after the Vienna premiere, with Lehmann in radiant voice, and comprising that kernel of the heroine's slightly odd psychology 'Er ist der Richtige nicht für mich', as well as the ensuing duet 'Ich weiss nicht wie du bist', with Kathe Heidersbach of the Berlin Opera as an appealing Zdenka.

To revert for a moment to Lehmann the Lieder singer.

Considering her towering achievements as a recitalist, this branch of her art is woefully under-represented on CD, but there is one disc which makes magnificent atonement, and that is RCA Victor *GD87809*. It is a bit of a musical mishmash perhaps, but Lehmann's recitals were by no means limited to 'das klassische deutsche Lied', so why should this disc be? From one inspired session on 13 March 1936 we are treated to eight numbers in four different languages. Several of these songs are by composers of whom I must confess to knowing absolutely nothing; but their very unfamiliarity establishes how marvellous Lehmann must have been at speaking to an audience through a song. For one thing you can hear every word, and if English happens to be your only language, just listen to what she does with a song lasting a minute and a half, called 'Midsummer', by a composer named Worth. The selection ranges from two exquisite lullabies, one Italian, one German, through the Hahn-Verlaine 'D'une prison', and the Gounod-Byron 'Vierge d'Athènes', to an ecstatic Mediterranean outburst entitled 'Canto di primavera', the final line of which, 'Udite! Aprite tutte le finestre al cor!' ('Listen! Open all the windows to the heart!'), could almost serve as Lehmann's credo, and culminates in a song, entirely new to me, to which I would feel inclined to hand the palm for the whole session. It was written by Lehmann's accompanist, Erno Balogh, it is called 'Do not chide me', and it fills me with regret that Lehmann never turned her attention, as her friend Tauber did, to the songs of Jerome Kern. Several of these numbers, incidentally, were never published on 78s.

There are many other delights on this disc, and even the songs from Lehmann's first Victor session in 1935 capture her vocal quality far more intimately than any of the earlier recordings. We are taken up to her very last commercial recordings, three Strauss songs in March 1949; and with the inclusion of three Wolf, three Schumann and five Schubert songs as well, we are given at least a glimpse of her approach to what has to be the core of any great Lieder singer's repertoire. Not for her the mere striving after technical perfection. She proves that as late as 1947 she was still quite capable of sustaining a line as taxing as Schubert's in 'Nacht und Träume'; but it is not to prove that point that she sings the song, it is to wrap around her listeners the mood of external tranquillity and internal longing, which the poem and the music engender. Every song in this selection – and they cover a well chosen variety of moods – has, as was Lehmann's avowed intention, its own story to tell. The disc closes most aptly with her deeply felt thank you to Music itself, Schubert's 'An die Musik', the song with which Lehmann ended her farewell recital in the New York Town Hall on 16 February 1951 when, choked with emotion, she was unable to sing the final line and stood with her hands covering her face while her accompanist played on alone.

There had been another widely publicized occasion in Lehmann's career when her emotions had overwhelmed her. At Covent Garden in May 1938 in the middle of the first act of DER ROSENKAVALIER she found herself simply unable to continue. She called out 'I can't, I can't', rushed sobbing into the wings, and dropped in a dead faint.* On that occasion, though, her breakdown was not caused by the sweet sorrow of parting, but by the intolerable strain of her existence after Hitler's annexation of Austria. Her husband was in a sanatorium in Switzerland, her stepchildren, who were half-Jewish, were trapped in central Europe as were so many of her dearest friends and colleagues, and she herself had lost her home and most of her possessions. Small wonder then that the festive atmosphere of the opening night of the season at the Royal Opera House with Lehmann singing the one role in all her repertoire most reminiscent of Vienna should have precipitated such a reaction. Lehmann herself was not Jewish, and had been brought under pressure by Goering, in his capacity as 'Kulturminister', to return to Germany and take her rightful place as one of the brightest pearls in the Herrenvolk's cultural crown. Indeed, the most amazing incident of any during a Lehmann performance must have been the interruption of one

---

* Luckily the Viennese soprano Hilde Konetzni happened to be in the audience and rescued the performance.

of her Lieder recitals in Dresden in 1934, when a terrified official kept trying to stop her in mid-song to tell her that the Herr Reichsminister in person was on the telephone demanding to speak to her. To the wretched official's consternation she insisted on completing her group of songs at the end of which the audience, instead of applauding, sat paralysed with fear. As Lehmann herself described it 'Only later did I realize why. They must have thought that I had fallen into disfavour, and expected me to be arrested at any moment.' It was in fact Lehmann's refusal to accept Goering's offer of an extravagantly favourable contract in Berlin which led to her being declared 'persona non grata', first in Germany and then in Austria, and eventually making her home in the United States.

Lehmann's career at the Met had started later than might have been expected, largely because Jeritza was firmly installed there and was on the friendliest of terms with the Chairman, Mr Otto Kahn. When he retired in 1933 Jeritza's contract was not renewed, and the way was at last open to Lehmann. She made her debut on 11 January 1934 as Sieglinde in DIE WALKÜRE, and in the words of *Time* magazine 'If the singer had been an Italian tenor who had spent his last nickel on the claque, the ovation could not have been bigger.' This had long been one of the most highly prized Lehmann roles at Covent Garden, and both in London and New York her habitual Siegmund was 'The Great Dane', Lauritz Melchior. In the summer of 1935 His Master's Voice brought off the remarkable coup of securing the two of them to record the whole of the first act with the Vienna Philharmonic Orchestra, conducted by Bruno Walter; and this classic set, on which so many enthusiasts of my generation cut our Wagnerian teeth, stands up resplendently to the test of time in its new incarnation as EMI *CDH 7 61020 2*. Of course modern stereo recordings have more to offer in terms of amplitude and detail, but this is a performance which can still make the skin tingle, and by the time the orchestra has swirled its way to the crowning glory of those final three bars, it is easy enough to see in the imagination the heavy curtains sweeping down and to hear the thunder of applause which invariably erupted from the audience on Lehmann-Melchior nights. It is, from all concerned, an intensely theatrical achievement, never more so than in Lehmann's delineation of Sieglinde as she blossoms from the downtrodden chattel of the brutal Hunding to the ecstatic 'Bridesister' of the heroic Siegmund. The revulsion in her voice as she remembers her enforced espousal, the almost girlish tone that she achieves as she describes Siegmund's strangely familiar features, the radiance of her dawning recognition, the total abandon of the final realization – all of this adds up to a Sieglinde who still speaks loud and clear over the gap of nearly sixty years.

The same can be said, but in a totally different way, of the other role on which Lehmann most deeply made her mark, the Marschallin in DER ROSENKAVALIER. She, to my mind, is a much more ambivalent figure than Sieglinde. How would we feel disposed nowadays towards a married lady enjoying all the privileges of wealth and rank, and approaching early middle age, who besports herself in the marital bed with a teenage admirer, pulls rank unashamedly when the going gets rough and indulges in a welter of self-pity at the thought that her toyboy days may be drawing to a close? I know that the same argument could be applied to married ladies who elope with their twin brothers, but somehow in the case of Sieglinde the greater distance of time lends its own suspension of disbelief. In any case, everyone who experienced Lehmann's Marschallin seems to have capitulated entirely to her dignity and charm. This was the role which the distinguished British critic Neville Cardus had in mind when he was asked who, in his opinion, were the three greatest actresses on the London stage, and named Lotte Lehmann alongside those two 'grandes dames' of classical drama, Edith Evans and Peggy Ashcroft. As Bruno Walter expressed it, Lehmann's Marschallin was 'one of the outstanding achievements of the contemporary operatic stage. Here, indeed, was that rare phenomenon of an artist's personality becoming wholly merged with a poetic figure, and of a transitory theatrical event being turned into an unforgettable experience.'

Well, how much of all this emerges from HMV's famous 1933 recording of a potted version of ROSENKAVALIER, with a classic cast, and now happily reissued by Pearl as GEMM *CDS 9365* (*two discs*)? The answer, I think, has to be a heartening amount. The general balance in this set was never as good as in the WALKÜRE recording – the rapid patter of conversation and its filigree underpinning in the orchestra seems to have been harder for the engineers to capture. After some slightly muddy opening pages, though, the voices do come through with increasing clarity, and in Lehmann's responses to Maria Olczewska's ardent *gaucherie* as Octavian we are immediately brought face to face with an emotionally very different creature from the Sieglinde discussed above. Funnily enough, on the surface these two characters have more in common than one might immediately suppose. They are both women who have suffered enforced marriages, the Marschallin admittedly in less primitive form than Sieglinde, but it is nevertheless on 'a girl fresh from the Convent and ordered into holy matrimony' that she looks back so wistfully. Like Sieglinde she longs for love and finds it outside marriage, but unlike Sieglinde she is destined for something much more circumscribed than elemental passion – a self-destructive Marschallin, after all, would be undignified, and not at all *comme il faut*. To me it is Lehmann's acceptance that everything in her life will have to exist under this patina of social dignity which so strongly characterizes her interpretation. It is as finite a form of resignation as the 'heut' oder morgen, oder den übernächsten Tag' ('today, tomorrow, or the day after that') with which she so accurately charts the journey of Octavian's affections. In every monologue the detail is beautifully observed; when Baron Ochs gets his come-uppance (he is shamefully treated, I always think) the necessary imperiousness is hers to command; and in the final trio her 'Hab' mir's gelobt' is sung with a dignified and moving eloquence. I have heard it said that with her one concluding phrase 'ja, ja', Lehmann was able to express more than other sopranos with the whole role, but those who feel it to be the case on this recording are deceiving themselves. With the trio safely wrapped up, and forgetting that there was still one bar to come, Lehmann went home – so Elisabeth Schumann saved the day by singing it for her!

Many singers, I know, will agree with me when I say that the approbation which means the most to us is that of our colleagues, and perhaps the ultimate accolade for Lehmann's Marschallin lay in Flagstad's reaction when she was asked if she would like to sing the role at the Met – 'I would love to, but after Lehmann – never!' It was the role in which Lehmann said her last good-bye to the operatic stage in Los Angeles in 1946, and thereafter, besides her continuing work as a recitalist, she plunged her energies into writing, painting, and her famous Master Classes, a form of instruction which was virtually her own invention. One red letter day in her latter years was the reopening of the Vienna State Opera in November 1955, when she returned for the first time to what had always remained her spiritual home. As she recalled it in a talk to the Opera Guild of Southern California shortly afterwards, 'The box was decorated with roses, and we were in a crossfire of popping flashbulbs. There we stood, Alfred Piccaver and I . . . He is now old, and I am old – but I certainly did not feel it at all at that moment.' When she died, at her home in Santa Barbara, California, the Vienna State Opera arranged for her ashes to be buried in that part of Vienna's Central Cemetery which is reserved for those who have attained outstanding honour in the Arts. On the stone was carved something which Richard Strauss had said of her – 'Sie hat gesungen, dass es Sterne rührte' ('She sang, and it moved the stars').

ALFRED PICCAVER

ENGLISH TENOR

b. Long Sutton, Lincolnshire, 25 February 1884
d. Vienna, 23 September 1958

I imagine that to English-speaking readers the name of Alfred Piccaver will be the least familiar in this book – which is ironical, as he was an Englishman who spent most of his early life in the United States. His true artistic home, however, was Vienna, and there his name is still legendary indeed. Vienna is a city in which there was always a better yesterday, and when I first went to live there in 1956 it was the 1910s, '20s and '30s that were looked back on as the Golden Age of the Vienna Opera; an age dominated by three glittering figures – Lotte Lehmann, Maria Jeritza and Alfred Piccaver.

In the case of Piccaver I have to plead a special interest; he was my first voice teacher, I owe him a great deal, and I was extremely fond of him. I first heard his voice on a gramophone record (it was Florestan's aria from FIDELIO) just at the time when I was wrestling with the decision to give up a safe job and study to be an opera singer. I was told that the owner of the voice was alive and well and took a few pupils at his home in Putney, so I decided to take my courage in both hands and seek his advice. I had been bowled over by the sound on the record – there was a heroic stature to the singing and a richness of timbre quite unlike any other that I had heard – and when I went to Putney I was expecting to be confronted by some leonine and intimidating character. The person who greeted me, however, was a small silver-haired gentleman of enormous courtesy and charm, kind, helpful and unassuming. He chatted to me about his garden and about Butch, his boxer dog, and I could see no connection at all between him and a vast portrait hanging in the hall of a fiery-eyed young man with a mass of raven curls, decked out in the trappings of some tremendous romantic role.* When he sat down at the piano and took me through a couple of scales the professional expert instantly emerged; but it was not until eighteen months later when I followed him to Vienna and saw for myself the magical effect which his name still had there that I really began to appreciate what a giant Alfred Piccaver had been.

He was born in Long Sutton in the county of Lincolnshire, and the unusual name (pronounced with the emphasis on the first syllable) may possibly be of Spanish origin, though the family have no hard evidence of this. Piccaver's grandfather had been an innkeeper who prospered sufficiently to buy a farm. Piccaver's father, being one of five sons, decided to widen his horizons by emigrating to America; Piccaver himself was not yet two years old at the time, and it was in America that he grew up. He was educated at the Albany High School in New York State, but from an early age singing came more easily to him than schooling. At his graduation party he was toasted by his fellow students with the couplet 'Here's to our singer, whose nickname is "Picc"; he has a fine voice, though he's full of Old Nick.' It may have been Old Nick who unsettled him during brief flirtations with the West Point Military Academy and Thomas Edison's electrical works, but in any case at the age of twenty-one he won a scholarship to the Opera School of the Metropolitan Opera, and from that moment singing became his life.

Armed with a free pass to the Met's standing room during the seasons of 1905–7 Piccaver listened to everything he could and fell completely under the spell of Caruso. He picked up some practical experience and some useful cash singing at social functions – on one occasion, for instance, thanks to an introduction from Heinrich Conried, General Manager of the Met, he was invited to

---

* I later established that the role was Dick Johnson in LA FANCIULLA DEL WEST.

oblige with some songs at the New York Southern Society Ladies' Night at the Astor Hotel; and at the Seventh Annual Dinner of the Manhattan Eye, Ear and Throat Hospital, as an old menu card still testifies, his contribution came next in the programme after the frozen Nesselrode Pudding. His first complete role on stage was Max in the Opera School's production of DER FREISCHÜTZ, performed at the Irving Place Theatre on 18 May 1907, when one of the critics wrote 'his voice, though small and timorous, is prettily coloured and agreeable' – praise which, I feel, could scarcely be fainter.

Later in that same summer, however, Piccaver's teacher, a Madame Jaeger, included him in a group of students whom she took with her to her summer school in the Austrian town of Hallstadt, and this proved to be the turning point in Piccaver's life. He was heard by Angelo Neumann, Director of the Deutsches Landestheater in Prague, who offered him a three-year contract. Neumann's reputation as a talent-spotter was never more fully justified than by his discovery of Piccaver. If ever there was a beginner, this was he – twenty-three years old, no repertoire, very little musical training, no apparent gift for acting, and no knowledge of the German language in which everything had to be sung. Within a couple of seasons, though, the surest way of selling out the house was to present Alfred Piccaver in one of the romantic roles of the French or Italian repertoire.

Piccaver worked harder during those early years in Prague than at any other time in his life. He made his debut on 9 September 1907, as Fenton in DIE LUSTIGEN WEIBER VON WINDSOR, when the critics, while welcoming his sympathetic appearance and attractive quality of voice, did not refrain from pointing out that he still had a lot to learn. He studied voice with Frau Professor Prohaska-Neumann, and he was also sent for several months to Milan, to work with a distinguished Maestro named Rosario. On the eve of his twenty-fourth birthday he sang his first Lyonel in MARTHA, and the tone of the reviews began to change. 'At last a role has been found which fits his outstanding voice like a glove', one of the critics wrote, and the familiar (but by no means easy) aria 'Ach, so fromm' had to be encored. Every season saw half a dozen new roles enter Piccaver's repertoire, many of them conducted by the young Kapellmeisters Otto Klemperer and Erich Kleiber, and by 1910 when his contract was renewed, though his stage-craft still left a certain amount to be desired, he had become an artist to reckon with.

In those days the legendary baritone Mattia Battistini used to tour Europe with his own Italian company, and in May 1910 they came to Prague to perform LA TRAVIATA. For some reason they were without an Alfredo; Piccaver assumed the role, and so impressed Battistini that he was asked to undertake the Duke in RIGOLETTO at their next port of call which was no less a place than the Vienna Hofoper – the Court Opera, later to become the State Opera. On 7 June 1910, at the age of twenty-six, Alfred Piccaver made his first appearance in the opera house with which his name was to become so closely associated, and the impact of his performance was immediate. As an old man he told me how alarmed he had felt as he sat on the train from Prague to Vienna, but he need not have worried. He was rapturously received by the public, and hailed as a major discovery by the press. As one paper put it 'He stands head and shoulders above all his German colleagues, and the Vienna Opera has no lyric tenor at its disposal today who is capable of singing like this.' Another complained 'while the Hofoper has been landed with the greatest tenorial problems, a couple of hours from Vienna by express train there was a young lyric tenor whose sweet smooth voice, and whose easy and well developed technique could have been a balm in our days of affliction.' The Director of the Hofoper, Felix von Weingartner, evidently agreed because Piccaver was offered an outstandingly favourable contract, to start in two years' time, when his obligations in Prague would be completed.

A contract with the Hofoper naturally gave Piccaver an entirely new status in the world of international opera. Further performances with Battistini in 1911 – RIGOLETTO again, DON

GIOVANNI and BALLO – added another layer of polish to the Italianism of his style, and the troupe's musical director, Maestro Arturo Vigna, Caruso's regular conductor at the Met, described Piccaver as superior to any Italian tenor of the time except Caruso himself. Another exciting development was that the Odeon Recording Company of Berlin had clearly decided on Piccaver as *the* up-and-coming lyric tenor of the day, because they sought him out in Prague before he had even started on his new career in Vienna, and they too offered him a remarkably flattering contract. Although their roster included many of the leading singers of the day, they undertook to pay nobody more than they paid Piccaver, and to bring out his records – a minimum of ten titles a year for three years – as 'a special series, with Luxury labels'.

A selection of eighteen of Piccaver's acoustic recordings covering his full eight years as an exclusive Odeon artist (1912–20), is now available on CD as *Lebendige Vergangenheit 89060*. The earliest of them is the cavatina 'Ah! lève-toi, soleil' from Gounod's ROMEO ET JULIETTE, and though it is sung in German, several of Piccaver's greatest virtues are immediately apparent. The voice at this stage was a purely lyrical one but very masculine in timbre and with a totally individual quality of sound – it is one of those voices which you recognize in the very first bar. The essence of the singing style is smoothness. There is no feeling of effort or attack, the legato flows on and on, and there is never a hint of a 'gear change' as the vocal line climbs into the upper register. Interestingly, although at this stage of his career Piccaver had no problems with the top of the voice, he recorded the aria a semitone down, with the climactic notes becoming A naturals instead of B flats. I imagine that it must have been to facilitate the magical and perfectly controlled diminuendo which he achieves on the second of these notes, retaining the full velvety quality of the voice even when he has reduced it to a pianissimo. This ability to move in and out of the so-called 'voix mixte' was very much a Piccaver trademark, not only in what one of the critics dismissively referred to as

the 'lemonade operas' (by which I take him to have meant those of
Messieurs Gounod, Thomas and Massenet), but also in the Mozart
and Verdi repertoires. In 1910 Piccaver's Tamino in Prague was
reviewed as being 'ever more gratifying, and already a thousand
times better than Slezak's in Salzburg'. When the Prague company
went to Berlin with RIGOLETTO and BALLO, it was Piccaver
who ran away with the notices, and in Prague itself he had become
a sort of cult figure. In appearance he was already stocky, and was
later to become what the Viennese call 'mollig' (chubby), and the
British call fat; but the boyish friendliness of his manner combined
with the sensuousness of his voice made him one of the teenage
idols of his day. Every Piccaver performance was packed with his
devoted admirers, a notable proportion of them being young and
female. Their unrestrained enthusiasm occasionally threatened to
become a nuisance but, as the *Tagblatt* recognized, 'There is no
getting away from it, Piccaver is now the Opera's trump card, at
least as far as the public is concerned. You only have to see his
name down for a new role, and a sold-out house is as good as
certain.'

When Piccaver bade farewell to the Prague Landestheater
with LA BOHEME in June 1912 the stage was already deep
in flowers by the end of Act III; and when the final curtain
fell the audience refused to leave until a piano had been wheeled
on stage and Piccaver had switched from Rodolfo to the Duke in
RIGOLETTO with a spirited rendering of 'La donna è mobile'. It
was with the Duke, once again, that Piccaver opened his account
as a fully-fledged member of the Vienna Hofoper, and later in the
same year he recorded the three arias, all of which are included
in the Lebendige Vergangenheit selection. Both 'Quest' o quella'
and 'La donna' are despatched with splendidly carefree bravura
(though even more points would be scored if the Italian were
really dead on target – but more of that anon), and Piccaver's
cadenza at the end of 'La donna' is the only one I know
which really challenges the speed and accuracy of Caruso's. It
is, however, the Act II aria 'Parmi veder le lagrime' which fully

demonstrates Piccaver's standing as a *bel canto* singer, and reveals why he should have garnered so rich a harvest of praise even in a house as exalted as the Vienna Hofoper. This is real Piccaver territory, with the vocal line, despite its awkward tessitura, easily and buoyantly sustained, rising to a fine manly forte at the climax and dropping back to an ideally poised *mezza voce* in the final bar.

The ultimate in smoothness of emission is to be found in two Donizetti arias, 'Spirto gentil' from LA FAVORITA and 'Deserto in terra' from DON SEBASTIANO. The latter in particular is a much more straightforward piece of music than 'Parmi veder le lagrime', and as Piccaver takes it a whole tone down from its punishing original key of D flat most of the aria flows easily along in the centre of the voice, rising up the scale at the end of each verse to a high A sharp. Listening to it you have the feeling that Piccaver is not so much producing the tones through any physical effort of his own as merely leaning into them and rolling them on their way. There is a lustrous, almost baritonal quality to the middle register, with no apparent change of placing as he rises to the top notes, and it was this kind of singing which inevitably led to comparisons, throughout Piccaver's career, between him and Caruso. Piccaver, however, had no illusions as to their validity. To the end of his life he revered Caruso – Battistini was the only other singer whom he considered worthy of being mentioned in the same breath – and I feel sure that it was his diffidence about coming into direct competition with his idol which led him to make what later emerged as having been a serious miscalculation. In 1912 Gatti-Casazza sent Piccaver a contract to sing seventeen roles at the Metropolitan Opera in the seasons of 1913–17, for the princely fee of $600, rising to $800, per performance.* For a twenty-eight year old tenor scarcely established in international opera this was a staggering offer, but Piccaver suffered a crisis of confidence and did not return the contract. The Met never

---

* Approximately equivalent to £4800 rising to £6500 at the time of writing.

approached him again.

In Vienna, in what turned out to be the last of that city's good old days, it did not take long for Piccaver to establish the same heady degree of popularity with the public that he had enjoyed in Prague. His regular partners were artists of a challenging calibre, and they kept him on his toes. There were long-established international stars such as Selma Kurz, she of the endless trill, a lady of whom Piccaver used to speak in old age with gratitude and affection; and, among the younger luminaries, the tempestuous Maria Jeritza, of whom he did not speak at all if he could help it. In 1913 the partnership of Jeritza and Piccaver stepped into the limelight when they were chosen to star together in the German-language premiere of Puccini's LA FANCIULLA DEL WEST. For some strange reason Caruso, who had created the role of Dick Johnson at the Met in 1910, never recorded the aria 'Ch'ella mi creda', but Piccaver did (in German) in 1914, and this too, along with several other Puccini arias, is on the Lebendige Vergangenheit CD. Puccini was probably the composer to whom Piccaver's voice and style were most ideally suited; he worked personally with Piccaver on several of his roles, and they provide so many opportunities for what Piccaver himself used to refer to as 'good straight singing'. In 'Ch'ella mi creda', as with Cavaradossi's first aria from TOSCA and Rodolfo's 'Che gelida manina' from LA BOHEME, Piccaver allows the sentiment of the music to speak for itself without resorting to extraneous sobs and gulps. For some tastes, I have no doubt, his approach would be too unemotional, and there are times when the lack of dramatic accentuation, or of Italianate thrill on the high notes, can leave one feeling slightly deprived. It was, however, absolutely not the roof-raising final note that was Piccaver's stock in trade, but rather the seductive flow of the whole *cantilena*. For the Viennese his voice held a sort of spell, and the quality which I have most frequently heard praised by older opera-goers in Vienna is its 'Weichheit', or softness – not in the sense of soft as opposed to loud, but in the sense of softness to the touch.

I recall one old lady, her eyes gleaming with the light of joys remembered, telling me during my student days 'His voice was like a great warm cloak – you could wrap yourself in it'; and many was the 'Wienerin' of over a certain age, who would blush delicately at the mention of his name and coyly admit that when she was a schoolgirl she used to sleep with his picture underneath her pillow.

Lotte Lehmann, after 1916 Piccaver's most regular partner, once wrote that when she performed with him she was happy to overlook his apparent lack of interest in the dramatic aspect of their scenes together because 'the caressing velvet of his voice was so unbelievably beautiful'. One of their most successful partnerships was as Manon and des Grieux, both in the Massenet and the Puccini versions, and the Puccini des Grieux is represented on the Lebendige Vergangenheit disc by the first act aria 'Donna non vidi mai', and by that searing passage from Act II, 'Ah, Manon, mi tradisce il tuo folle pensier'. The former, however mellifluous it may be, lacks the surge of passion which this particular aria especially demands, but the latter is one of the most beautiful of all Piccaver's recordings. It is fascinatingly different from Björling's performance which I applauded in the opening chapter of this book. There is no anger in Piccaver's des Grieux as he reproaches the feckless Manon with the catalogue of degradation to which she has reduced him; there is hardly any bitterness either, even in so desperate a phrase as 'Fango nel fango io sono', 'Dirt in the dirt am I'. The quality which steeps the whole agonizing recital is an infinity of resignation and regret, expressed, even on the high B flat entry at 'la scala dell' infamia', 'the ladder of infamy', without a hint of a break in the melodic flow, or a trace of vocal effort. No wonder that Puccini, when he wrote to Piccaver after hearing him for the first time as des Grieux, addressed him with the words 'Carissimo Signor Piccaver'.

Piccaver's French repertoire is well represented on this same disc, albeit sung in every instance in German. His celebrated *mezza voce* is mesmerically deployed in 'Adieu, Mignon' and 'Elle ne croyait pas' from Ambroise Thomas's MIGNON, although recording techniques in 1914 were apt to be caught out by soft singing, and in any case both of these arias seem to have been taken from disappointingly poor originals – I fear that one needs to be something of an 'acoustic record nut' to appreciate these two tracks, wonderfully well though they are sung. Werther's two solos, 'O nature' and 'Pourquoi me réveiller', have been considerably better captured, with the latter rising to a fine pitch of intensity; and in 'O Dieu de quelle ivresse', from Offenbach's LES CONTES D'HOFFMANN, Piccaver demonstrates once again what is meant by legato. The disc is completed by two rarities from the German repertoire – an ornate and demanding, but musically not very interesting, aria from Weber's SILVANA, and one of Piccaver's concert favourites, 'So leb' ich noch' from Cornelius's DER BARBIER VON BAGDAD.

By the time Piccaver had lived in Vienna for four or five years, he had become one of the city's characters. In 1917, a fortnight before his thirty-third birthday, he was appointed 'Kaiserlicher und Königlicher Kammersänger', Royal and Imperial Court Singer, by the Emperor in person, an exceptional honour for a foreigner, especially one so young. At that time Piccaver still had American nationality, and when the United States entered the First World War he made an attempt to leave the country fearing that he might be interned. He was briefly detained at the border until a typically Viennese arrangement was devised whereby Herr Kammersänger Piccaver, enemy alien, would be allowed to roam free, on parole, provided that he continued to discharge his duties at the Court Opera. Vienna has always been a place with its own way of doing things, and there was something about Piccaver's nature which made him and the Viennese click. Universally known as 'Picci', he was unaffected, easy-going ('gemütlich') and overweight, three qualities the Viennese appreciate. In 1913 he had married a Hungarian pastor's daughter who was widely regarded as the most beautiful girl in Vienna – so much so that picture postcards of Marietta Johanny-Piccaver could be bought in every 'Tabak-Trafik'. It was not a happy union, however, and was soon dissolved, though not before a 'Skandal' hit the newspapers, when a jealous rival attempted to mar Frau Piccaver's beauty by confronting her in the Sacher Hotel and trying to throw acid in her face. Piccaver did not remarry until 1926 – his bride, once again, was an outstandingly beautiful girl, a dancer from the city of Brünn, by whom he had one son.

In the same year, to add to his title of Kammersänger, Piccaver received a still more remarkable accolade, when he was made an 'Ehrenmitglied' of the State Opera – a 'Member of Honour', a distinction rarely conferred, and a kind of operatic equivalent to the Freedom of the City. His relationship with the management of the Opera was not, however, without its stormy interludes, and the pattern of their altercations was fairly consistent. They always made headlines in the Austrian press, and were characterized by demonstrations of loyal affection at his farewell performance, soon to be followed by further demonstrations of loyal affection when a penitent management brought him back again.

The cause of these upheavals usually revolved around cuts in salary or reductions in the number of his performances, both of which inevitably occurred in depressed inter-war Vienna, but which were not always tactfully introduced. The squabble which the public followed with the greatest glee, however, was not an instance of Piccaver versus the management, but a head-on crash between him and the Opera's resident femme fatale, Maria Jeritza. She was a thorn in most tenors' sides, and on one occasion, during a performance of CAVALLERIA RUSTICANA on 19 May 1925, Piccaver decided that he had had enough. At the end of the quarrel scene Jeritza used to indulge in one of her great *coups de théâtre*, whereby the Turiddu had to give her a push, and she would fall headlong, with tremendous dramatic effect, down the steps of the village church. On this particular evening, though, Piccaver simply crossed his arms and stood there. Jeritza had to take an unmotivated tumble, in her opinion ruining her performance. At the end of the opera she refused to join Piccaver in front of the curtain, and when his solo bow was greeted with louder applause than hers it was the last straw. She stormed into the office of the Director, Franz Schalk, announcing that she would never sing with Piccaver again. For a while the diva's command was obeyed, but within a year they were back on stage together as Tosca and Cavaradossi.

It was generally during his temporary tiffs with the Opera that Piccaver cast an eye further afield. On 31 December 1923 he made his American debut, in the familiar role of the Duke, with the Chicago Opera. He received glowing reviews, with *Musical America* in particular going into ecstasies about his voice, and describing his contribution to the quartet as 'almost unbelievably rich and lovely'. His Turiddu was even more rapturously received, and the following season he repeated both roles in Chicago as well as adding a Cavaradossi, partnered by the soprano whom he once described to me as 'the greatest of all my Toscas', Claudia Muzio. It is interesting that his acting, too, came in for considerable praise, as it did when he appeared at Covent Garden in between his two Chicago seasons. *The Times* wrote of his Cavaradossi 'His voice is full and round in quality, and of great power; even at the biggest moments one felt that he held in reserve quite as much as he gave out.' When he appeared three days later as the Duke, with Maria Ivogün as Gilda, *The Times* informed its readers 'Mr Piccaver imparted a swagger to the character of the Duke that fits the part . . . In the sheer power of fine phrasing he gets subtleties as well as broad outlines from his voice, and is not limited merely to playing on the two emotional strings of love and bravura.' Ernest Newman, however, availed himself of every critic's privilege, and wrote the exact opposite – 'His phrasing lacks finesse,' he complained. 'Somehow he never moves me.'

In view of the overwhelming enthusiasm of the press (Mr Newman excepted), both for his Covent Garden and his Chicago appearances, it is strange indeed that Piccaver never returned to either of these two houses. He had been enough of a success with the London public to be engaged for an Albert Hall concert in the following year, 1925, and that went so well that the Management promptly invited him to fill a gap in the hall's bookings and give a second one the following week. In the audience on the first occasion sat Luisa Tetrazzini and such was her enthusiasm that at the end of the concert she rushed up on stage, embraced the astonished Piccaver and handed him a large bunch of violets which she happened to have with her at the time. No less entranced was the critic of the *Daily Sketch*. 'His voice has improved since he was at Covent Garden last summer,' he wrote, 'and he was a great tenor then. The words "Caruso's successor" have often been misused. He has now arrived. The greatest tenor in the world is an Englishman.'*

Piccaver's Vienna concerts tended to be colourful occasions too. Even in the 1930s, when he had been singing regularly in the city for twenty years and one might suppose that the public had heard enough of him, any Piccaver concert was a guaranteed sell-out. He was not a Lieder specialist like Lehmann or Schumann, but his programmes often included a few of Richard Strauss's songs, as well as operatic arias and English drawing-room ballads, and there was usually something of a family atmosphere about the evening – Alfred Piccaver and a thousand of his friends. After one particular concert in October 1924, on the eve of his departure from Vienna to undertake his second Chicago season, the public refused to go home, and the manager of the hall had the lights turned out. At this the audience redoubled its clamour, so the manager called for the lights to be turned on again, only to find that the electrician had gone home taking his keys with him. In the end Piccaver borrowed a torch, came back on stage, and sang seven encores. On another occasion, when Piccaver gave a joint recital with Elisabeth Schumann, the audience would not leave until they had sung the BOHEME duet which was on the printed programme. The manager explained to them that the pianist had brought the wrong music, which was why they had

---

* Piccaver had elected to resume his British nationality in 1923.

been treated to the BUTTERFLY duet instead. As this still did not do the trick the manager resorted to asking the public 'Is there a BOHEME in the house?' 'I've got one!' called a voice from somewhere up in the gallery; so the score was passed to the pianist, Schumann and Piccaver sang the duet, and everyone went home happy.

For those who like to put singers into pigeon-holes, Piccaver is a somewhat confusing case – neither in vocal quality, nor in the roles that he sang, does he quite fit into any specific compartment, as, for instance, does a Gigli or a Melchior. Primarily a Verdi/Puccini man, he also made considerable incursions into the German and the Mozart repertoires. His Don Ottavio in DON GIOVANNI was one of the highlights of the Salzburg Festival of 1927 and when he was unable to return the following year (or unwilling – it clashed with holiday time), Richard Strauss, in his capacity as Director of the Festival, wrote to him 'You must come, or I shall look ridiculous. You are one of the few real Mozart singers of today.' Earlier in the same year of 1927 Piccaver had undertaken his first Florestan in a new production of FIDELIO marking the centenary of Beethoven's death, and Franz Schalk, who had conducted the performance, wrote to him the following day 'You have long been known as one of the greatest singers of your time, and now you have proved your mastery of an artistic and musical task, of which only the fewest are capable.' Piccaver's partner on this occasion had been Lehmann once again, and they were to sing many a FIDELIO together, in Salzburg and Paris as well as in Vienna. Visually, as old photographs reveal, they strained credulity, with Lehmann a generously contoured youth and Piccaver a conspicuously unemaciated jail-bird, but vocally it was by all accounts a lavish feast.

By this stage of his career Piccaver's voice had developed into a darker instrument than it had been in the days of his early Odeon recordings but even when he tackled roles such as Florestan and Lohengrin, normally the province of more dramatic voices, his style remained entirely lyrical. Four examples of his

Lohengrin are included in a Piccaver CD issued by Pearl (GEMM *9412*); they consist of the 'Grail Narration' and the 'Farewell', together with the duet 'Wenn ich im Kampfe' and the opening of the Bridal Chamber scene, in which Piccaver's partner is the Hungarian-born soprano Margit Angerer, a young lady who was noted for her beauty but whose voice on records sounds somewhat pale and colourless. Piccaver's Lohengrin is a million miles from anything one would be likely to hear in Bayreuth. It is Lohengrin lightly touched by the wand of Puccini, with the same honeyed flow as a des Grieux or a Cavaradossi, and though phrases such as 'Nie sollst du mich befragen' ('Never are you to question me') may lose their sword-clanking imperiousness, there are others which gain surprisingly. When Lohengrin tells of the dove which appears every year from Heaven ('alljährlich naht vom Himmel eine Taube'), no other tenor in my experience has made that dove sound quite so charming a bird; and when Lohengrin bequeaths his ring to Elsa's brother, his 'doch bei dem Ringe soll er mein gedenken' ('but with the ring may he think of me') becomes the stuff by which tears are jerked.

All the recordings on this CD were made between 1928 and 1930, which brings us into the electrical era and in many ways represents easier listening than the old acoustics. The unique quality of the voice is better revealed but in the Italian arias it becomes evident to what an extent the growing breadth and weight of the middle register had detracted from the extreme top. In Dick Johnson's 'Ch'ella mi creda' the two high B flats have faded in body and focus, and the two Verdi arias, 'Ah, si ben mio' from IL TROVATORE and 'O tu che in seno' from FORZA, suffer from a lack of 'grip' on the climax notes. To my mind though, the greatest artistic deficiency in Piccaver's work always lay in his sloppy use of text. As an Anglo-American regularly singing French and Italian operas in German, he became a jack of all tongues and master of none. His Italian, like Björling's at the beginning of his career, is never idiomatically articulated and often downright wrong; and although his German is a lot better than that, in all his years in Vienna he never really mastered the complexities of the language. It is as if words as a means of communication simply did not interest him – as if the production of beautiful tone was all that mattered. Certainly by the time I knew him it could not really be said of Piccaver that he spoke any known language at all. He expressed himself in a very charming and initially somewhat bewildering mixture of English and German, delivered with traces of an American accent. It took me a little while to catch on to advice such as 'You'll never get your tones out if you keep your Mund tight zu'; and I remember him one day after a lesson in Putney, as he saw me into my old Morris Minor car, coming out with the splendidly idiosyncratic utterance 'One of my pupils has a kleiner Renault, but it's too klein for to schlüpfen hinein' – by which he meant that it was too small for an elderly gentleman to slide into with any degree of ease.

Having said all this, however, far be it from me to dissuade anyone from sampling the Pearl CD – it includes much that is marvellous. That caressing quality which the Viennese loved so much shows up best, I think, in the sweeping phrases of Vasco da Gama's aria from Meyerbeer's L'AFRICAINE, a piece which Piccaver undertook for the first time on stage as late in his career as 1935; and in the two TOSCA duets, and the Garden Scene from FAUST, again with Angerer as the soprano, the famous legato unfolds with all its magic. Most of the older Viennese whom I knew back in the 1950s, if asked which single aria they regarded as being most essentially Piccaver's private preserve, would have chosen the Dream from MANON, and this, too, is included in the Pearl CD, along with des Grieux's 'Ah, fuyez', and Werther's 'Pourquoi me réveiller?' (all sung in German). Here I would like to quote Lotte Lehmann once again. 'I myself,' she wrote after Piccaver's death, 'have "The Dream" from MANON, which he sang with such unearthly beauty in our many performances. But I do not find that this record does full justice to the charm of his voice. People often complained that his technique was too nasal – and I could notice this on the recording far more than I ever did in real life.' This is an interesting point. Was Piccaver's voice one whose faults showed up more clearly on records than in performance? As far as the nasal quality is concerned there is a much greater tolerance of nasal singing in Vienna than in most other places (the Viennese dialect contains many essentially nasal sounds), and I remember one Viennese Kapellmeister saying to me of Piccaver 'Ach, wie herrlich der Mensch genäselt hat!' – a basically untranslatable remark, meaning 'How gorgeously the chap used to sing in his nose'. In London however, where nasal tone is not a fault which people tolerate readily, the critics never mentioned it – can Piccaver have 'genäselt' in one place, and not in another?

The Pearl CD closes with two numbers from the lighter end of Piccaver's repertoire. There is Tosti's 'Addio', imbued with something of the same quality of resignation which I commented on in connection with des Grieux's 'Ah, Manon'; and finally there is a recording to which I am particularly devoted – 'Pale Hands I Loved', one of Amy Woodforde-Finden's 'Indian Love Lyrics'. Many an Edwardian drawing-room echoed to the memorable question 'Whom do you lead on rapture's roadway far, before you agonize them in farewell?' but I am confident that it never sounded like this. This is the real Piccaver timbre, call it creamy, call it velvety, or call it, as the tenor Helge Roswaenge did in his memoirs, 'a shower of gold drifting gently down onto the public'. It is a sound like the sound of no other voice that I have heard, and a sound which lingers in the ear.

'Pale Hands' was one of the songs which featured in Piccaver's programme at the London Palladium when he topped the bill there for a fortnight in January 1932 during one of his periods of coolness towards the management of the Vienna State Opera. He almost failed to make the opening night on time because the Orient Express, with Piccaver on it, was snowed up somewhere in Central Europe, a fact which the Palladium's press officer milked for all it was worth – **CAN ANYONE TRACE THE MISSING TENOR?** the headlines screamed. In the event he arrived in time to perform, but not to rehearse, and his opening night had to be accompanied by piano rather than orchestra. During the last decade of his career Piccaver made several forays into the world of lighter music, including a run as Schubert in DAS DREI-MÄDERLHAUS in the Vienna Stadttheater, two musical films and a highly paid month in Vienna's leading Variety theatre, the Ronacher. At the Palladium his main supporting act had been the great British comedian Will Hay. At the Ronacher he had to compete with a singing sea-lion.

Piccaver's path, however, always brought him back sooner or later to the State Opera. In 1936 LA FANCIULLA DEL WEST was revived, and in the opinion of the critics Piccaver at fifty-two was well able to sustain the comparison with himself when young. Despite his reputation as a canceller – he would try out his voice in the morning and if it did not seem to be running smoothly he would ring up the Opera and pull out of the evening performance – his popularity never waned. On 2 June 1937 a certain Herr Simon Rosenheck got himself into trouble with the Viennese police because, as their charge sheet put it, 'He committed an offence, namely causing a disturbance, in that he did at 8.15 in the State Opera, during a performance of TOSCA, cry in an overloud manner "Bravo" and "Long live Piccaver".' Piccaver paid Herr Rosenheck's ten Schilling fine for him, which must have made him feel less hard done by, but what neither Herr Rosenheck nor anyone else knew at the time was that he had been applauding Alfred Piccaver's last appearance on the stage of the Vienna Opera.

At the time of Hitler's annexation of Austria Piccaver happened to be in London, and he decided that it would be sensible to stay there. His family and all his belongings (including his beloved Bechstein grand piano, autographed inside the lid by Enrico Caruso) were brought over from Vienna and, for the first time in over fifty years, he became a resident of his native land. It was an abrupt end to an illustrious career. In Vienna he could have gone on singing for a few more years and then settled comfortably into the role of Revered Public Figure but in London, at the age of fifty-four, he was in a sort of vacuum. He renewed a contract with the Decca record company for a series of English ballads,* he made an appearance on the infant television service from Alexandra Palace, and he participated in a charity concert at the Albert Hall, but in general little notice was taken of his presence in the country. No doubt a pushier, more flamboyant operator than Piccaver could have carved out something more impressive for himself, but this was not Piccaver's way. On 17 January 1943 he gave a Celebrity Concert in the Wimbledon Town Hall,† and he never performed in public again.

It cannot have been easy for Piccaver to acclimatize himself to such an anonymous existence. In Vienna the police used to stop the traffic when they saw his car approach – in London tradesmen could not spell his name. In Vienna, though, he had not been forgotten. In 1954, on his seventieth birthday, he received an official letter from the Bürgermaster, ending with the words 'Please accept these greetings from the city of your triumphs. Let them be an expression of what your name still means to us, and of the emotions which are stirred by the memories of your unforgettable performances.' Then, in the Autumn of 1955, came the invitation to attend the opening of the rebuilt Vienna State Opera as one of the official Guests of Honour. This was much more than a merely artistic occasion. The Russian occupation of Austria had only just ended, and the re-opening of the Opera really marked for the Viennese the beginning of a new era. For Piccaver it was like a homecoming, and he never returned to London.

I have many memories of Piccaver during the two and a half years of my studies with him in Vienna. During my lessons he never sang out full voice, but he could still manage a

---

*   His recording of 'There'll always be an England', made in October 1939, provides a touching parallel to Caruso's 'Over There', recorded in similar circumstances in 1918.
†   The audience on this occasion included the twenty-year-old Earl of Harewood, who, many years later, recalled in his memoirs the spell of Piccaver's seamless legato.

mezza voce two-octave scale, C to C, with complete ease and remarkable beauty of tone. It was difficult to set him talking about the old days – he seemed to dread living in the past – but occasionally a cunningly expressed question would unlock the door and elicit an anecdote or two. After the opening of the Opera he made a point of staying out of the limelight, and led a totally retiring life, though one rather touching occasion remains with particular clarity in my mind. A colleague from his time at the Opera had died, and Piccaver asked me if I would drive him out to the Central Cemetery for the funeral. Before the service we strolled amongst the many singers' graves which occupy that corner of the cemetery, and we paused longest, I remember, at that of Selma Kurz. Not many famous names attended the funeral – so many of them had been scattered to the four winds by the coming of Hitler – and most of those present were long retired singers of supporting roles. As they greeted each other with a quiet 'Servus, wie geht's?' I felt strongly that the real question in all of their minds was 'Which of us will be next?'; and sadly, it was to be Alfred Piccaver.

Piccaver died on 23 September 1958 and was accorded a State Funeral. The centre of Vienna was closed to traffic, and the procession halted in front of the Opera House, while from the balcony above the main entrance the Vienna Philharmonic Orchestra played the Funeral March from Beethoven's 'Eroica' Symphony. Piccaver's widow and son generously invited me to walk with them behind the coffin, and when I saw the crowds of people lining the streets I could not help thinking how strange it was that all this was in honour of an Englishman who had not sung a note in Vienna for over twenty years and whose death would have passed unnoticed had he died in his native land.

Opera singers, though, do sometimes acquire a very different status in certain continental countries than they do in Britain. In Vienna, as also previously in Prague, Piccaver had belonged to everybody, not just to the opera public. How else, in the spring of 1912, shortly before Piccaver's final performance in the

Landestheater, could a leading Prague newspaper have written as follows?

> Round the hearts of the girls of Prague a wistful sorrow is stealing. Soon, too soon, will come the time of parting. As yet, they are still happy. Out there, in the beautiful gardens of the city, the lilac is in bloom; in the streets at midday a gentle sun shines down. The air is as light and gay as the new dresses that they are wearing – and Alfred Piccaver is still within the city walls.

EZIO PINZA

ITALIAN BASS

b. Rome, 18 May 1892, d. Stamford, Connecticut, 9 May 1957

As I mentioned in the chapter on Alexander Kipnis, the roles as-signed to basses tend to fall into a few distinct categories – senior citizens of extreme solemnity, black-hearted villains and comic cari-catures. Not many singers have the versatility to master all three types, but one who did, and even managed in the process to establish himself as the most glamorous figure in international opera, was the Italian, Ezio Pinza.

Pinza was born into a working-class family in Rome, and his parents wanted him to be christened Ezio. When their local priest pointed out that this had been the name of a pagan Roman general, and would not therefore be smiled upon by the church, they settled for the name Fortunato – it was however as Ezio that the boy was universally known.* When Pinza was two years old the family moved from Rome to Ravenna. His father, who was illiterate but thoroughly worldly wise, was a carpenter, and as a boy Pinza used to help him with odd jobs and also pick up a bit of extra pocket money performing such tasks as delivering bread for the local bakery. As he grew older and stronger he graduated to work on a railroad, before indulging his real ambition which was to be a racing cyclist. In this capacity, as his father put it, 'he covered a lot of ground, achieved a muscular figure and never won a race' – though I have no doubt that it did nothing but good to his lung-power. As it gradually became evident that Pinza possessed a more than usually attractive singing voice he decided to try

---

* By a strange coincidence the original Ezio was to make a brief appearance in Pinza's recorded repertoire, via the trio from Verdi's ATTILA.

a change of tack and presented himself for an audition at the Conservatory in Bologna. He did so with considerable diffidence because, unlike many of the great Italian opera singers, he had never been in a church choir as a boy, and music was a foreign territory to him. Nevertheless his natural talent made such an impression on the examiners that he was granted a scholarship with a small sum for daily expenses on the side. Added to this he was assigned to a voice teacher named Alessandro Vezzani, who was sufficiently generous and far-sighted to waive his fees, on the understanding that Pinza would repay him as soon as he could – a debt which Pinza in due course was happily able to discharge.

After only two years in the Conservatory he had made such strides that he was ready to risk a professional debut. This took place in one of Italy's obscurer opera houses in the little town of Soncino, not far from Cremona, with Pinza as the first of a long line of religious dignitaries – the Archdruid Oroveso in Bellini's NORMA. It went well enough to bring him several offers from other provincial theatres; he appeared in the Tuscan town of Prato, then in the Sicilian capital Palermo, and the future looked bright. Unfortunately, though, the year was 1914, and his next engagement, like it or not, was with the Italian army; he was drafted into an artillery regiment, served on the Alpine front and rose to the rank of captain. It was not until 1920 that he could discard his uniform and pick up the pieces of his budding operatic career, but from then everything was (as far as anything ever is in opera) plain sailing. He was engaged as a company member by the Teatro Costanzi in Rome, where he was able to concentrate on building up a repertoire, and such was his success that within two years Toscanini fetched him to Milan to become one of the principal basses of La Scala.

Pinza was one of those charismatic people who make an instant impression. He was gifted with a voice of highly individual beauty, and though he was not a well trained musician he was a strongly instinctive one – he may have had to work hard in order to learn his roles but, once learnt, he knew how to bring them vividly to life in performance. It was of course of inestimable advantage to him during his artistically formative years that he should have as potent a mentor as Toscanini, and in a ghosted autobiography, posthumously published, Pinza was to pay tribute to the Maestro's influence. 'It's impossible to describe Toscanini's contribution to my development,' he declared. 'Suffice it to say that he taught me most of what I know about style in operatic singing. He was a teacher by the grace of God.'

It was during his days at La Scala that Pinza's recording career was launched, and EMI have issued an outstanding CD (*CDH 764 253-2*) in their *Références* series, to mark the centenary of his birth. It consists of nineteen titles, recorded between June 1923 and December 1924. Technically, the Italian studios were not as far advanced at that time as their counterparts in London and New York, and as a good many of these tracks are of ensemble numbers, with no less than eight of them involving chorus, they sometimes sound rather overloaded and even more 'historic' than they actually are. Pinza's voice, however, comes over with remarkable splendour and with that arresting immediacy, which was so characteristic of his work. His debut role of Oroveso is twice represented, and a couple of phrases are enough to reveal why he rose so rapidly to the top of his profession. The voice has all the richness and body of a true bass, but it is used lyrically and flowingly – he never digs into the tone or allows it to become bogged down in the weight of its own sound. The incisiveness of his diction, particularly the splendid roll of the 'rs' on the ends of words, makes his every utterance gripping and vital – basses at the serious end of the repertoire are much given to portentous announcements, and without this vividness of delivery there is the constant risk of pomposity. In Raimondo's narration from LUCIA DI LAMMERMOOR Pinza fairly relishes his gothic tale of the ghastly moans he has heard emerging from the bridal chamber and the blood-bespattered scene that has confronted him within it. His audience of wedding guests (hardy folk though they must have been, brought up in the Scottish castles of three hundred years ago) could be forgiven if they felt a shiver or two by the time Pinza has come to the end of his grisly recital, and the fact that they respond to such flesh-creeping stuff by swinging into a catchy waltz tune is Donizetti's fault, not his. When he turns his attention to the aria 'Cinta di fiori' from I PURITANI, Sir George Walton's more restrained description of his niece's lapse into insanity, Pinza is all sympathetic concern, noble and dignified, with a smoothness of legato to satisfy the most demanding hankerer after the good old days of true *bel canto*. We are treated to one tremendous piece of vindictive rhetoric, Cardinal de Brogni's Curse from Halévy's LA JUIVE (sung, like everything else on the disc, in Italian) in which the force of the declamation never spills over into a loss of tonal splendour; and the nobility of the same character's prayer to the Lord for the enlightenment of the Unbelievers provides a neat opportunity for a straight comparison between Pinza and his great Russian contemporary, and occasional rival, Alexander Kipnis. To prove that Pinza, like Bottom, could also 'roar you as gently as any sucking dove', there is the lullaby 'De son coeur', sung by the old minstrel Lothario in Ambroise Thomas's MIGNON, one of Pinza's most moving stage characterizations. In music of this kind Pinza capitalizes most effectively on the very quick vibrato which was a feature of his voice and which, far from degenerating into the wobble that can affect so many basses, lent it a tension all of its own. Goethe, on whose *Wilhelm Meister* MIGNON was based, is further invoked by four numbers introducing Pinza as Mephistopheles, two each by Gounod and Boito. That mighty German polymath can hardly have realized when he wrote *Faust* that it would make him the patron saint of theatrically-minded operatic basses, but in these four tracks, Pinza, like Chaliapin before him and so many others since, has a field day.

For musical distinction, however, as opposed to theatrical flamboyance, the patron saint of Italian basses is surely Giuseppe Verdi, and this disc provides ample evidence that in his early thirties Pinza was already *the* Verdi bass of the inter-war years. There is an intense dramatic bite to Fiesco's recitative 'A te l'estremo addio' from SIMON BOCCANEGRA, followed by an exemplary rendering of the grief-stricken aria 'Il lacerato spirito'. As the Padre Guardiano in LA FORZA DEL DESTINO, hurling his cries of 'Maledizione' at anyone who might dare to disturb the hapless Leonora in the solitude of her eremitic cave, Pinza displays an upper register which would be the envy of many a dramatic baritone – but with every note still sumptuously encased within the velvety timbre of the true *basso cantante*. As the garrulous Ferrando in IL TROVATORE, Pinza, with his remarkable articulation, comes as near as anyone could to lending intelligibility to the complex story of the baby and the bonfire; and in the bass solo 'Confutatis maledictis' from the REQUIEM (the original 78 evidently did not quite allow time for the final phrase) several glorious touches of vocal colouring, such as the reverential 'piano' on 'voca me cum benedictis', may, I suspect, reveal the direct influence of his 'teacher by the grace of God'.

Several of the tracks on the EMI disc are conducted by Carlo Sabajno, who had started his career as Toscanini's number two back in the Maestro's days as musical director in Turin, and in 1927 Sabajno conducted a full recording of the Verdi REQUIEM with Pinza as the bass soloist. It is now to be found on *Pearl* GEMM *CD 9374*, and it reveals Pinza at the absolute peak of his powers. He does, however, dwarf the other three soloists, and the full forces of the orchestra and chorus of La Scala gave the engineers of 1927 some pretty testing moments. Most people, I imagine, would be happier with the more spacious sound of the famous 1939 recording of the REQUIEM, now available as EMI *CDH 7 63341 2*, with the forces of the Rome Opera under Tullio Serafin, in which Pinza is joined by three other soloists of similar status – Maria Caniglia, Ebe Stignani and Beniamino Gigli. The theatricality of Gigli's contribution, with his sobs, interpolated aspirates and penchant for downward *portamenti* is not to everyone's taste (it worries me less than some), but Pinza, as one would expect of a singer so adept at playing men of God, is vocally, musically and stylistically impeccable. Indeed, it is interesting to note that he recorded the 'Confutatis' more often than any other individual number in his repertoire, and a comparison of the various versions reveals another of his many virtues as an artist – a most remarkable consistency.

Though Pinza seldom sang in any other language than Italian (his occasional forays into French sound like some obscure dialect from the Provençal hinterland, and heaven alone knows how he would have tackled German*), his repertoire was not limited to Italian works. He made his debut at La Scala as Pimen in BORIS GODUNOV, and several Wagnerian roles such as Pogner and König Marke (Ré Marco) swelled the list of his personal successes. It was as Gurnemanz in PARSIFAL that he made his first important overseas debut – in the Teatro Colón, Buenos Aires, in 1925 – and the following year, after Giulio Gatti-Casazza had heard him singing at La Scala, he found himself for the first time on the stage of the Metropolitan Opera. He was presented to the New York public as yet another high priest – the Pontifex Maximus in Spontini's LA VESTALE – and this turned out to be the first of fifty-one roles which he was to sing with the company over a period of twenty-two years. Like so many other European singers he made his home in the United States, and it was there, in the late 1920s and early 1930s, that he made many of his finest recordings – the voice still sizzles with the ardour of youth, and the advance in the technical sound quality since the earlier Milan group shows it off to considerable advantage. Eleven of these New York recordings (along with ten of the Milan tracks already discussed on the EMI *Références* disc) have now been reissued on *Pearl* GEMM CD 9306. There is another imposing selection of the great Verdi arias, and I would have difficulty in deciding whether to award the palm to Silva's 'Infelice' from ERNANI, or Procida's 'O tu Palermo' from I VESPRI SICILIANI, both of

---

* Since this was written Pearl have issued an interesting Pinza/Rethberg disc (GEMM CD 9958) on which he sings two items in a German which is painstaking and charming, but very much his own.

which offer the broad sweep of Pinza at his most majestic. King Philip's lament from DON CARLOS over the lovelessness of his marriage is taken a little faster than ideal – it was always too long an aria to lend itself comfortably to any format of 78 rpm discs – but it remains a noble depiction of regal vulnerability. There is a fourth 'Confutatis maledictis', possibly the finest of them all, and we hear from yet another high priest, Ramfis in AIDA – never, I find, a very interesting figure, but the role which Pinza sang most frequently in his entire Met repertoire. There are a couple of comparative rarities, too, in the Invocation from Meyerbeer's ROBERT LE DIABLE, in which Pinza's mephistophelean side is once again given free rein, and the Drum Major's song from Ambroise Thomas's LE CAÏD. This is a jaunty, swaggering, bravura number, in which flexibility is the *sine qua non* and, although Pinza does not quite display the same virtuoso command of rapid coloratura as his famous predecessor Pol Plançon in a recording of many years earlier, it does allow him to indulge in all sorts of unpriestly vocal high jinks.

After this bracing excursion into the frivolous, nothing could emphasize Pinza's versatility more succinctly than the three tracks devoted to Mozart. First we hear him as the archetypal *basso profondo*, and the most sublime of all operatic high priests, Sarastro in DIE ZAUBERFLÖTE. His 'O Isis und Osiris' (in Italian, of course, and sadly without the support of a chorus), is a gorgeously mellifluous piece of singing, orotund and reverential, with a rock-like low F to round it off. Then he turns his attentions to a very different figure, and the one with whom his name will probably always be most closely linked in any history of opera in the twentieth century – Don Giovanni. He first undertook the role at the Met in 1929. It was regarded as an exclusively baritone preserve, and the critics, usually unstinting in their praise of Ezio Pinza, were sceptical. The darkness of timbre, they felt, made the Don too satanic a figure and disturbed the balance of the male voices, while the company's baritones were predictably up in arms. They were all, however, overlooking a vital point. There was one essential element in which Pinza left the competition entirely in the shade, and that was personal magnetism, or, to express it more blatantly, sex appeal. He was an actor of brilliance (Virgil Thomson called him 'the finest singing actor I know'), and a dashingly handsome man whom women found hard to resist – a distinct advantage for a Don Giovanni. The impact of the Pinza charisma was perhaps most neatly summed up in the memoirs of Bruno Walter. Walter was due to be conducting the Salzburg Festival's first Italian-language production of DON GIOVANNI in 1934, and he had made it a condition of his doing so that a singer should be found for the title-role who, in addition to all the necessary artistic attributes, also possessed 'that immediately convincing personal fascination, which is an essential of the part'. While the casting was being finalized, Walter happened to be in New York accompanied by his wife and, as Pinza had been recommended to him as a vocally and musically resplendent Don, Walter invited him to call so that he could assess for himself whether or not Pinza also had the necessary *je ne sais quoi*. 'We had taken with us to New York,' Walter wrote, 'our Bohemian cook, an efficient, but quite unimaginative middle-aged person. There was a ring, and Anita went to answer it. She came rushing back flushed, confused and excited, and whispered to my wife: "Ma'am, there's such a beautiful man outside." I said to my wife "I think I've found my Don Giovanni for Salzburg." I had.'

I would imagine that Pinza's ten-inch 78 with Don Giovanni's Serenade on one side and the so-called Champagne Aria on the other must have featured in the record collection of almost every opera-lover of my generation. My copy certainly worked overtime, and it is a treat to hear these two old friends come up again as fresh as ever on CD. Whether he is turning the tap of suave seductiveness in 'Deh, vieni alla finestra', or swashbuckling his way through 'Fin ch'han dal vino', Pinza is a singer who puts his mark on things. There is an energy, a totality about the impersonation which leaves a heavy imprint on the listener's memory. In the eyes of those lucky enough to have seen him play

the role on stage, his portrayal doubtless gained in conviction
from his widespread reputation for playing it off stage as well.
When Pinza and the German soprano Elisabeth Rethberg undertook a joint concert tour of Australia followed by a nationwide
tour of the United States, his first wife, an Italian lady named
Augusta Cassinelli, brought a $250,000* suit against Rethberg for
'alienation of affection'. Pinza suddenly became an object of
interest to newspaper readers all over the United States whether
operatically inclined or not and, although Mrs Pinza was
persuaded to withdraw her allegations, the marriage did not survive. Pinza was then on the loose for eight years, and the gossip
columnists had him marked down as a potentially rich source
of copy. When a dewy-eyed Californian beauty named Olivia
Picchioni tried to sue him for breach of promise she filed for the
sum of $200,000, and reporters had a bit of fun conjecturing why
the market value of Pinza's heart should have suffered a twenty
per cent reduction. In any case Pinza's lawyer managed once
again to talk him out of trouble. 'It is Mr Pinza's Italian background,' he explained. 'Sometimes people think he is being
romantic when he is just being gentlemanly.' The American
journalist Winthrop Sargeant once wrote that 'when Pinza is
seated at a restaurant, the entrance of a good-looking girl will
throw him into a trancelike condition like that of a well-bred
hunting dog that has scented quail'; and Louella Parsons, referring
no doubt to the crowds of ecstatic youngsters who used to picket
the stage door on DON GIOVANNI nights, came up with the
doubtful compliment of 'Bobby-sockers [sic] have discovered
in Met bass Ezio Pinza the Frank Sinatra of long-hair music.'
National polls rated him variously as one of the ten best-dressed
men in the United States and fourteen most glamorous men in the
world, and in newspaper photographs he was generally portrayed
wearing casually elegant tweeds and a spotted bow tie, often
with a pipe between his teeth, and sometimes with a Clark Gable

---

* Approximately the equivalent to £1,200,000 at the time of writing.

hat set at a rakish angle on his head. Many a tale would be told within the Met of romantic notes passed under ladies' doors at night when the company was touring the States by train, and I remember the words of one long-retired soprano, talking to me a few years ago in New York – 'I came from rather a sheltered background, and I made it my business to avoid Mr Pinza in the darkness of the wings.'

In 1940 Pinza lost some of his appeal to the gossip columnists when he married one of the dancers at the Metropolitan, a dentist's daughter named Doris Leak, who in the course of time bore him three children (he had one daughter, a talented soprano, by his first marriage), and steered him into the calmer waters of a settled domestic life. There was, however, one temporary leap back into public notoriety during the Second World War when it was suddenly announced, on 13 March 1942, that Pinza had been arrested by the FBI as a potentially dangerous enemy alien and incarcerated on Ellis Island. It was alleged that he had persistently boasted of a personal friendship with Mussolini, and he was kept under lock and key in the middle of the Met season for eleven weeks. This was generally supposed to have been the work of a certain American bass who had his eye on Pinza's roles but, be that as it may, after his release Pinza took pains to establish himself as a patriotic American with his heart on Uncle Sam's sleeve. He sang for the Treasury Department to promote the sale of war bonds, and he posed in pictures for the blood donor service. He was photographed in his car with a sign saying **I CO-OPERATE BY NOT PARKING IN CITY STREETS** and on his bicycle, announcing that he would be pedalling to save gas. In any case, the incident did nothing to damage his popularity with audiences at the Met, and his career continued to thrive while that of his machiavellian rival did not.

Despite this proclivity for appearing on the non-artistic pages of the nation's press, in all matters to do with his work Pinza was a deeply serious professional – nobody would have got very far with Toscanini or Bruno Walter by messing around.

He was an easy-going man, and the nearest he ever came to an
outburst of temperament was when he turned to a little boy in
the front row at one of his recitals and asked him very politely
'Little boy, please stop to waggle your foot: it interfere with
my tempo.' Luckily the long collaboration between Pinza and
Bruno Walter led to a group of Mozart recordings with the
orchestra of the Metropolitan Opera which now form part of a
Pinza recital, everything dating from the mid-1940s, on CBS *MPK
45693*. (They also feature in a three-disc set of Walter conducting
Mozart, on SONY *SM3K 47211*). In the opening number Pinza
discards the rich accoutrements of Don Giovanni and adopts
the unfamiliar guise of his servant Leporello with a superbly
self-satisfied rendering of 'Madamina'. Walter laid great store
on having Mozart's Italian roles sung by actual Italians, and the
relish with which Pinza serves up every lascivious little detail in
the Don's catalogue certainly justifies that view – he really plays
with the text, and a prurient chuckle lurks behind every note. Had
he not been a natural Don Giovanni, Pinza would clearly have
been a Leporello in a million, but when we move on to that other
great Mozartian servant-figure, Figaro, we meet a very different
sort of fellow. This was always one of Pinza's most trenchant
impersonations, both at the Salzburg Festival and at the Met,
and the bitter, potentially dangerous side of Figaro's nature was
never far from the surface. There is a scarcely concealed anger
both in 'Se vuol ballare' and in 'Aprite un po' quegl'occhi', and
in the recitatives which precede them it is once again the bite of
the truly Italianate delivery which scores point after point. It
would, of course, be hypocritical to claim the same degree of
'echt'-ness for Osmin's 'Ha, wie will ich triumphieren' from DIE
ENTFÜHRUNG, or Sarastro's 'In diesen heil'gen Hallen' from
DIE ZAUBERFLÖTE, when both of them are sung in Italian;
nor would it be true to say that Pinza's voice in 1946 had quite
the same regal sheen to it as in 1927 when he recorded Sarastro's
'O Isis und Osiris'. These are, nevertheless, intensely compelling
performances, the one erupting with animosity and rancour and

the other authoritatively dignified and serene.

Of course in this matter of vocal quality and the passage of time the ageing bass has a distinct advantage over the ageing tenor. An Alfredo in LA TRAVIATA or a Rodolfo in LA BOHEME has to sound young, or he will sound wrong. On the CBS disc the 54-year-old Pinza may not display quite the same glorious timbre as Fiesco in SIMON BOCCANEGRA, or Cardinal Brogni in LA JUIVE, as he did in the recordings of 1923 which I discussed earlier; but as long as the breath control remains unimpaired, the legato remains firm and the range is still attainable, all of which was the case with Pinza, the actual quality of the voice is theatrically more suitable to venerable figures such as these. As Colline in LA BOHEME Pinza does sound undeniably mature, but his farewell to his ancient overcoat is a skilful and moving performance, a worthy memento of the many times that he sang the role at the Met, often in such starry company as Lucrezia Bori, Beniamino Gigli and Giuseppe de Luca. It was also a role which he sang at Covent Garden in 1935 and 1936. He had made his debut there in 1930, as Oroveso once again, to the Norma of Rosa Ponselle, and during the next eight years he was an ever welcome guest. Apart from his all-conquering Don Giovanni, his two outstanding successes in London were in the comic Rossini repertoire, first as Don Magnifico in LA CENERENTOLA, and then as Don Basilio in IL BARBIERE DI SIVIGLIA. He sang Basilio on 29 May 1935, as part of King George V's Silver Jubilee celebrations, and the critic of the *Daily Herald* was moved to speak out loud and clear. 'One singer stole the show at Covent Garden last night,' he wrote. 'Ezio Pinza as Don Basilio stood head and shoulders (and hat) above the rest of the cast. Pinza is the greatest Italian singer – comic or serious – who has been heard in London since Battistini. His performance last night was an experience we shall not forget.' Apart from his singing of these roles, Pinza was an outstandingly brilliant stage comedian. Like Feodor Chaliapin he was fascinated by what could be done with make-up – certainly, as photographs prove, by the time he had modified the famous profile with the addition of Don Basilio's nose, chin and various other attributes, there was little left to interest Louella Parsons' bobby-sockers – and his stage technique went way beyond the 'hands on stomach and bent-knees walk' which so often passes for comic operatic acting.

The first act of that gala performance was relayed over the radio by the BBC, and the *Radio Times* for that week contained one immortal paragraph, indicative of opera's position in the scheme of things. 'In this month of Jubilee,' listeners were informed, 'the King, ever among the first to encourage the Arts,* did not forget Music. The season of great singing at Covent Garden, in its colour and glitter and social significance a Royal Ascot of Music, will reach its climax when the curtain rises on the happily chosen gay and witty BARBER OF SEVILLE, to be sung by a brilliant and international cast, to a brilliant and international public.' Whether the brilliant and international public appreciated Pinza as much as did the critic of the *Daily Herald*, I am not able to say; but the version which he recorded in New York ten years later of Don Basilio's moment of glory, 'La calunnia è un venticello', is riproaringly dispatched on the CBS disc, and though it is taken down a semitone, it would certainly be enough to bring a rousing cheer from any public which was not *too* busy being brilliant and international.

This same disc also includes one sample of Pinza's Boris Godunov, the monologue which is usually translated into English as 'I have attained the highest power', sung once again, as it was when Pinza sang it at the Met, in Italian. This was one role in which Sir Thomas Beecham was desperately anxious to secure Pinza's services for Covent Garden, but to no avail. He wanted him to spend four weeks in London for only three performances, but even at a fee of £125† per performance, this could not be fitted into Pinza's schedule. The recording under discussion was

---

*   He did not attend himself, but sent the Duke and Duchess of York instead.
†   Approximately £3000 at the time of writing.

not made until a decade later, in 1944, but it still finds Pinza in superbly dramatic voice. Chronologically the last of the tracks on the CBS disc, however, Don Giovanni's Serenade, recorded in 1947, presents a noticeable contrast with the old favourite made back in 1930. The tone is drier and less pliant and, despite the cleverness with which Pinza sustains the teasingly high line, the listener does become aware that cleverness is now required.

Pinza could assuredly have remained in opera for several more years, abandoning the Don, no doubt, and picking his roles with increasing circumspection as time went by. He chose, though, to take a different route into his vocal twilight, and in doing so he achieved a greater fame than he had ever known before. Over the years he had been approached on several occasions with suggestions for something of a more popular nature than Grand Opera, and when, in 1948, the Rodgers and Hammerstein partnership came up with the suggestion that he should create the role of the glamorous middle-aged Frenchman Emile de Becque, in a musical which they were planning based on two of the stories from James Michener's novel *Tales of the South Pacific*, Pinza seized the opportunity. Inevitably he was accused in some quarters of prostituting his talent, but that is not a view with which I am able to feel any sympathy. A singer likes to sing, and he likes to have an audience, but he dreads the words 'You should have heard him in this role when he was young.' If Pinza had sunk to peddling musical rubbish I would doubtless feel differently, but the score of SOUTH PACIFIC was a very long way from being that. In 'This nearly was mine' and 'Some enchanted evening' Rodgers and Hammerstein offered Pinza two of the finest romantic numbers ever to be heard on the light musical stage, and Pinza did them proud. After try-outs in New Haven and Boston the show opened on Broadway on 7 April 1949, shortly before Pinza's fifty-seventh birthday, and suddenly he found himself being fêted as the most glamorous male star on Broadway. His acting came in for almost as much praise as his singing – as one journalist put it 'Pinza took the theater away from the boys and gave it back to the men', and in the words of another 'Mr Pinza not only fluttered feminine hearts in his audience but stirred hope among thousands of other middle-aged men that their lives, too, might just be beginning.' Pinza stayed in SOUTH PACIFIC until the end of May 1950, but sadly he did not come with it, as his partner Mary Martin did, to London. I was lucky enough to secure two tickets for the opening night at the Drury Lane Theatre, on 1 November 1951 and, after having feasted my ear so often on the splendour of Pinza's Emile de Becque on the original cast recording, it was with a sad sensation of anti-climax that I listened to the role being sung by just an ordinarily excellent performer. Now that that recording is available on CD (*Columbia CK 32604*), it is nice to have my memory of it confirmed – Pinza, with his luxuriant low notes, his cunningly spun soft high ones, his expansive phrasing and his Mediterranean English (his Emile is definitely an Emilio, but who cares?) puts his stamp on Rodgers and Hammerstein just as he had on Mozart and da Ponte.

SOUTH PACIFIC brought Pinza a rich harvest of show business awards and was followed by three Hollywood films – *Mr Imperium* with Lana Turner, *Strictly Dishonourable*, and *Tonight we Sing*, the life story of the impresario Sol Hurok, in which Pinza gave a spirited performance as Feodor Chaliapin, a task for which he was well qualified, having sung Pimen to Chaliapin's Boris at the Met a quarter of a century before. He returned to Broadway in 1954 to play the role of César in FANNY, a musical by Harold Rome, which attempted to combine the plots of the three Marcel Pagnol films, *Marius*, *Fanny* and *César*, but Rome was no Richard Rodgers and, to quote the *Herald Tribune*'s review of Pinza's contribution, 'The color, the warmth, the command all come from this mature and magnificent personality.'

After several months as César Pinza handed over the role to Lawrence Tibbett, and took his family to Italy on a holiday. While they were there he suffered a heart attack, and reluctantly he had to accept that, apart from lullabies for his five-year-old daughter, his singing days were done. Back in the States he appeared in one or two straight plays and on radio and television, but his health never fully recovered, and shortly before his sixty-fifth birthday he died at his family home in Stamford, Connecticut. His unique position in the musical life of America was reflected in the choice of honorary pallbearers at his funeral. They included a number of celebrities whose paths would never normally have crossed – from the world of the Broadway musical, Richard Rodgers, Oscar Hammerstein and the director Joshua Logan, and from the world of grand opera, Edward Johnson, the retired general manager of the Met. Mary Martin was prevented from attending the funeral by a professional engagement in distant California, but one sentence in her press statement summed up the essence of Pinza's artistic personality – 'He was the most electric human being I have ever appeared with on any stage.'

ROSA PONSELLE

AMERICAN SOPRANO

b. Meriden, Connecticut, 22 January 1897
d. Green Spring Valley, Baltimore, 25 May 1981

It reads like the script of a bad Hollywood musical. The plain and dumpy daughter of humble Italian immigrants loves to sing while washing the dishes, and eventually leaves home to scratch a living in the New York music halls. One day she is heard by a stout gentleman in an expensive suit. 'The time will come, my child,' says he, 'when you will stand upon the stage of the Metropolitan Opera, and you will stand beside me – Enrico Caruso!' Within months his prophecy comes true, the audience stamps and cheers, the critics rave, and a star is born. The main thing wrong with this as a film script is that it has already been done – give or take the odd touch of poetic licence it is the story of Rosa Ponselle.

Her parents – their surname was Ponzillo – had emigrated from Caserta in southern Italy to the industrial town of Meriden in Connecticut where her father continued to pursue his old career running a grocery and café. When Rosa was fifteen the Star Theatre in New Haven, which showed silent films, found itself in need of someone to play the piano during the picture and to play and sing while the reels were being changed. Rosa got the job, and did so well that by the time she was eighteen she had graduated to a purely vocal stint in New Haven's Café Malone, a familiar spot to many a Yale man, where she sang tasteful ballads from a balcony. Meanwhile her elder sister, Carmela, was chancing her arm as a vaudeville artiste in New York, and as there was a vogue at that time for sister acts she summoned Rosa to join her. Carmela lured a vaudeville producer named Mr Hughes to an evening meal in the boarding house where the two of them lodged, but much as he enjoyed the sisters' pasta, when asked if he could help Rosa get a foot into the vaudeville door Mr Hughes replied succinctly 'She's too fat.' He did agree though to listen to her voice, so she sang him 'Kiss Me' from Victor Herbert's MADEMOISELLE MODISTE whereupon her size suddenly seemed less of a problem, and he signed up both girls on the spot. They opened in another Star Theatre, this time in the Bronx, and they were billed as 'The Ponzillo Sisters: Those Tailored Girls', because they could not afford evening dresses, so performed in street clothes. They opened their act with the Barcarolle from THE TALES OF HOFFMANN, then came Carmela with Musetta's Waltz Song, Rosa's all-conquering 'Kiss Me', 'Comin' through the Rye' as a showy coloratura duet, and a final medley of operatic excerpts, culminating in the trio from FAUST – though which of them sang two lines at once I am not quite sure. For three years they plied the circuit, giving their programme four times a day; they made it to the top, too, by appearing in that Mecca of vaudeville, the Palace in New York. It was Carmela who first felt the urge to move a rung or two up the musical ladder, and she sought the advice of a fashionable teacher named William Thorner, who was known to have many influential contacts in the world of opera. He accepted first her and then Rosa as pupils; it was the early Spring of 1918, Rosa had just turned twenty-one, and this was the first vocal tuition she had ever received.

Thorner lived up to his reputation as far as the important contacts were concerned, and it was in his studio that the fateful encounter with Caruso took place. After one glance at Rosa he addressed her as 'Scugnizza', something akin to 'little urchin' in Neapolitan dialect, and asked her 'Do you know you look like me?' She later claimed to have answered 'If I could sing like you I wouldn't care what I looked like', but I somehow doubt whether in the circumstances she could have commanded that much presence of mind. In any case, she sang for him, he liked her, and he did make that famous remark about singing at the Met. More important still, he went to Gatti-Casazza, the all-powerful Manager of the Met, and told him that she would be perfect for Verdi's LA FORZA DEL DESTINO, which Caruso was desperate to sing for the first time but to which none of the Met's sopranos seemed to be quite suited. A couple of days later Rosa was summoned to audition for Gatti, after which he asked her to come back in a week bringing Leonora's aria 'Pace, pace' from FORZA and the appallingly taxing 'Casta diva' from NORMA. The poor girl worked herself into the ground, skimping on both food and sleep to crack these two formidable nuts, and at her second audition, after giving a good account of herself in the 'Pace, pace', she fainted dead away in the middle of the 'Casta diva'. She naturally assumed that that was the end of the road, but no. Gatti took her into his office, presented her with a contract to sing the FORZA Leonora in five months' time with Caruso, de Luca and Mardones, and the die was cast. The five months were spent on a programme of intensive coaching with a man who became and remained one of the pillars of her professional career, Romano Romani, and on the evening of Friday 15 November 1918 the Met public was introduced for the first time to LA FORZA DEL DESTINO, starring the greatest tenor in the world and a totally unheard-of 21-year-old, billed as Rosa Poncelle. Now Leonora is not by a very long chalk a beginner's role, and to add to her other worries Ponselle (as she soon became) had been made aware by Gatti that much more than her own future hung in the balance. She was the first American soprano without European training and experience ever to be presented to the New York public. If she succeeded the whole status of American singers would change overnight. If she failed the same risk would probably never be taken again. When her mother and Romani led her into the wings before that first performance she was literally speechless with nerves. She was sure that Caruso would manage to bolster up her courage, but she was wrong. He completely failed to notice her, so busy was he with his own first-night jitters, banging his forehead with his fist and shouting in Italian 'Never again! This is the last time! No man should be asked to go through this!' Ponselle went on stage, her head filled with the thought 'I am going to die

– oh my poor mother!' – and gave a performance which instantly established her as the most gifted soprano in living memory.

Back in 1984 I was in New York to do some interviews for a radio programme which I was presenting for the BBC on the life of Maria Jeritza. One old lady to whom I spoke was Nanette Guilford, a distinguished soprano with the Met between the wars, and I asked her the question 'How would you compare the quality of Jeritza's voice with that of, say, Rosa Ponselle?' The reply came back like a bullet. 'Would you compare Woolworth with Cartier? Ponselle had the most beautiful soprano voice anyone has ever heard!' – and that is certainly the impression one gains from her recordings. One of the first of these, Butterfly's 'Un bel di', recorded a few months after her triumph in FORZA, is featured on a Nimbus disc, 'Divas 1906–1935' *NI 7802*, and immediately reveals why the hard-boiled New York critics should have used expressions like 'vocal gold, dark, rich and ductile', or 'one of the most voluptuous voices ever heard'. There is not a lot of characterization in this early sample of her art, but the purple, velvety sheen on the voice makes it quite unlike any other, and she sustains the full amplitude of this lavish quality from the low D flats of 'I nomi che mi dava' right up to the final ecstatic high B flat. The sound which she achieves on the word 'Vedi' ('Look') as she pictures Pinkerton's return cannot be described, it has to be heard. The notes are F to G, Puccini has marked them 'ritenuto, con passione', and what Ponselle does with them is enough in itself to justify the view of that very exacting connoisseur Walter Legge that 'This was the most glorious voice that ever came from any woman's throat in the Italian repertory.'

Nimbus have also devoted one whole disc in their Prima Voce series to Ponselle (*NI 7805*) consisting of eleven operatic tracks and five songs. The earliest of the arias, Aida's 'O patria mia', dates from 1923, and as a hardened trouper of twenty-six Ponselle had come on a long way in terms of textual inflexion and dramatic thrust. As she appears to have mastered virtually every aspect of the art of voice production too – line, breath control, phrasing, the projection of every vowel sound, open or closed, with the same wealth of lustrous tone, the ability to pluck soft high notes out of the sky, and anything else one can think of – it is hard to see how this aria could possibly be more magnificently performed. To add to her vocal mastery the overweight Miss Ponzillo had transformed herself into a svelte and glamorous young lady, whose face in many of the photographs appears to consist largely of two huge and challenging dark brown eyes. But no singer in my experience has ever quite been given everything, and at Ponselle's christening the Wicked Fairy had evidently laid upon her the dreaded curse of Shaky Nerves. Though not always as terrified as she had been at her debut, she was frequently to be seen walking round and round the Met before she could summon up the courage even to enter the building, and though I think everyone in the operatic profession would agree with Caruso that 'the singer with no nerves is no singer', to suffer as Ponselle did must be a hideous burden. Funnily enough the 'O patria mia', dispatched on this recording with such sovereign ease, became one of Ponselle's mental Waterloos. One evening when she had risen from a sick bed to sing Aida in the Brooklyn Academy she failed to sustain the high C as long as she meant to and from then onwards never felt confident in the part – despite, of course, peppering high Cs all over the house with uninhibited abandon in so many of her other roles. Another AIDA excerpt on this same disc is of particular interest because for some inexplicable reason the Victor Company never published it. It is a resplendent account of the Nile Scene duet, with Giovanni Martinelli in noble voice, and Ponselle ideally encompassing the transition from the shrewish 'D'uno spergiuro non ti macchiar!' ('Do not stain yourself with a falsehood!') to the seductive cooing of 'Là, tra foreste vergini' ('There, amongst virgin forests'). Indeed, her skill in twisting this macho military man round her very feminine little finger calls to mind Ernest Newman's review of her in Montemezzi's L'AMORE DEI TRE RE – 'If as a divorce-court judge I had heard her one "Ritorniam" breathed to her lover I would have given her husband a divorce without hearing further evidence.'

Femininity of a more innocent brand pervades her highly sensitive renderings of Desdemona's 'Willow Song' and 'Ave Maria' (sadly she never sang the role on stage), while her more monumental style is arrestingly represented by 'Suicidio!' from LA GIOCONDA, one of her great successes both at the Met and at Covent Garden. When we come to the antics of Elvira's show-stopping rumpty-tum outburst from ERNANI there is only one word to be used of Ponselle's performance – that very dangerous one 'unique'. In the history of the gramophone, and I suspect in the history of singing, there has been no other soprano who could carry that warm viscosity of sound from the mezzo-like lower register straight up into the realms of coloratura, crowning it all with a long trill whose precision would shame most of the specialist 'canaries' with one tenth of Ponselle's splendour in their voices. It was this boundlessness of Ponselle's vocal panoply which set Gatti-Casazza's heart on the realization of one of his pet dreams – NORMA, which had not been seen at the Met since Lilli Lehmann last sang it there in 1892. Gatti was wary, though, of rushing his and Ponselle's fences, and with the active support of Maestro Tullio Serafin he decided first to present her in Spontini's LA VESTALE (aptly described by Francis Robinson, later Assistant Manager at the Met, as 'a kind of B-picture NORMA'). Like Norma, the heroine is a priestess who lives to regret her vows of chastity, and Ponselle sings her two main arias with classical severity of style but with plenty of smoulder lurking in the tone. We have now advanced into the era of electrical recordings – this was 1926 – and though, to my ear at least, the engineers sometimes had greater difficulty in capturing a big voice like Ponselle's on the early electrics than they had had on the late acoustics, the two VESTALE arias with their staid and steady *cantilena* fare better than most. By the time Ponselle made her two celebrated NORMA recordings, 'Casta diva', and the 'Mira, o Norma' duet with that fine American mezzo Marion Telva, the technicians had their new toy under better control.

NORMA had eventually been unveiled at the Met on 16 November 1927. Ponselle's personal triumph was immense, and she chose the role for her Covent Garden debut in 1929. Londoners were very honoured because apart from her Covent Garden seasons and three performances of LA VESTALE in Florence she refused ever to sing with any company except that of the Metropolitan Opera, apparently worried by the many stories she had heard about the claques, the intrigues and the venal critics in so many European houses. She had been reassured that Covent Garden was a mannerly establishment, an impression confirmed by a conversation shortly before her debut there with her girlhood idol, that erstwhile uncrowned queen of the place, Dame Nellie Melba. 'My dear, don't expect Covent Garden to be like your Metropolitan,' Melba told her. 'Above all, don't expect applause after "Casta diva". A London audience wouldn't clap the Angel Gabriel himself until the curtain came down.' To quote Francis Robinson once again 'Ponselle must have outdone Gabriel, for after the aria the public could not hold its enthusiasm. There was a thunderclap that split the roof. The next time they met, Dame Nellie was not so solicitous.' Anyway, suffice it to say of Ponselle's 'Casta diva' that it must surely be taken as one of the landmarks of recorded vocal artistry. It is an alarmingly difficult piece – I recall that Callas, then in her days of contented tubbiness, and vocally more secure than later on, could not keep it in tune at her Covent Garden debut in 1952 – but Ponselle makes it sound a totally natural vehicle of self-expression and beautifies it with a hundred subtle touches. In the duet she is glowingly partnered by Telva, their voices an ideal blend.

The last operatic number on this disc is taken from the piece which always meant more to Ponselle than any, LA FORZA DEL DESTINO. It is 'La vergine degli angeli', the end of the long scene with the Padre Guardiano, of which she claimed in later days that it had been more difficult for her than any single part of any opera in her repertoire. 'By the time I got to the "Vergine degli angeli",' she said, 'I was in seventh heaven, for

I knew the worst was behind me. In that scene Leonora has to be a lyric, dramatic and near-mezzo soprano. She must express fear, fatigue, piety, desperation, remorse, relief and a dozen other assorted emotions – all in phrases placed all over the stave, and below and above it as well.' Perhaps it was this determination to get under the skin of a role that gave Ponselle her ultimate layer of greatness; in any case the singing of 'La vergine degli angeli', with Ezio Pinza at his most orotund, is certainly more stamped with piety than with desperation.

After this miraculous display of operatic splendour the disc is delightfully rounded off by a group of five songs. The first two are Neapolitan: de Curtis's 'Carmé' and di Capua's 'Maria Mari!', and with them Ponselle waves a golden salute to the land of her fathers. Whether they are as idiomatic as Caruso's Neapolitan recordings I am not able to say – he was born a genuine 'Scugnizzo' after all – but when truly great singers let their hair down with this sort of song I always adore the results. Tullio Serafin used to say that though he had in his time worked with many wonderful singers he had only encountered three giants – Caruso, Ruffo and Ponselle. It so happens that all of them recorded a number of Neapolitan songs, and in every instance the natural timbre of their voices was as tellingly displayed as by anything else they sang. Ponselle's last three songs are in English. One, an acoustic recording of touchingly personal quality, is a sentimental ballad called 'A Perfect Day' with text on the poetic level of a greetings card and melody to match; the other two are Arensky's 'On Wings of Dream' and Rimsky-Korsakov's 'The Nightingale and the Rose', both accompanied by her invaluable Romano Romani. They were recorded in Hollywood in 1939 and, as you would expect from a soprano of only forty-two with a voice as sound as a bell, no aspect of her art shows the remotest sign of deterioration. And yet the extraordinary fact remains that by that time Ponselle had retired from professional life, and the manner of her departure from the Met had been a lamentable anticlimax to such a meteoric career.

During her nineteen years with the company Ponselle had been required to tackle quite a number of rather out of the way roles – operas like OBERON, LE ROI D'YS, L'AMORE DEI TRE RE, LA NOTTE DI ZORAIMA, L'AFRICAINE, and even LA VESTALE make up an odd list for someone who never got around to Tosca, Mimi or Butterfly. She had always unquestioningly accepted what Gatti-Casazza decreed, and despite some carping voices amongst the reviews of her Carmen and her Donna Anna she had always won glory for the Met as well as for herself. When the 1937–8 season was being planned she agreed to the four roles that were offered her, but she also, for the first time, put in a request of her own. She had set her heart on playing Cilea's ADRIANA LECOUVREUR, recently put back onto the European map by Toscanini. She even offered to sing it for nothing, but Edward Johnson, successor to Gatti-Casazza who had retired in 1935, turned her down. The combination of this rebuff, the constant strain on her nerves and the fact that she was just about to marry the son of the Mayor of Baltimore made her feel that the game was not worth the candle and it was time to settle for a quiet life. On 17 April 1937 she appeared as Carmen in Cleveland during the Metropolitan's annual visit, then she packed up, went home and never appeared in public again. After a year without her the management of the Met did all they could to lure her back, but by then she had settled into a new life and that was that.

Another invaluable disc devoted to the art of Rosa Ponselle is RCA Victor *GD87810*. Seven tracks coincide with Nimbus – the Rimsky song, the ERNANI aria, the Willow Song, Aida's 'O patria mia', the second VESTALE aria, 'Suicidio' and 'Casta diva' – but there are nine tracks which do not. There are two more of the 1939 recordings, a French song called 'A l'aimé', which displays the full richness of her lower register, adorned by two seamless diminished octave swoops up to perfectly poised high Gs, and a touching little ballad called 'When I Have Sung My Songs'. This opens with the words 'When I have sung my songs to you I'll sing no more', and by an ironical coincidence it was part of Ponselle's contribution to a Sunday night concert on 14 March 1937, which, though no one knew it at the time, was her very last appearance on the stage of the Metropolitan Opera. The disc's operatic tracks, those which we have not already encountered *chez* Nimbus, consist of Aida's Act I aria 'Ritorna vincitor' (one of the most striking instances of Ponselle's ability to soar like a very expensive lift from the ground floor to the penthouse without apparently having to press any buttons), Selika's 'In grembo a me' from L'AFRICAINE, in which I confess to feeling that even her inspired vocalism cannot rescue an idiotic piece of music, and two excerpts from LA FORZA DEL DESTINO. The first of these is Leonora's aria 'Pace, pace' ('Peace, peace'), which meant so much to Ponselle that when she and her husband built their dream house in the Green Spring Valley they called it the Villa Pace, and had the opening notes carved in stone by the gate; and the second is the finale to the whole opera, in which she is joined by Martinelli and Pinza. Despite the fact that these were always uncomfortable recordings – electrics of 1928, so they should have been better – the performances are so vibrant, and the piece is so intertwined in the whole life story of Ponselle that no anthology of her art would be complete without them. They do, however, emphasize what a shame it was that she and Caruso never recorded together. Much as I admire Martinelli, his is a very 'straight' voice, without the opulent overtones which made Caruso's and Ponselle's so endlessly fascinating, but as the two giants were contracted to different recording companies we are left having to imagine what this marriage in Heaven must have sounded like.

One of the remaining tracks on this RCA Victor disc may seem initially like a bit of a cheat, because for the first half of the recording we are not allowed to hear the Ponselle voice at all. It is the Bach-Gounod 'Ave Maria', which is played straight through by a violinist named Mischa Schmidt, after which the diva joins in and it becomes a duet. The final result, though, is a rather special display of certain of the Ponselle hallmarks. Mischa Schmidt, about whom I know nothing, was evidently a violinist with an impeccable legato technique and bags of soul in his tone, but even so Ponselle finds him an easy act to follow. To say that she spins out her contribution like some equally impeccable cellist would be to tell only the half of it; she provides the richness of a cello, but it is always with the brilliance of a violin on the front of the stream of sound. I suppose it is simply that no man-made instrument could be expected to provide the wealth of colour, the chiaroscuro, inherent in a voice like Ponselle's.

After her retirement Ponselle revelled in the joys of country life, and the Villa Pace stood in enough ground to provide space and to spare for horses, cattle and innumerable dogs. She had always been a fresh-air fiend. During her time at the Met it was a house rule that on Ponselle nights the heating had to be turned off in the corridor of ladies' dressing rooms, and occasionally she even insisted on having the huge scenery doors opened right onto the street. Ezio Pinza was once deputed by his colleagues to lead a delegation of protest to Gatti-Casazza but it did no good, and a tenor in the company is said to have threatened to sue her if he caught a cold. Anyway, in Green Spring Valley Ponselle was able to turn her back on New York and breathe her fill, but though her days before the public were over she never gave up singing for her friends, her few carefully selected pupils and herself. In October 1954 she was persuaded to make some recordings in the Villa, and two of them complete the RCA Victor disc. They are songs in folk style, one called 'Carmen-Carmela', sung in Spanish, the other called 'Amuri, amuri', and sung in Italian to her own piano accompaniment, with a variety of dramatic effects thrown in. Much of the old quality is still there, and a good deal of the old control. Had she wished to, or had she needed the money, she could obviously still have been packing out concert halls anywhere.

There is one other Ponselle recording available on CD which certainly merits a mention though, for reasons that will become apparent, I think it is likely to remain of largely specialist interest. As a reward to the Covent Garden Management and public for taking to her Norma with such un-British lack of reserve in 1929, she promised them a special treat for the following year – her first Violetta in LA TRAVIATA. This was a project very dear to her heart. One night in February 1930, sitting up in bed after singing a concert in Washington, she penned a delightfully chaotic letter, full of underlinings and exclamation marks, to Colonel Eustace Blois who had assumed command at Covent Garden. 'I hope you'll give us plenty of stage rehearsal for Traviata,' she wrote, 'as I won't have a chance to prepare it here. *You will won't you*??? I *do want to do it well* you know . . . I do want to put it over *big* – don't we?? you!!!!!' After details of her requirements concerning the set – she wanted it as her famous predecessor Gemma Bellincioni had had it, and the walls in the bedroom scene were to be 'if possible please a real mysterious lavender more on the orchid shade' – she turned to the musical side. 'Another great favour I ask of you', she continued, 'is to get after the *orchestra pitch* – Have your German director keep pulling it down until you get it to 435 and *keep* them down – get them to *adjust their instruments* before beginning your season . . . of course using the *435* new clarinets.' Whether the Colonel obeyed orders I do not know; it is a matter of operatic history though that her Violetta conquered London as decisively as had her Norma. The most authoritative Verdian amongst the English critics, Francis Toye, was moved to write 'I do not think I have heard anything to surpass or perhaps even to equal it', and he was not alone in his views.

Thereafter Violetta entered Ponselle's repertoire at the Met, and the Pearl recording to which I refer (GEMM *CD 9317*) is of a live performance in May 1935. The reason for the caveat expressed above is that the quality of the recording is very poor indeed, nowhere near what one would normally call an acceptable commercial standard, being a CD taken from a tape taken from acetate discs taken from a radio broadcast! *But* it does give us one of Ponselle's most legendary roles in the white heat of performance, and it is a role from which she did not record a single number in the studio. I must confess that when I first heard this CD, after doubting during the Prelude whether I would persevere, as soon as Ponselle came on I was hooked. Out of the mush and through the clicks it is recognizable that somewhere in the distance she is indeed 'Putting it over big'. By my reckoning she takes the 'Sempre libera' down a full tone, but the combination of opulence and flexibility bemuses the ear and defies any attempt to put a label on the voice. By this stage of her career she had become a deeply subtle vocal actress too; the flashes of insight are simply too many to enumerate. Given patrician support by the eloquent Germont of Lawrence Tibbett she makes a heart-rending experience out of their Act II duets; and in that melting passage after the quarrel scene: 'Alfredo, Alfredo, di questo core non puoi comprendere tutto l'amore' the naked grief in her voice must have reached many more hearts than just Alfredo's. Verdi marks the vocal line 'con voce debolissima e con passione'. Not everyone can sing 'with the weakest of voices *and* with passion' – but Ponselle could. The tenor, Frederick Jagel, is a somewhat inflexible Alfredo and has pitch problems in 'Parigi o cara', but the conductor, Ettore Panizza, gives a searing account of the piece. Most of the traditional cuts are made, and Pearl have found room on the second disc for the two NORMA numbers discussed above.

Ponselle became something of an all-American folk heroine – she must have reached one of her widest audiences when she sang 'The Star Spangled Banner' at President Roosevelt's inauguration – and the inexplicability of her early retirement was the stuff of which myths are made. She was no recluse though, and in her old age, apart from keeping open house to friends and admirers from all over the world, she put much time and energy into guiding the fortunes of the Baltimore Civic Opera. As milestone birthdays came and went, seventy, seventy-five, eighty, the press never lost their interest in her, and the story of that FORZA debut back in 1918 was told and retold like some Homeric saga. There is one aspect of the story though which leaves me with a niggling sense of waste – surely she would have been the greatest Tosca of them all? She visited Puccini in Viareggio in 1924 shortly before his death. She sang him the 'Vissi d'arte', and when she had finished asked if she could sing it again in an entirely different style. After the second version Puccini sat with his head in his hands saying softly 'If only I had heard her earlier!' If he had, or if he had had a few more years to live, to what might that miraculous sound have inspired him! For miraculous it was. As legend has it, Lotte Lehmann once turned with a sigh to Geraldine Farrar and posed the rhetorical question 'How does one get a voice like Ponselle's?' Back came the answer – 'By special arrangement with God.'

TITO SCHIPA

ITALIAN TENOR

b. Lecce, 2 January 1889 (?), d. New York, 16 December 1965

To me, Tito Schipa stands outside the mainstream of Italian tenors. The rest of them, whether dramatic, *spinto*, lyric, or *leggiero*, always seem to have some quality in common, but Schipa is different. His vocal timbre does not lend itself to any neat categorization. I can understand people describing him as a singer's singer or as an acquired taste; I can even (with an effort) understand people not liking him. The voice does not have the roundness that some may look for, it does not have the robustness in which others delight. What it does have, though, is something indefinable, all of its own, and those who love their Schipa, myself among them, love him very much. One Italian critic came up with a nice phrase to describe him – 'Un gusto clavicembalistico applicato al canto' ('A taste of the harpsichord applied to song') – but to me if voices were to be compared with orchestral instruments, and if one voice were to be equated with the trumpet, say, or another with the clarinet, Schipa's instrument would be the oboe. It is slightly reedy in quality, pleading in tone, more dangerously poised on the breath than beefier voices, and thus more miraculous as the tenuous line spins on and on. 'Ah,' the knowledgeable might say, 'he's describing the archetypal *tenore di grazia*'; but I am not, because here again Schipa declines to fit the specification. When did a *tenore di grazia* ever make a famous Cavaradossi? Can a *tenore di grazia* handle Werther's dramatic outbursts? Let us simply settle for the fact that Schipa was Schipa, and not try to put a label on him.

Over his birthday another question hangs. Often given as 2 January 1888 but equally often as 2 January 1889, it is possible that the last day or two of December 1888 might actually be correct, and that his father fudged the record to make things work out better as far as military service was concerned. Be that as it may, the happy event definitely occurred in Lecce, right down in the heel of Italy, and it was not very long before the child revealed himself as the possessor of an exceptional soprano voice. When he was only eight, the music master at his primary school wrote a hymn for a special service in the local church, and Schipa was entrusted with a solo. This won him his first press notices, and his first chance on the operatic stage, singing the line 'Vo' la tromba il cavallin!' in the second act of LA BOHEME, which happened to be in the repertoire at Lecce's Teatro Greco. It was a few years later, though, that his voice changed the course of his life, when another solo in an important religious festival brought him to the attention of the visiting Bishop, Monsignor Gennaro Trama. Hearing that 'the boy with the voice of an angel' came from a poor family and would soon be leaving school to go in search of some menial job, the Bishop suggested that he should be offered secondary education in the Seminary, and moreover at the Bishop's expense. Schipa's time as a seminarist was followed by vocal studies with a certain Maestro Garunda, who was so confident of the boy's talent that after three years he organized a benefit concert, the proceeds of which paid for Schipa to travel all the way to Milan and complete his training with one of the city's foremost teachers, Maestro Emilio Piccoli. Piccoli soon had him ready for an official debut (BOHEME did not count!), which took place in 1910 in the opera house of a town in Piedmont called Vercelli, as Alfredo in LA TRAVIATA.

Schipa was not the sort of performer around whom many anecdotes collected, but there was one incident during that first TRAVIATA which he used to recall with particular enjoyment. His partner, the ailing Violetta, was built as provincial divas are traditionally supposed to be – large. He was built like Falstaff back in the days when he was page to the Duke of Norfolk – 'sottile, sottile', very slight. After letting rip with a particularly passionate 'Amami, Alfredo' in Act II, this formidable lady grappled Schipa to her bosom with such determination that a voice was heard calling from the gods 'Don't damage the poor boy, we want to hear him sing!'

Despite this hazard, Schipa's debut was enough of a success to see him launched on the Italian provincial circuit. Happily Lecce was on the list, along with Palermo, Bologna, Parma, Trento, Perugia, Ancona and several more, and by the time he reached his first really important theatre, the Teatro dal Verme in Milan, during the season of 1912–13, he already had nearly twenty operas under his belt. It was in 1913 too that he made his first recordings, and another of the Nimbus company's admirable discs (*Prima Voce N17813*) offers us three of these early titles as part of a well balanced selection extending to the year 1937. They are the off-stage Serenade from CAVALLERIA RUSTICANA, the Duke's scena 'Ella mi fu rapita' from RIGOLETTO, and Edgardo's 'Tu che a Dio' from LUCIA DI LAMMERMOOR, all of which display the quality which was pre-eminently Schipa's calling card throughout the whole of his long career – elegance. The voice itself has a vernal freshness to it, as one might expect from a tenor still in his mid-twenties. Less to be expected are the polish and stylishness which were already at his command. Schipa was always an exceptionally fastidious, musicianly singer, and even at this stage of his career he clearly did not allow youthful impetuosity to disturb the purity of his vocal line. I cannot myself pretend that at the heavier end of his repertoire I always see eye to eye with his characterizations. His Duke of Mantua, for instance, I find an insufficiently dangerous fellow. When a phrase like 'E dove ora sarà quell'angiol caro?' ('And where now may that dear angel be?') is sung with such exquisite delicacy of tone and sincerity of expression, we are left feeling that the Duke has lost the love of his life rather than just another plaything for a night; the 1926 'Questa o quella' on the same disc, a delightfully frothy piece of vocalization, also leaves me feeling that his Duke is nothing much worse than an amusing playboy. However, as he enjoyed regular triumphs in RIGOLETTO in many of the world's largest houses (Covent Garden, to its eternal shame, was one of the few which never invited him) evidently his view of the role met with few disappointed customers. People did not come to Schipa nights looking for the magnificence of a Caruso or the open floodgates of a Beniamino Gigli. Where Caruso's singing assumes the listener's capitulation and Gigli's demands it, Schipa's requests it, very politely; and if, to my personal taste, this approach is a little too melancholy for 'Ella mi fu rapita', it strikes me as entirely suitable to the aria from LUCIA. Edgardo, after all, really did love Lucia, and she has been more irrevocably removed than Gilda. This number also establishes that for all his delicacy Schipa could ride a climax when he needed to; indeed, I remember the Italian conductor Giuseppe Morelli telling me what a surprise it was, when Schipa appeared in LA TRAVIATA in the Rome Opera, that his was the voice which dominated the huge Act II finale.

This Nimbus disc does also provide many examples of the kind of music which, once you have heard the Schipa version, your ear cannot ever quite dissociate from him, so strongly does he put his individual mark upon it. The MANON Dream, for instance, with its ravishing diminuendi on the high notes, and with Schipa's directness of communication commanding the listener's total attention; the two MIGNON arias, gentle, eloquent and persuasive; 'Sogno soave e casto' from DON PASQUALE, a winning example of how Schipa sees his deprived lovers not as angry, vengeful men, but sad and lonely ones; or Almaviva's 'Se il mio nome' from IL BARBIERE DI SIVIGLIA, a role in which Schipa, during his prime, had very little competition. The immaculate articulation seems always to be right on the lips and the tip of the tongue; you could take dictation from him – he was once warned by the chief administrator of the Teatro dal Verme that the sellers of libretti were becoming his implacable enemies because on Schipa nights nobody needed to buy one – and yet the flow of the vocal line is never even momentarily interrupted. I imagine, too, that Schipa must have been a recording engineer's dream, using as he did a comparatively limited dynamic range, a smooth and constant projection and a tonal quality which is never aggressive but is always carrying and incisive.

The year 1913 saw another important 'first' in Schipa's career, when the Teatro dal Verme presented him in partnership with Amelita Galli-Curci. These two were ideally suited to one another, and appeared together with enormous success, not only in Milan but also seven years later in Chicago, where they became the absolute darlings of the Civic Opera. Off stage they were also the greatest of friends, with Galli-Curci becoming godmother to Schipa's daughter Elena. (The godfather was Titta Ruffo – no record has been kept of the standard of singing at the christening.) In any case, for the kind of Bellinian or Donizettian love duet in which the soprano and tenor lines twine dreamily in and out of each other in thirds and sixths, it would be hard to imagine a more seraphic pair, and of the many recordings which they made together I feel that Nimbus have picked the most magical, the 1922 version of 'Tornami a dir' from DON PASQUALE. How suitable that these two should warble to each other 'La voce tua si cara' ('Your voice so dear') – certainly the effect of these two 'voci si care' is pure moonlit enchantment. The only other duet on this disc also ranks among my personal favourites – the Cherry Duet from Mascagni's L'AMICO FRITZ, recorded with Mafalda Favero. This time it is sunlit enchantment, with Schipa as the middle-aged bachelor whose heart is less impervious than he supposed to the combined effects of spring in the air and Suzel up a cherry tree. I really would urge anyone who is not able to follow Italian to try to lay their hands on a translation of this duet. The conversation, starting with Schipa's utterly natural and unconcerned 'Suzel, buon di' is the essence of charm and, though Favero can be a touch squally on her high notes, and Schipa, most uncharacteristically, is caught out by a couple of soft high tones at the end, it is an irresistible performance of a scene which, for my money, represents the peak of Mascagni's achievement.

The rest of the nineteen tracks on this disc are solos. There is an impassioned 'Ah! non mi ridestar' from Schipa's favourite role, Werther; there is the 'Lamento di Federico' from L'ARLESIANA in which that pleading quality in Schipa's voice, to which I referred earlier, must have brought joy to Cilea's heart; there are two arias from L'ELISIR D'AMORE, including of course 'Una furtiva lagrima', after which, on the occasion of Schipa's Met debut in 1932, as the New York critic Olin Downes reported, 'the audience not only applauded, but shouted its approval'; and 'M'appari' from MARTHA, which once sparked off an almighty row in Chicago when the conductor, Maestro Cimini, was compelled by the public to break the rigorous ban on encores and was sacked for his troubles, whereupon Schipa declared 'If he goes, I go too', and much fat was in the fire. We also have three other tracks, each a gem – des Grieux's Saint Sulpice aria from MANON, redolent to Schipa, no doubt, of his own days in the Seminary – less tortured, one hopes, than des Grieux's; his celebrated rendering of Arlecchino's Serenade from PAGLIACCI; and an exquisite account of 'Quando le sere al placido' from LUISA MILLER.

EMI has released a Schipa CD in its *Références* series (*CDH 7 63200 2*), and this too can be warmly recommended. Half the numbers double with those on the Prima Voce disc, but those which do not include some valuable additions, notably three songs by Alessandro Scarlatti. One of them, which Schipa habitually sang in his concerts, is a splendidly jaunty number named 'Violette' (at least that is what he used to call it – EMI correctly list it as 'Rugiadose, odorose' from the opera PIRRO E DEMETRIO), and it finds the tenor with a very happy smile on his voice. A less happy experience is the orchestral introduction to 'Che farò senza Eurydice' from Gluck's ORFEO – (all swoops and slithers nowadays!) – though Schipa comes as near to sounding right in the role as any tenor could. We are treated to another two soprano/tenor duets, the first being 'Prendi, l'anel ti dono' from LA SONNAMBULA, ideal Schipa territory if ever anything was. When the opera was revived in Chicago in 1919 specially for Schipa and Galli-Curci, though critics found the plot puerile and the music excuse enough in itself for the heroine's somnolence, no praise was enough for the two protagonists. On this 1933 recording, though, Schipa's partner is Toti dal Monte, and I must admit that I do miss that insouciant quality of Galli-Curci's in music of this kind. I miss it even more in the second duet, our old friend 'Tornami a dir' from DON PASQUALE. It is not that there is anything wrong with this later version, but I do not quite feel the magic of the spring night as I do in the other; I miss the scent of the lilacs.

By a happy chance EMI offers us an almost entirely different selection from Nimbus of the old 1913 recordings. Schipa sets about the broad sweep of 'Cielo e mar' from LA GIOCONDA with an assurance astonishing in one so young, but interestingly he is far less successful with 'Che gelida manina'. LA BOHEME was in his stage repertoire but the aria just does not seem to be his cup of tea. He puts it down a semitone (plenty of people have done that), but he has to compensate by lifting one of the lower notes, and even in the transposed key he doctors the climax to unconvincing effect. His reputation as a Puccini singer is rescued, though, by the two TOSCA arias (Puccini's regard for him was demonstrated four years later when he was selected to create the tenor role in LA RONDINE), which in a way pay more eloquent tribute than anything else to Schipa's artistic stature. He was, after all, fighting on a modern battleground with old-fashioned weapons. His was a voice of Rossinian or Donizettian mould, in an era of *verismo*, when roof-raising was more in vogue than refinement. Yet here he was, competing with voices twice the size of his own, in one of the most popular of all veristic roles, and proving that Cavaradossi could be as effectively portrayed using the old virtues of *bel canto* as it could in the newer style of blood and thunder. It was indeed shortly after he made these recordings that Schipa featured in a remarkable incident during a TOSCA performance at the San Carlo in Naples. His poetic rendering of 'E lucevan le stelle' earned him an encore, at the end of which the public naturally applauded him again. When they had quietened down, the conductor, Leopoldo Mugnone, universally recognized as one of the grumpiest of all Maestri, to the astonishment of Schipa and of the public, called up to him in his thick Neapolitan dialect and using a local diminutive of the tenor's name, 'Little Schipa, sing it again – but this time,' with a gesture of his thumb to the auditorium, 'not for that lot, but for me!' Certainly this 1913 recording of the aria would deserve an encore in any company, and interestingly it ends with what I believe to be a unique example of Schipa indulging in a Gigliesque sob. In fact, though one might not imagine it from the fastidiousness of his singing, Schipa was an uninhibited stage performer – he was also once referred to by a Chicago critic as 'the handsomest man in opera' – and he was proud of having on one occasion struck fear into the heart of the legendary baritone Mattia Battistini. It was TOSCA again, in Monte Carlo, and Battistini was so convincing as the sadistic Scarpia that Schipa found himself really hating the man. When the announcement was made in Act II of the victory at Marengo Schipa's exultation overcame him, and so violent were his attempts to get at his supercilious tormentor that Battistini was heard to hiss at his henchmen Spoletta and Sciarrone 'tenetelo, tenetelo', ('hold onto him, hold onto him').

Besides this solo disc EMI have one other trump up their sleeves. In 1932 DON PASQUALE was recorded in its entirety, with the Chorus and Orchestra of La Scala Milan under Carlo Sabajno, and Schipa as Ernesto, a role which had become virtually his private property. The rest of the Scala cast were naturally no slouches – Ernesto Badini upholding the best Italian *buffo* traditions in the title-role, Afro Poli a suave Malatesta, Adelaide Saraceni a zestful (though occasionally shrill) Norina – but Schipa emerges as the undisputed star of the show. As we have seen, he had already recorded a couple of the more famous numbers, but to have his participation in the ensembles and his masterly delivery of the recitatives is a treat indeed, and in general the sound quality of this much-loved old set comes up as bright as a new pin (EMI

CHS 7 63241 2 – two discs).

Considering how many Schipa CDs there are on the market, it is remarkable how little they conflict with one another. The compilation on RCA Victor *GD 87969* is another splendid one because although several of the operatic titles cross with Nimbus and EMI, they are almost all different versions – an electric 'Ella mi fu rapita', for instance, instead of the 1913 recording, and with the Duke's 'Vendetta' sounding a bit more 'formidabile'. We are also treated to three more duets with Galli-Curci, 'Un di felice' from LA TRAVIATA (of which more anon), 'Son geloso del zefiro' from their familiar partnership in LA SONNAMBULA, and 'Verranno a te' from LUCIA DI LAMMERMOOR, which may seem small in scale compared with the more full-throated approach of Callas and di Stefano, say, or Sutherland and Pavarotti, but which proves that music of this period can be made to work in more ways than one. Two tracks which, to me, do not work at all are the DON GIOVANNI arias – a curiously uninvolved 'Dalla sua pace' and an orchestrally truncated and musically dubious 'Il mio tesoro' – which is strange, because this was another of his famous stage roles, though it is true to say that he made these recordings before he had sung the part under Bruno Walter. One most attractive feature of this Victor release, though, is that it presents a rounded portrait of Schipa by including a selection of his favourite songs. Early in his career Schipa established himself as something of a popular hero in Spain – one politician is said to have remarked 'What the people want is bread and Schipa' – and he seldom gave a recital without including at least one or two popular Spanish numbers. On this disc 'Princesita' and 'Amapola' demonstrate his knack (one which he shared with Richard Tauber) of finding a kind of perfection in such trifles and thus serving them up as jewels in their own right. The same applies to his Neapolitan songs, amongst which his 'Chi se nne scorda occhiu' has to rank as a classic – a performance of considerable vocal virtuosity allied, as I am assured by friends from that part of the world, to a classically idiomatic command of dialect. Certainly there can be no doubting the authenticity of the final track on the disc, a Neapolitan song composed by Schipa himself. This is no mere 'one-off', like Caruso's 'Dreams of Long Ago', because Schipa was a prolific composer with two operettas to his credit as well as numerous songs and even a Mass dating back to his early days in Lecce. It is worth noting, too, that this track is chronologically the last of any to be reissued on CD. It dates from 1955, and bears remarkable testimony to the state of Schipa's voice in his late sixties.

There are some more of these miscellaneous items on Pearl's two Schipa volumes, GEMM *CD 9322* and *9364*, as well as various valuable additions to the operatic list, including in the first volume two more items from RIGOLETTO – 'La donna è mobile' which he toys with 'qual piuma al vento' – like a feather in the wind – and a seductive account of the 'E il sol dell'anima' duet, teamed once more with Galli-Curci – and in the second his exemplary 'Fantaisies aux divins mensonges' from the now neglected LAKME. On the popular front we have in Vol. I a gorgeously rumpty-tum bit of espagnolerie called 'Valencia', and an even dottier number about the girls of Trieste entitled 'La campana di San Giusto'. It is such a comfort to know that the oh-so-artistic Signor Schipa was as happy to sing lucrative rubbish as anyone else, and I am only sorry that no room has been found so far on CD for the various catchy bits of nonsense which a composer named Bixio used to write for Schipa's films. Schipa was a dedicated film buff and indeed from 1928 until his return to Italy in 1941 he made his main home in Hollywood. He chose Ramon Novarro as one of his second daughter's godparents, he wrote the theme tune for an early sound picture called *Seventh Heaven* starring Janet Gaynor, he dashed off a tango for Douglas Fairbanks Senior in *The Gaucho*, and he himself starred in such epics as *Vivere, Tre Uomini in un Frak* (*Three Men in a Tailcoat*), and *Terra di Fuoco*. But to return to Pearl's 'pops', in Vol. II we have two of the more hackneyed Neapolitan songs (nothing wrong in being hackneyed – songs get that way because people like them) in 'Santa Lucia' and 'Vieni sul mar', better known to English listeners as 'Two lovely black eyes', as well as several other less well known examples of the genre, over which Schipa pours his authentic Southern brand of nostalgia.

To me, though, the greatest service which Pearl performs is that in Vol. I they have reissued both sides of an old 78 which mercifully outlived most of its fellows in the wartime HMV catalogue, and was originally responsible for my addiction to Tito Schipa. This was *DA 1133*, Schipa and Galli-Curci in the two TRAVIATA duets, and people can tell me what they like about Galli-Curci being past it and singing flat and heaven knows what else – I do not care. From the first bar of side one, with Schipa as the shy and hesitant Alfredo breathing his first declaration of love, through to the magical diminuendo on the E natural before that heart-stopping melody 'Di quell'amor', then on to the opening of the 'Parigi o cara', the merest whisper but urgent and vital nonetheless, and up to the *mezza voce* A flat (all right, Verdi marked it forte, but for a change he was wrong – who raises his voice in a sick-room?), then back to a gentle murmur for the final bar, this is the kind of singing that turns listeners into fans.

It was certainly a great moment for me when, in 1951, I saw to my absolute astonishment a poster announcing that Tito Schipa was coming to sing in the Festival Hall. I had simply assumed that he, like so many names on old 78s, belonged to times gone by, and I awaited the evening of the concert with mounting excitement. Alas for such high hopes! The dreaded Man in a Dinner Jacket came on stage. Mr Schipa was suffering from a heavy cold but rather than disappoint us he would try to sing. He did try but it was no good. He had a microphone brought on but that was no good either. I could have killed some wag behind me who asked 'Why doesn't he try a loud-schipa?' – and then, almost in tears, my hero left the stage. Such is the enthusiasm of youth that I immediately sent him a letter begging him to come again. I remember writing that my generation had never had a chance

to hear him sing and surely he would not deprive us of it now?
I received a charming reply and an autographed photograph, and
I will not pretend that it was any of my doing, but some time
later he *did* come again, and what an evening it was! Whatever
the truth about his birthdate he was well into his sixties. One
or two of the more taxing arias (MARTHA, I remember, and
WERTHER) were sung in lower keys than of yore, but the voice
was the voice I knew from *DA 1133*, and he could still mesmerize
us with his artistry. It was not the end of the road for him either.
As late as 1957 he undertook, incredibly, his first tour of Russia,
and it was not until 3 October 1962, when he was seventy-three
(or seventy-four?) that he finally said good-bye to his public in
the States.

Schipa's honeymoon with the American concert public had
begun back in 1917, with a recital in New York's Town Hall. (It
was attended by Caruso, who had heard glowing reports of the
new tenor but who quietly slipped out after the first few songs.
When asked if he had not enjoyed them he replied 'Oh yes, he
sings beautifully, but I have nothing to worry about.') There
was a nasty hiccup in 1941 when Schipa suddenly announced
from South America, where he enjoyed enormous popularity,
that he was cancelling all of his obligations in the United States
to return, at the urgent request of Mussolini's son-in-law and
Foreign Secretary Count Ciano, to his native Italy. When the
war was over and he reappeared at Carnegie Hall it was to the
unfamiliar spectacle of a half empty house, but by the time he
took his final bow, back in the Town Hall, all had been forgotten
and forgiven. As if by some pre-arrangement, as the short and by
now stocky figure appeared on stage, the whole public rose to
greet him. But what, after fifty-two years of professional singing,
did he still have to offer? According to Harold C. Schonberg of
the *New York Times* 'Nothing – and everything. His production
is unsteady, his pitch often uncertain, his breath control nil. But,
and this is a big but, his singing still has style . . . he managed
inimitably to put across song and aria, and to convince his audi-

ence that a great man was before it.' At one point, during 'Una furtiva lagrima', a sudden cry of 'Bravo' rang through the hall like a pistol shot. With commendable dignity Schipa raised an admonishing hand and continued singing. As one of the other critics put it 'Tito Schipa in Town Hall last night was like a king who had come out of retirement to find himself still monarch of all he surveyed.'

LUISA TETRAZZINI

ITALIAN SOPRANO

b. Florence, 29 June 1871, d. Milan, 28 April 1940

COPYRIGHT 1911- I
KIRKLAND
DENVER

All of us who make a living in opera are aware that our world teeters permanently on the edge of the absurd; how else could there be such a thriving industry in operatic disaster stories? Buxom Toscas bouncing happily back into view after the death-fall from the battlements of the Castel Sant'Angelo; magic swans gliding gracefully from the stage before Lohengrin has had a chance to climb aboard; cast-iron anvils falling apart one bar before Siegfried strikes them – the list is endless. I believe, though, that for many of those people who are disposed to scoff at opera rather than fall under its spell the ultimate emblem of absurdity is the four-square coloratura soprano, who portrays the moribund heroine, her lungs wasted with consumption, by firing cascades of dauntingly healthy high notes like bursts of shrapnel into the furthest corners of the auditorium; and in this category of singer one name stands unchallenged at the top of the twentieth century's role of honour – Luisa Tetrazzini.

Tetrazzini must surely have been the most naturally gifted vocalist of any Italian soprano in the gramophone era. She was born in Florence on 29 June 1871. Her father was a prosperous military tailor, and the family was able to afford such luxuries as regular visits to their local opera house, the Teatro Pagliano. Her sister Eva, nine years older than herself, was a professional soprano – a good enough one, indeed, to create the role of Desdemona in the United States – and she gave Tetrazzini her first voice lessons. For a short time – reports vary between three months and one year – Tetrazzini also studied under Eva's teacher, Maestro Ceccherini, at the Istituto Musicale in Florence; but whichever version is correct, that was the sum total of her formal training, and for a singer in the most technically demanding of all vocal categories it amounts to a singularly sketchy one. And yet in 1890, at the age of only nineteen and in the most bizarre of circumstances, Tetrazzini succeeded in launching herself on a career which was, from A to Z, unlike that of any other soprano before or since. It happened like this. Just as a performance of Meyerbeer's L'AFRICAINE was due to begin in the Teatro Pagliano the distraught conductor came before the curtain and announced that it would have to be cancelled, as the soprano who was cast in the role of Inez had succumbed to a sudden but violent indisposition. Without a moment's hesitation Tetrazzini leapt up on her seat and called out that there was no need to cancel – she knew the role by heart. After a lively discussion, in which numerous members of the audience took part, it was decided that she should be given two days to rehearse and to prove her capability. This she did. Two days later the performance duly took place, and such was the success of the unreluctant debutante that she was promptly invited to repeat her Inez later in the same season in the Teatro Argentina in Rome. Here word of her precocious talent reached the ears of Queen Margherita, who summoned her to sing in the royal palace. The Queen requested music from her own favourite opera, and although that happened to be as far from the Italian coloratura repertoire as anything one could possibly imagine – it was Wagner's TRISTAN UND ISOLDE – Tetrazzini was happy to oblige.

This spontaneity of Tetrazzini's, this determination to have a go and devil take the consequences, was to characterize everything she did in her life and it was backed up by an unassailable sense of humour, almost of self-mockery. The public, while of course principally bowled over by her vocal acrobatics, sensed behind them a special kind of recklessness, and they adored her for it. Within two years of erupting so spectacularly into the operatic arena, years spent building a repertoire on the Italian provincial circuit, she set sail for South America with her own company, organized by the first of her three husbands. This was in 1892, when she was still only twenty-one, but for several years she enjoyed an unprecedented popularity all over the South American continent, and most especially in Argentina with its vast population of immigrant Italians. For an account of those early years – an account, be it said, that must be taken not with a pinch of salt but with about a ton of it – Tetrazzini's memoirs make hilarious reading. Inevitably she became involved in a revolution, as well as in frequent brushes with brigands, blackmailers and other assorted undesirables, but as she herself expressed it 'It is too much to expect to go through life on the top of any profession without having to fight against malicious onslaughts. Even the great and good General Gordon, even Abraham Lincoln and Garibaldi did not entirely escape.' Later famous for her *embonpoint*, in those days, as photographs testify, she was by no means unattractive – on the plump side, certainly, but no more so than many of the young ladies who brought gleams to the eyes of the Edwardian 'Stagedoor Johnnies' – and one of her most ardent admirers was the President of the Argentine. On the occasion of her fiftieth triumphant Lucia di Lammermoor in Buenos Aires he decreed that a lavish gala should be given in her honour, and her personal influence with him was considerable. When she was approached by the relatives of a young naval officer, who had been languishing in jail for nine years after a trial of dubious validity, she had no hesitation in taking up his cause, and his family could not have found a more effective advocate. 'I have ordered a new trial,' the President assured Tetrazzini, 'and I can tell you before it takes place what the result will be. He will be found innocent and immediately released.' Typical of the adventures in which Tetrazzini found herself involved was an episode which occurred while she was staying with friends on their huge estate somewhere in the Argentinian hinterland. One day she was suddenly confronted by her host's wild-eyed son of twenty, brandishing a silver-handled dagger. 'Signorina Tetrazzini,' he cried, 'I love you and if you do not kiss me I shall kill myself.' The diva decided to play for time. 'We Italians,' she answered, 'never kiss anyone unless we know them very well. Now suppose you give me that lovely dagger of yours, then I will go out on the lawn and tell you presently if I like you well enough to kiss you.' To cut a long story short, Tetrazzini survived the episode unkissed *and* retained the silver-handled dagger. 'For fifteen years,' she observes with some satisfaction, 'in all parts of the world, I used this same dagger when singing Lucia.'

During her South American period Tetrazzini earned staggering sums of money, quite apart from the jewellery heaped upon her by many an impetuous admirer. She tore herself away, though, for occasional trips to Europe, appearing in Lisbon, Madrid, Naples and St Petersburg. She sang Musetta in Russia's first LA BOHEME to the Rodolfo of Enrico Caruso, another sunny soul, with whom she predictably struck up a warm and lasting friendship. In 1903 she toured Mexico and conquered it as she had the Argentine. Again she led her own troupe, again run by her husband – a different troupe this time and a different husband – and in the same year, for an Italian company called Zonofono, she made her first recordings.

These are now great rarities but, as one would expect from the products of a small company as far back as 1903, they are technically primitive and musically crude, with the accompaniments provided by a distinctly honky-tonk piano. The heyday of Tetrazzini's recording career really lay between 1907 and 1914 when she was one of the best-sellers for the London Gramophone Company and for the Victor Talking Machine Company of New York. An excellent selection of nineteen titles from this period is available on Nimbus's Prima Voce *NI 7808*, all with the voice well forward, and all evidently taken from remarkably well pre-served 78s. You only have to listen to a couple of these tracks to hear immediately what the fuss was about – the coloratura singing is dazzlingly spectacular. Under the umbrella of that word colo-ratura, of course, lurks many another technical subdivision, and the expert who wishes to befuddle the ordinary listener can lay about him with *fioriture*, *gruppetti*, *appoggiature*, *acciaccature*, *mordenti* and a great deal else besides. Suffice it to say that for Tetrazzini vocal ornamentation of almost every variety appeared to be second nature. In several familiar warhorses of the operatic repertoire – 'Una voce poco fa' from BARBIERE, the second half of the Mad Scene from LUCIA (did she take the silver-handled dagger into the studio with her, I wonder?), the Bell Song from LAKME, 'Merce dilette amiche' from I VESPRI SICILIANI, the Polonaise from MIGNON, and so on – she launches herself with joyous abandon into an unquenchable riot of runs, trills and other vocal fireworks. During 'Saper vorreste', the cheeky little number from BALLO in which the pageboy Oscar refuses to reveal to the murderous Renato what costume his would-be victim is wearing to the masked ball, she releases into the stratosphere an astonishing row of staccato high Ds, every one a beefy little note in its own right. Indeed, one of Tetrazzini's most amazing attributes is the ability, after an exhausting display of whizzing up and down and all around, to cap an aria with a high note, be it a B, a C or even something higher, which is taken with the full meat of the voice and which she is apparently able to sustain for as long as she feels inclined. In the various non-operatic numbers, whose sole raison d'être is to show off the performer's agility and flexibility, and which featured prominently in Tetrazzini's concert repertoire – the Nimbus CD offers us Proch's Air and Variations, Venzano's Grande Valse and Eckert's 'L'Eco' – she flits about with almost insolent ease and, indeed, her ability to perform these feats was something which she did take very much for granted. The interviewer's inevitable question 'How on earth do you do it?' would be regularly brushed aside with the dictum 'Either you are born with a flexible voice or you are not'; and on one occasion, when asked about the high E flat which she used to interpolate as Lucia, swelling and diminishing it to the ecstasy of all, she replied 'Oh, as to that, no soprano ever sings that scene exactly as it is written. She adds what she can do, and as much as she can, and I do the same' – a true enough comment in its way, though it did rather gloss over the difference between what lay in her powers and in those of ordinary mortals.

At this stage I should perhaps confess that when the heroine of a nineteenth century opera brings the action to a full stop in order to stand by the prompt box and indulge in a coloratura tightrope act, usually pursued by at least one desperate flute, my attention tends to wander. With Tetrazzini, though, it is different. For one thing, the voice itself does not have the somewhat pallid, squeaky quality which often characterizes the coloratura soprano. It is one of great warmth and femininity, and her recordings reveal no trace of the 'infantile' tone in the middle and lower registers, for which she was brusquely hauled over the coals by one or two of the critics when she first appeared in New York. The manner in which she tackles these bravura scenes, too, is so much more than mere display. In Lucia's 'Regnava nel silenzio' for instance, the narration about the ghost which emerges from the fountain in the still small hours of night, the legato is firm and flowing, the voice is capable of many different shadings, and when the vocal elaborations begin they are grafted onto the melodic line with such ease and spontaneity that, far from interrupting it, they simply seem to extend its natural flow. In the TROVATORE aria 'Tacea la notte' it is interesting to note how many breaths Tetrazzini needs in the middle register of the voice compared with the apparent inexhaustibility of her lungs when she soars above the stave, but her general handling of the piece makes it credible that her stage repertoire should have stretched to roles as heavy as Aida and Leonora in LA FORZA DEL DESTINO (both of which are represented in the more extensive sets discussed below). The same steadiness of *cantilena* makes her 'Ah, non credea mirarti' from LA SONNAMBULA one of the most impressive of all her recordings. This is the mournful aria which the heroine sings while she is actually somnambulating, and while her subconscious is giving her much to grieve over; but when the clouds have passed and she signals the arrival of the happy ending with her second set piece, 'Ah! non giunge', Tetrazzini is enough of a vocal actress to cavort through her expressions of bliss with a totally different sheen on the voice.

Another of her most regular stage triumphs, Gilda in RIGO-
LETTO, is also represented by two tracks on the Nimbus disc.
The first is a miraculously poised 'Caro nome', and the second
is the great Quartet, in which she sails effortlessly along the top
line, capping the proceedings with a vintage high D flat, while
the lower levels are entrusted to the mezzo Josephine Jacoby,
the baritone Pasquale Amato and the king of Dukes, Enrico
Caruso. This was recorded in 1912, and later in that same year
Tetrazzini and Caruso were billed together for a RIGOLETTO
performance at the Metropolitan Opera, which was, surprisingly,
their only joint appearance on the operatic stage after their early
days in Russia. Whether it was felt that as either of them singly
could sell out any house it was therefore superfluous to pay two
astronomical fees in one evening, I do not know. In any case, the
effect of the announcement that they were to appear together was
unparalleled in the entire history of the Met. Although every
reservable seat had been sold days ahead, some five thousand
people surrounded the building in the hope of securing one of
the 450 so-called admission tickets which were to be issued on
the evening of the performance. In the words of one New York
newspaper:

> Not until mounted policemen had charged the crowd was
> Broadway open for traffic, and not until other policemen on
> the beat had used their nightsticks was there anything resembling
> peace and order in the lobby of the opera house. The treasurer,
> Mr Earl R. Lewis, opened his box-office window at half-past
> seven and sold the first admission. In about a minute the line
> of buyers broke and there was pandemonium. The window was
> slammed down, the policemen leaped into the fray and tried to
> coax order into the musical mob. Not until the nightsticks were
> drawn did the line form again.

(The same paper goes on rather delightfully to report the distinguished quality, not of the performance, but of the audience.
'In Colonel John Jacob Astor's box, No. 7, were Mrs William

H. Force and her daughter, Miss Katherine Force, and a party of young men. Mrs Force was in white satin veiled with black tulle. Miss Force wore white brocade' – and so on round the Diamond Horseshoe.)

Lest it should be supposed that Tetrazzini was only capable of the showiest effects the Nimbus CD also includes two examples of her in a mood of remarkable vocal restraint. One is Brahms's 'Vergebliches Ständchen', or rather 'Serenata inutile', in a garishly non-Teutonic orchestral arrangement, but both sung and characterized with great charm. The other is a rather touching song called 'Tre giorni son che Nina', attributed to the eighteenth century composer Ciampi, in which she displays a positively classical refinement of style and abjures all temptation to fling in any woodnotes wild.

Of course all of Tetrazzini's showpiece roles did also contain passages in which it was the solid virtues of legato singing which were required rather than vocal acrobatics, and none more so than Violetta in Verdi's LA TRAVIATA, which proved to be a milestone in her career, and which is represented on the Nimbus disc by her dying lament for the happiness of days gone by, 'Addio del passato'. To turn the clock back for a moment to Tetrazzini's early triumphs in South and Central America, though they brought her local fame and financial fortune, it was noticeable that they did not prove to be a passport to the really prestigious European houses such as La Scala and Covent Garden. Toscanini, who had conducted her in Russia, was known to dislike her – 'Soprano pirotecnico', he snarled, as he waited for her to complete one of her more extended embellishments. That was probably enough to close the doors of La Scala, and Covent Garden in the heyday of Nellie Melba was a hard nut for any other soprano to crack. Tetrazzini did manage to get a toehold in the United States in 1904 when she went to the Tivoli Opera House, San Francisco, whose Director, William H. Leahy, had heard her singing in Mexico. (The Director of the Metropolitan Opera, Heinrich Conried, tried to impose an injunction against her San Francisco appearances on the grounds that he had been negotiating with her for a United States debut under his aegis the following year. As no contract had been signed, he failed in his attempt.)

Though Tetrazzini was taken as warmly and as instantly to the hearts of the San Franciscans as she had been to those of her audiences south of the border there was still no sign of a European thaw until, in 1907, she received an invitation from Covent Garden to come and sing Violetta. It was a grudging invitation. Her brother-in-law, Cleofonte Campanini, who was chief conductor of the Italian repertoire at Covent Garden, had repeatedly recommended her to Percy Pitt, the Musical Director there, and to Harry Higgins, the General Manager. They were trying to put together an experimental autumn season of Italian opera to follow the Grand Season in the summer, and to quote Pitt's memoirs, 'as it was impossible to secure the services of any well-known artist for the latter half of the season, and as Tetrazzini happened to be available, it was decided to approach her.' The first half of the season, however, was a box-office flop – for London society opera in the autumn was not the done thing – and Higgins cabled to Tetrazzini, trying to cancel the contract. She ignored his first cable, and to his second she replied that she insisted on her rights. In Pitt's words once again 'She arrived for four days of rehearsals with a certain air of deliberation which was very distressing for us all', then on Saturday 2 November, a chilly and cheerless evening, when the fog for which London was in those days justly famous not only descended onto the streets but actually found its way into the auditorium, Tetrazzini made her Covent Garden debut. Despite the fact that hundreds of complimentary tickets had been handed out the place was still half empty, and when the curtain rose to reveal the dumpy figure of the heroine there was nothing in the sight to relieve the general air of gloom. As Violetta is a role which starts with snatches of disjointed conversation it is not one with which an instant impact can be achieved. Early in Act I, though, comes the Brindisi, and that made the more discriminating members of the audience sit up and listen. The duet with Alfredo, 'Un dì felice', confirmed the impression that this was not just any provincial soprano. When Tetrazzini was left alone on stage to close Act I with Violetta's great solo scene, excitement was running high. By the end of the aria 'Ah fors' è lui' she had her listeners on the edge of their seats, and when she crowned a brilliantly and recklessly executed 'Sempre libera' with a high E flat which was not only dead in tune and as solid as a rock but opulent and gorgeous too, they were on their feet, shouting and yelling and waving their programmes in the air. Tetrazzini was a lady with a point to make, and she had made it.

After that one evening her status as an artist of world class was assured. Unknown to her, the moment Harry Higgins heard the first cadenza of her final scene of Act I and realized that he had on his hands, as he put it, 'a real "leggiero-spinto" with breadth and purity of tone such as I had dreamed of all my life', he rushed to the telephone and rang every influential newspaper in Fleet Street. By the time Act II began numerous reporters had tumbled out of their cabs and into the auditorium, and the next day the phenomenal new star was on every front page. On the Monday morning the manager of the Gramophone Company was on her doorstep. (She kept him waiting because she had been nettled by a previous incident in New York, and as that great pioneer of the record industry, Fred Gaisberg, once wrote, 'This trait of never forgetting or forgiving was most pronounced in the lady.') Covent Garden made amends for its lack of courtesy by mounting a special series of Sunday concerts – it was the only way to satisfy the public's clamorous desire to hear her – and plans for the Grand Season the following summer were changed so that she could open it with her Violetta. She returned for the next five summer seasons, and in 1911 she was accorded the ultimate honour of selection for the Coronation Gala. The operatic portion of the programme consisted of Emmy Destinn in the Triumph Scene from AIDA, Nellie Melba in Act II of ROMEO ET JULIETTE and Tetrazzini in the final scene of BARBIERE. The auditorium was decorated with 100,000 rose blooms, and during the course of the evening the strength of their scent caused many tightly corseted ladies to swoon elegantly away.

Another immediate result of Tetrazzini's belated leap into the top flight of international prime donne – she was, after all, thirty-six in 1907, and had been singing for seventeen years – was an invitation from Oscar Hammerstein to join his Manhattan Opera Company in New York. He was losing money heavily and was badly in need of a singer who could create a real sensation. Tetrazzini demanded a fee of $2500 a performance (equivalent to about $100,000 today, and around five times as much as she had been paid at Covent Garden), but it was the best investment Hammerstein ever made. Thanks almost entirely to the popularity of his new star he showed a large profit at the end of the season and succeeded in establishing his company as serious competition for the Metropolitan Opera.

Once again it was as Violetta that Tetrazzini came, was heard, and conquered. She bowled the New Yorkers over as deftly as she had the Londoners, despite the crop of carping reviews to which I have already referred. While acknowledging her extraordinary dexterity in the upper regions, one or two of the more exacting critics complained that the different registers of the voice were not properly fused together and that the tone quality lower down was simply not up to scratch. When one listens to her records this is difficult to understand, but it is perfectly possible that when she first made the breakthrough into houses which were used to the degree of perfection represented by singers like Melba and Sembrich, not to mention the legendary Adelina Patti, there were gaps in Tetrazzini's technical and stylistic armour, and that they were gaps which she had no difficulty in filling when she realized the need to do so. It was certainly one of the most gratifying moments of her life when Patti came to her dressing room after a Covent Garden Violetta and congratulated her on the extent of her success. By now there are not many people left who heard

Tetrazzini before the First World War, but one who did, and who is blessed with total recall of everything he heard during his early years, is the British singing teacher Rupert Bruce-Lockhart. He has told me that Tetrazzini was as moving in the Act II duet with Germont as she was electrifying in the final scene of Act I, and that is something which can only be achieved by perfect control in the middle of the voice.

My one disappointment with the excellent Nimbus disc is that that Act I final scene is not included, but it appears in two different versions in EMI's outstanding three disc set of the complete London recordings (*CHS 7 63802 2*), to which a third version is added in a five disc set entitled 'Luisa Tetrazzini, the Complete Known Recordings', which the Pearl Company has issued under the number GEMM *CDS 9220*. It is obvious that any complete collection is principally aimed at the specialist listener. Out of sixty-five titles on EMI and ninety-six on Pearl some are inevitably of lesser interest, and several of the Pearl tracks are taken from less than perfect originals. Pearl also believes in a 'warts and all' approach to re-recording, and listeners who are unaccustomed to the full 'fried egg' surface hiss and crackle of the earliest 78s may occasionally wonder, as in the case of the Zonofono titles, what was going on in the studio while the fat lady sang. There are, however, many rarities here which will be of great interest to the serious collector, and the full gamut of Tetrazzini's recordings clearly demonstrates the versatility of her voice. She once told one of her successors at the Met, the German-born soprano Frieda Hempel, who enjoyed a most jocular friendship with her, that her voice had originally been a contralto. When Hempel was sceptical about this, Tetrazzini gave a brief but convincing demonstration. 'Ah, Luisa,' said Hempel, 'what a voice! Is there anything you cannot do?' Tetrazzini laughed, and looking down at herself (she was by then *extremely* stout) she answered 'Well, Friedelina, some singers hava da figure – but Tetrazzini gotta da voice!' Most people, I think, who are only familiar with the coloratura recordings would be likely to share Hempel's incredulity, but when one hears

a number such as 'Carceleras', by that prolific 'zarzuela' composer
Ruperto Chapí, in which the fullness and flexibility of Tetrazzini's
lower register really come into their own, one has little alternative
but to agree – she did indeed getta da voice.

These two sets, including as they do practically every familiar
aria in the nineteenth century Italian coloratura repertoire, several
of them recorded more than once, also emphasize what a streak of
musical inventiveness Tetrazzini possessed. She was well known
for seldom singing a cadenza quite the same way twice running,
and when juggling with embellishments as complex as those which
Tetrazzini revelled in, a soprano needs to keep her wits about her.
She needs an exceptional sense of rhythm too, or things can come
badly unstuck, and again and again, as in the MIGNON Polonaise or in Benedict's 'Carnevale di Venezia', the rhythmic drive
of Tetrazzini's performance adds almost as much to its impact as
do the acrobatics.

Doubtless out of these many tracks everyone will have his
or her personal favourites. Two of mine are the Tosti songs
'Aprile' and 'Serenata' with Percy Pitt at the piano, (on EMI and
Pearl, but with the latter *chez* Pearl taken from a rather clicky
original), and another is her stupendously sustained rendering of
'The Last Rose of Summer' (Pearl only), sung, as one occasionally
becomes aware, in English. This was the item with which she
opened her programme on one of the most remarkable occasions
even of her remarkable career. It was an open-air concert which
she gave on Christmas Eve 1911, free of charge, to the populace
of San Francisco, a city which occupied a special place in her
affections, having given her her first opportunity to sing in the
United States. It was said that Oscar Hammerstein, wanting her
to appear exclusively for his company in New York, had forbidden
her to give guest performances in the San Francisco Opera House,
whereupon with typical vim she had replied 'When I wish to sing
to my beloved San Franciscans I shall do so, even if it means singing in the street' – and this remark reputedly reached the ears of an
influential San Franciscan, who thought it a great idea. Whether

that is fact or fiction the concert most assuredly took place, and a crowd thought to number some 250,000 people (to judge from photographs that was probably no exaggeration) turned out to hear her. The chosen spot was in front of the Chronicle Building and Lotta's Fountain. The Municipal Board of Works had erected a stage strong enough to sustain an orchestra, a choir and Madame Tetrazzini, and when she made her entrance, stepping forward into the full glare of a spotlight wearing a white dress and a white cartwheel hat, there was a momentary breathless silence followed by a thunderous roar. She raised her hand for silence, and then sailed into 'The Last Rose of Summer', followed by the waltz song from ROMEO ET JULIETTE. Her voice was not amplified in any way, but even those who were too far away to be able to see her were said to have heard every note.

During the seasons of 1913 and 1914 Tetrazzini sang with the Chicago Opera Association, but when war broke out she went back to Italy where she applied herself to various charitable causes and sang in concerts for the troops. She never went back to the operatic stage, partly because she could earn more money for less effort on the concert platform, and partly because it would have been asking a great deal of the operatic public to go on accepting her as the winsome maiden which so many of her roles portrayed. If the passage of time had not reduced her physical proportions, though, neither had it laid any withering hand on the pristine freshness of her famous voice. In 1919, when she returned for the first time to the States and opened her tour with a concert in New York, it was the old triumphant story all over again. To quote the *New York Herald*: 'The ovation which Mme Tetrazzini received was breath-taking. Mr Caruso led the cheering from his box. It is marvellous how beautiful her voice still is. In the vicinity of high C her tones are thrillingly large and lovely. In the middle register there was more fullness and color than in earlier years.' This assertion that the voice, far from deteriorating, had actually gained in quality, was repeated by critics right across the States – wherever she appeared the plaudits were unanimous and unstinting.

Another area of Tetrazzini's art which had in no way abated was her skilful handling of publicity. As she expressed it in her memoirs, 'I soon realized how great a power is the Press in making more remunerative the business side of a Prima Donna's work', and one of her most effective headline-grabbing antics during her 1919 tour was to take to the air for the first and last time in her life. The occasion was an exhibition of stunt flying at the Tanforan Race Track, sponsored by the *San Francisco Examiner*. The big attraction was a barnstorming young aviator named Ormer Locklear, who had gained a daredevil reputation by being the first man to change planes in mid-air and by walking on the wings of planes in flight, and it had been announced that anyone who contributed fifty dollars to the *Examiner*'s Christmas Fund would receive one complimentary ticket for a ride as his passenger. Thousands of people packed the grandstands, and thousands more were scattered around the surrounding hillsides. To quote one journalist's report: 'Waving fifty dollars in bills the ample queen of song wended her way through the throngs to center field' where she was assisted into a warm coat, a flying helmet and a pair of goggles – and eventually, with slightly more difficulty, into the passenger seat of the plane. She did not stay up for long because of the potentially dangerous effect of the chilly slipstream on her valuable throat but long enough to hold a press conference about it later that afternoon in which she indulged in such gems as 'I wondered as we skimmed out over the grass if it indeed would be goodbye.'

On a later visit to the States another publication sought her views on prohibition. They were straightforward. LUISA TETRAZZINI CALLS PROHIBITION RIDICULOUS announced the banner headline, and her recipe for restraining excessive drinking was straightforward too. 'You know, if American men did not have that genial habit of – what you call it? – buying a drink for Tom, Dick and Harry, prohibition wouldn't have come. In Europe there is not so much treating, and because each one pays for his own drink there is not so much consumed.' Simple, really.

In Britain Tetrazzini's popularity as a concert artist ran every bit as high as in the States. Her regular accompanist on her British tours was Ivor Newton, whom I have already quoted in my chapter on Jussi Björling, and once again his memoirs provide vivid glimpses of the star in action.

> She would cross herself before making her entrance, and then set off for the stage at a brisk run, arriving before the audience breathless and panting. Invariably the audience had overflowed onto the platform, and Tetrazzini, struggling to regain her breath, would walk round the semi-circle they made and greet them warmly, shaking hands with some of them and kissing any very young child who might be there. Her friendliness and warmth would bring the entire hall to a state of excitement before she had sung a note. There was never any sense of insincerity about these effusive ceremonies; she was behaving with complete naturalness. A long rope of pearls always hung round her neck; when at last the social preliminaries were over she would take the end of the rope and throw it over her shoulder. That was my signal to begin.

Tetrazzini did not believe in long concerts. 'Always leave them wanting more' was her motto, and although she was of course the chief attraction she habitually had supporting artists to fill up the evening. This way she continued for several years to earn enormous sums of money without unduly taxing her vocal resources, and it would be nice to be able to report that in due course she settled down to the leisurely enjoyment of her staggering wealth. In reality, though, the final chapter of the Tetrazzini story is no traditional happy ending. She had always been thoughtlessly extravagant, never bothering to see whether the tip she handed the doorman was a pound note or a fiver. Her secretary, a fine figure of a man – thought not, as far as anyone knew, actually able to write a letter – wore a platinum watch with a pearl-encrusted chain. Her house in Rome was decorated and furnished in a challengingly lavish style – the less decorative items of plumbing were cunningly concealed behind a covering of the rich Spanish shawls which she had worn as Rosina in IL BARBIERE – and lace curtains embroidered with her portrait draped the windows of her limousine. This penchant for the flamboyant would not in itself have been enough to run through the million pounds which she was reckoned to have earned in her career, but her disastrous choice of financial advisers and her flirtations with spiritualism did nothing to help. At the age of fifty-two, moreover, she took a third husband, twenty years younger than herself, and film clips of the ceremony make melancholy viewing. One would have to be deeply charitable to believe that the slick young bridegroom had formed a genuine passion for the formidable figure at his side, and within a short time the union came acrimoniously adrift. Lawsuits were filed by each against the other, and on and on they dragged year after year, he trying to wrest from her the control of her financial affairs, and she counter-suing him for extortion. In 1932 she tried to make good some of her losses with a final trip to the United States, appearing neither on the operatic stage nor on the concert platform, but in Variety at the Paramount Theatre, New York – 'At 4.30, 6.30 and 8.30 Tetrazzini Sings!' Though she still had a surprising amount to offer, both in voice and in bravado, the venture was not a success. 'She was a ponderous woman,' one of the newspapers wrote, 'a caricature of a diva, and she festooned herself with ostrich plumes.' Her farewell to London, with an Albert Hall concert in 1934, was a worthier affair, and when she launched into one of her most celebrated tours de force, the Mad Scene from HAMLET, many happy memories were aroused. She retired to Milan where she lived in humble circumstances, taking both pupils and lodgers, and she died there on 28 April 1940, aged 68. All the money was gone, and all the jewels, and she was buried at the state's expense.

In the circumstances it would be natural to assume that after the glories of the past Tetrazzini must have died a sad and embittered old woman. That, however, was not the sort of person she was. By all accounts her indomitable sense of humour held up to the end, and she was never short of friends who would drop in and enjoy a good chat. Inevitably she would be asked what sort of state her voice was in, and her response would be to waddle to the piano, strike a chord, and let fly with a rocketing arpeggio, capped by a high C of triumphant quality. 'Ah!' she would chuckle when she saw the look of astonishment on everyone's faces, 'sono vecchia, sono grassa, sono brutta'; and then, with all the old *grandezza*, 'ma sono sempre la Tetrazzini!' – 'I am old, I am fat, I am ugly – but I am still Tetrazzini!'

EVA TURNER

BRITISH SOPRANO

b. Oldham, 10 March 1892, d. London, 16 June 1990

Nowadays British opera singers appear with gratifying frequency in leading houses all over the world. Between the two world wars there was only one of whom that could be said – Eva Turner. She was born in 1892 in the Lancashire town of Oldham, but when she was ten her father, the chief engineer in a cotton works, changed jobs and the family moved to Bristol. It was there that she heard the Carl Rosa Company perform IL TROVATORE, and decided that opera would be the life for her. She received the unfailing support of her parents, and they paid for her to take lessons with Daniel Rootham, who had been teacher to Dame Clara Butt. At the age of nineteen she started a four year course at the Royal Academy of Music, and towards the end of her time there she auditioned for Walter van Noorden, General Manager of the very company which had so fired her imagination. As she recalled many years later, his verdict was 'I cannot give you a principal's contract, because you have not walked the stage' (she used to be full of these charming old-world expressions), but he did accept her for the chorus with a strong hint that solo roles might follow. She was assigned a place at the back and made a firm resolve to work her way to the front. With typical determination (she remained very proud of being what she called 'a down to earth Lancastrian') she told her parents that they could discontinue her allowance – with a salary of thirty-five shillings a week she could now stand on her own two feet. This was raised by a further five shillings when she was promoted to being a Page in TANNHÄUSER, a task which was evidently mastered to Mr van Noorden's satisfaction (and to that of the very strict Musical Director, Eugène Goossens) because soon such heavy responsibilities as First Lady in THE MAGIC FLUTE began to come her way.

Perhaps it will give some idea of the progress which Eva Turner made once she had started 'walking the stage' to say that in 1920, her fifth year with the Carl Rosa Company, during a three week season at Covent Garden she gave nine performances in six different leading roles: Santuzza in CAVALLERIA RUSTICANA, Musetta in LA BOHEME, Elisabeth in TANNHÄUSER, Leonora in IL TROVATORE, Giulietta in THE TALES OF HOFFMANN and the title-role in MADAM BUTTERFLY. The following year she capped this with nineteen performances in twelve different roles, adding to the previous list the WALKÜRE and SIEGFRIED Brünnhildes, Fricka in DAS RHEINGOLD, Elsa in LOHENGRIN, Jeanette in a short-lived piece called LE CHANT FATALE, and the title-role in AIDA. Admittedly the 1921 season ran for seven weeks, but twelve huge roles in under two months is not a workload which many sopranos would be willing or able to undertake. I should also emphasize that this is only a list of the roles which Eva Turner happened to sing during the company's stint at Covent Garden. There were plenty of others too, such as Donna Anna, Tosca, Nedda, Fidelio, Marguerite in FAUST, to name but a few – and who on earth nowadays would reckon to sing Marguerite *and* Brünnhilde?

In 1924 Eva Turner was suddenly transported from the somewhat rough-and-tumble life of a British touring company to a very much headier existence. The Italian conductor Ettore Panizza was in London to conduct at Covent Garden, and he heard Miss Turner sing Butterfly in the Scala Theatre, Charlotte Street. He felt that she would be better suited to the rather more elevated Scala in which he held a position as assistant to Toscanini, so off went our stalwart Lancastrian to audition for the great man in Milan. 'Bella voce, bella pronuncia, bella figura', he declared, and promptly offered her Freia in DAS RHEINGOLD and Sieglinde in DIE WALKÜRE. From then on her international stature was assured. She found her presence requested not only by most of the other leading houses in Italy but by Vienna, Munich, Lisbon (where she sang Minnie in LA FANCIULLA DEL WEST, which must have been very much up her street), Rio de Janeiro, Buenos Aires, and Chicago.

Within eighteen months of her debut at La Scala Eva Turner was accorded the considerable honour of being chosen to lead the massed forces of the company in two recordings which now re-emerge as the earliest tracks on EMI's CD 'Dame Eva Turner – Opera Arias and Songs' (*CDH 7 69791 2*). These are the great ensemble 'Gloria all'Egitto' from the AIDA Triumph Scene, and the less familiar but equally massive 'Già ti veggo' from Act III of LA GIOCONDA. In fact, when I say that she led the forces, I should add that she did so in the best traditions of the Duke of Plaza-Toro, from behind. The engineers had such difficulty in matching her voice with those of her colleagues that she was temporarily relegated to her old position in the back row; but as she herself says in a delightful spoken introduction to this disc, 'I don't think you will have any difficulty in hearing me.' Perhaps it awakens some dormant spirit of John Bull within me, but I love this idea of Miss Turner from Oldham so easily overtopping the entire company of the crème de la crème of Italian opera houses. Indeed, the first thing that is bound to strike any listener is that her voice was one of phenomenal power. On the recordings it emerges as a wonderfully sturdy instrument, but characterized at the same time by a vibrant brilliance of timbre. Lord Harewood describes it very aptly in his memoirs when he says that he can think of no other soprano 'with that blend of opulence and blade', and though in the theatre she was occasionally criticized for insufficient variety of tone colour (certain disrespectful members of the Covent Garden chorus used to call her 'the steam whistle'!), there is always a deep commitment to the mood of the music. It may be expressed on a statuesque scale, but her singing is by no means simply fortissimo all the way. The grand sweep of her phrasing in 'D'amor sull'ali rosee' from IL TROVATORE is matched by a touching tenderness; the high notes are taken with enviable ease, in no way overblown, and there is plenty of flexibility in the cadenza.

This and her compelling account of Santuzza's anguished outburst from CAVALLERIA RUSTICANA, both dating from July 1928, were conducted by Sir Thomas Beecham, with whom she got along famously – 'We were both Lancastrians, you know, and had the same sense of humour'. Perhaps she does not quite respond with Sicilian warmth to the 'con grande passione' called for by Mascagni on Santuzza's first climactic phrase, but she certainly hits the final 'con disperazione' right in the middle of the target. In the TOSCA 'Vissi d'arte' she may not assay the pianissimo re-attack after the crowning high B flat, which can be such a million dollar moment with a singer like Renata Tebaldi, but the vocal quality is lustrous and appealing and Tosca's vulnerability is effectively expressed through the immaculate articulation of the text.

The TOSCA aria is sung in English, as are her hitherto unpublished versions of Elsa's Dream from LOHENGRIN and Elisabeth's Greeting from TANNHÄUSER, and though the translations may smell of mothballs they will give listeners who do not speak German or Italian a lively impression of Eva Turner's treatment of words in opera. The diction may sound old-fashioned, with its rolled final 'r's' and its lingering final 'l's'; indeed it is reminiscent of the way in which actors of the Donald Wolfit school used to articulate the lines of Shakespeare or Marlowe, and even back in the early 1950s some people derided that as dated. But – one *understood* it, and to listeners who feel that they prefer not to understand phrases such as 'I saw in splendour shining a knight of glorious mien', I can only say that long stretches of Wagner's original text are in no way preferable. Certainly Turner's exultation on Elsa's 'I give him all I am' and the élan with which she launches Elisabeth's 'All hail to thee' are the sort of thing guaranteed to make any audience sit up and take notice, and it is much to be regretted that these are the only recordings which she made from her wide Wagnerian repertoire. On the other hand we are much indebted to some extraordinary technical wizardry on the part of EMI that the TANNHÄUSER track exists at all, because Eva Turner herself possessed the only test pressing, and it was broken into three neat pieces. In its resurrected form it is still inevitably a bit crackly, but the treasury of Turner's recordings would be very much the poorer without it, and it seems remarkable that such a fine piece of singing should have mouldered for so long amongst the Columbia Company's unpublished items.

Another of the vocally most distinguished numbers on this disc is 'Suicidio' from LA GIOCONDA, but it is one of the 1926 Milan recordings in which Turner's exceptional vocal scope was not as well captured as it was by the engineers in London. In Aida's great solo from the Nile Scene, recorded in the Central Hall, Westminster in July 1928, the regal superiority of her singing comes across with stunning effect. This aria, with its long and mercilessly exposed climax, is a famous graveyard for sopranos whose technique is less than rock solid, or whose confidence can desert them under pressure. Turner's technique, though, *was* rock solid (she attributed much of the credit for this to daily lessons with an Australian singer named Richard Broad whom she first met when he was in an administrative position with the Carl Rosa Company and who became her manager and coach), and her voice possessed the very rare characteristic of appearing to grow both in size and in ease as it mounted the scale. Where some other sopranos can be heard to start doubting themselves as that Nile Scene high C looms nearer, Turner audibly revels in the prospect, and it is of course a wonderful feeling for the audience, too, never to have to worry for a singer. A couple of weeks before making this recording Turner had sung Aida for the first time at Covent Garden as a star of the Grand Opera Season, a big step up from singing it there seven years earlier in English as a contracted member of the Carl Rosa Company. The Covent Garden public was to hear her Aida another dozen times before the outbreak of war brought matters to a temporary halt, and the last of these occasions, on 8 June 1939, was one which she never forgot. Sir Thomas Beecham had to withdraw at the last moment, and the baton was handed to Wynn Reeves, the

Leader of the London Philharmonic Orchestra, who acquitted himself most nobly. As is often the case when some unusual circumstance puts the cast particularly on its mettle, everyone sang up a storm, and as the final curtain fell the Radamès, Beniamino Gigli, grabbed Eva Turner by the hands and swung her round and round in his excitement. Just a few years before her death I remember Dame Eva giving me another delightful little insight into that performance. 'Mr Gigli was always such a deeear,' she told me with her usual infectious enthusiasm. 'Do you know, when I came onto the stage for our final duet in the Tomb Scene he made a charming gesture to me to sit down on a stone bench before singing the "O terra addio", and he whispered in my ear "Prego, Signora, s'accomodi" ("Please, Madam, take a seat"). Always so *courteous*, Mr Gigli.'

Impressive as Eva Turner's Aida must have been, it is on the last of the roles represented on this disc that her fame principally rests. When Puccini's final opera, TURANDOT, was unveiled at La Scala in its unfinished form on 25 April 1926, the title-role was given to Rosa Raisa. Eva Turner was in the audience, and when she herself first undertook the part some months later in Brescia the composer Franco Alfano, who had been entrusted with the task of completing Puccini's score, told her that in his opinion hers was the ideal interpretation. This view was shared within a short time by audiences in many parts of the world, and though the Covent Garden Management took a while to accept that home-grown talent could possibly be the best in the business – they gave the first Covent Garden performances in 1927 to a soprano named Bianca Scacciati, and the show was duly stolen by Lotte Schöne's Liù – they did turn to Turner for the revival the following year, and soon discovered how wrong they had been. She astonished both press and public, and listening to her great scene 'In questa reggia', recorded shortly after the Covent Garden performances (and on the same day as the AIDA aria discussed above) it is not hard to see why. It had been widely felt that Puccini had gone too far this time, and that the role of Turandot was inhumane and unsingable, but here was Eva Turner, late of the Carl Rosa, actually making it sound easy! The riveting brilliance of tone on the words 'Quel grido e quella morte' as the vengeful princess describes the murder of her ancestress; the utter disregard for the superhuman demands of Puccini's vocal line as she hurls her defiance at her own would-be vanquisher 'Mai nessun m'avrà!' ('But no one will have *me*!'); the punishing phrase 'Gli enigmi sono tre, la morte una!' ('The riddles are three, death is one!'), which climbs up step by step to what is probably the most dreaded high C of all – there was not a soprano in the world at that time, and with the possible exception of Birgit Nilsson there has not been one since, who could rival Eva Turner's majestic dismissal of these fearsome hazards.

To judge from the very different repertoire which completes the EMI CD – six highly romantic songs – I would guess that the thawing of the Ice-girt Princess was also in safe hands with Eva Turner. Grieg's 'I love you', Tosti's 'Goodbye' and Ronald's 'O lovely night', though monumental in concept compared with the warblings to which they must have been subjected in ten thousand Edwardian drawing-rooms, are nevertheless permeated by a warm humanity. (Is it mere fancy, or might that old association with Clara Butt's teacher have coloured Eva Turner's delivery of ballads?) D'Hardelot's two classics, 'Because' and 'Sometimes in my dreams', are dealt with in the grand manner; and as for del Riego's 'Homing', when Eva Turner delivers the opening line 'All things come home at eventide' we have no alternative but to believe her. This is the voice of authority. I have already mentioned elsewhere in this book how I often feel that one comes closest to singers as people when they are singing some quite trifling piece in their own tongue, and in these songs I detect much of that stalwart straightforwardness which so characterized Eva Turner.

To return, though, to her operatic career. Apart from her popularity in Italy she established herself as a great favourite in the Teatro Colón, Buenos Aires, and with the Civic Opera in Chicago. Strangely enough she submitted to an audition at the Met (she even protected her reputation by using the anagrammatical pseudonym Maria Rentur), but it never led to an engagement. Covent Garden though, having discovered what it had been missing, asked her back with commendable regularity, and the peak of her British career was probably marked by the TURANDOT performances during the Coronation Season of 1937 when she was partnered by Giovanni Martinelli, singing Calaf for the first time, and making a welcome return to Covent Garden after an inexplicable absence of twenty-three years. The same season did contain one rebuff for Eva Turner though, or so many people saw it. On the actual evening of the coronation, after the King's speech had been relayed live to the Covent Garden audience, Eva Turner led all present in what must have been a memorable rendering of the National Anthem. This was followed, however, by a gala performance of AIDA in which the title-role was not given to the one British soprano considered good enough to sing it in the great houses of the world, but to a visiting Italian, Gina Cigna. Perhaps the management felt that with three Turandots just behind her it would have been too much of a scramble, perhaps it was not possible to fit in the necessary rehearsals – nobody ever quite knew. There were those, of course, who felt that if her name had been less of a dyed-in-the-wool English one, and if she had cultivated more of the mystique of the international star she would have been more regally treated in her native land, but at least nothing could detract from the glory of those Turner/ Martinelli TURANDOTS. Luckily the proof that they were truly glorious has been preserved for us, because at two of the three performances certain excerpts were recorded live, and after spending fifty years gathering dust somewhere, they were issued for the first time by EMI as *CDH 7 69791 2*. It is, one has to say, a slightly odd selection because we have the same four scenes (Calaf's two arias, Turandot's 'In questa reggia' and the Riddle Scene) twice each, with Liù's 'Signore, ascolta', appealingly sung by Licia Albanese, thrown in once for good measure. Neverthe-less, it is a fascinating experience to hear Eva Turner and Giovanni

Martinelli, not to mention the conductor, John Barbirolli, in the white-hot atmosphere of an actual performance. However tremendous 'In questa reggia' may sound in a studio recording, to hear it on stage, with the climax taken up by so authoritative a tenor, and to hear the awesome power with which Eva Turner sustains the voltage of the aria right through the posing of the riddles and beyond – this is to eavesdrop on operatic history. I particularly relish the venom with which, when the Unknown Prince guesses Hope as the first answer, she spits out the words 'Si, la speranza che delude sempre' ('Yes, Hope which always disappoints'), and if the soloists have to share the honours with sundry coughs and thumps and with a highly conscientious prompter, that is how live recordings were, and often still are.

This TURANDOT disc gains still more in importance when one thinks that apart from Pearl's reissue of the original cast of Vaughan Williams's 'Serenade to Music', with Eva Turner contributing a brief but typically soaring soprano line (GEMM *CD 9342*), nothing else of hers exists on CD. This does not mean, though, that her career ended with those pre-war seasons at Covent Garden – far from it. When the war began on 3 September 1939 she was stranded in Switzerland, but she succeeded in making her way home because problems of that sort were not going to prevent her from appearing as contracted at Sir Henry Wood's Covent Garden concert on 25 September. When asked by a journalist if she felt up to performing in wartime conditions, she replied very pertinently 'Why not? It was how my career began,' thinking back no doubt to all sorts of discomforts while touring the provinces during the previous conflict. When the war was over, and a new Covent Garden Company was formed, memories of old glories were rekindled in its first two seasons by the re-engagement of Eva Turner as Turandot. She sang it fourteen times in London and another fourteen on tour, and at the age of fifty-five she found that the part still held no terrors for her. There was no reason for her to retire, and it was never really her intention to do so, but in 1949 she received an invitation from the University of Oklahoma to undertake a year's professorship. Gradually the one year expanded into ten, and among many other pleasant things, this new phase of her life provided her with one of her favourite anecdotes. It was the period in which Rodgers and Hammerstein's OKLAHOMA was changing the face of the American musical and, as Eva Turner herself related the story to me, her friend Dame Myra Hess, meeting a mutual acquaintance in London, enquired 'What is Eva up to? I haven't seen her for ages.' Receiving the reply 'Eva is in Oklahoma', Dame Myra asked with some surprise 'Really? In which role?'

The anecdote used to gain greatly, of course, from Eva Turner's own emphatic delivery, and at this point I would like to revert to the first track of the EMI recital disc, the spoken introduction, to which I briefly alluded earlier on. I cannot pretend to have been a member of Eva Turner's intimate circle of friends, but I did have the pleasure of chatting to her on many happy occasions, and to anyone who came within the orbit of that heart-warming personality the sound of her speaking voice will bring her back as nothing else could. In 1962, belatedly as many people felt, Eva Turner was made a Dame of the British Empire, and it was as 'Dame Eva' that she gradually became a Great British Institution. This was not merely because of her tireless work teaching, advising and adjudicating. It was because, right up to the time of her final illness, she retained a passionate interest in everything and everybody in the world of opera. She never seemed to forget a voice or a face and when she spoke about other singers, whether of her own day or of more recent vintage, it was always with generosity, never with malice. I well remember how, after I myself had been singing in a certain opening night, which for various reasons was an especially important occasion to me, I heard to my delight that unmistakable voice ring down the stone corridors of the Sadler's Wells Theatre with the question 'Can you tell me please where is the dressing room of Mr Nigel Douglas?' 'Oh, my deeear!' she said, as she came in, 'you were maahvellous! You gave me an evening of grrreat joy!' Anyone listening to her message on the

CD will be able to imagine for themselves the articulation, the brio, the *slancio* with which these utterances were delivered, and it was typical of her that I had at that time only met her once, quite a while before, and at the sort of large party after which you do not expect anyone, particularly an octogenarian celebrity, to remember who on earth they have been talking to. But – on that occasion she had said she would come to my first night, and come she did. When Dame Eva reached her ninetieth birthday it was celebrated on an unprecedented scale, and the special gala programme arranged for the occasion at Covent Garden included affectionate contributions, some spoken, some sung, by Tito Gobbi, Ljuba Welitsch, Victoria de los Angeles, Isobel Baillie, Sir John Gielgud and several star singers of the younger generation. After Dame Eva's death, at the age of ninety-eight, a memorial service was held in Westminster Abbey, at which her voice rang out once again in Turandot's 'In questa reggia'. She would have been tickled, I think, to know that once again there had been a scramble for tickets and she was singing to a full house.

I remember a friend of mine once telling me that in his opinion people could be broadly divided into two categories, life-diminishers and life-enhancers. Dame Eva was a life-enhancer if ever there was one.

FRITZ WUNDERLICH

GERMAN TENOR

b. Kusel, Rheinland-Pfalz, 26 September 1930
d. Heidelberg, 17 September 1966

Few singers would disagree with me, I think, when I say that the greatest tragedy to strike the operatic profession since the end of the Second World War was the early death, following a trivial domestic accident, of Fritz Wunderlich. Both vocally and musically his was the most blazing talent of my generation, and just as that talent was reaching maturity it was suddenly extinguished.

Wunderlich was born in the little country town of Kusel, which can perhaps best be pinpointed by saying that it lies some forty miles from the frontier of northern France, in the middle of that part of Germany which is bordered by the Rivers Saar and Mosel to the west, and the Rhine to the east. Officially, Wunderlich bore the imposing first names Friedrich Karl Otto – he once remarked in an interview that it was presumably because he was a late arrival in the family that his parents felt sufficiently elated to name him after quite so many Kaisers – but he was universally known as Fritz. His parents were both musicians of modest attainment. His father had been a military bandmaster, and his mother played and taught the violin. At the time of Fritz's birth they were the tenants and managers of an establishment called Emrichs Braustübl, which doubled the functions of a beer-house and a cinema, and they enhanced their modest income by providing the musical accompaniment for the dancing that went on in the one, and the films which were shown in the other. They were hard times in Germany, and for the Wunderlich family they became harder still when the Braustübl was declared to be structurally unsound, which removed at a stroke both home and employment. The coming of the Nazis made things even worse.

Wunderlich's father was known to have allowed a rival political party to run an office on the premises of the Braustübl, and it became harder and harder for him to find work. Eventually, a few weeks after his son's fifth birthday, he took his own life.

By the time the war began it was a desperate task for Frau Wunderlich to make both ends meet. She took to going round the neighbourhood with a little hand-cart, collecting food, clothes and coal as payment for the music lessons which she gave. At the age of twelve Wunderlich himself assumed the role of assistant breadwinner, by playing the accordion and trumpet in local dance bands, and his schooling dropped into second place. The main thing was to survive – survive the poverty, the shame, the hunger, the cold and, for one devastating period, the bombs. Wunderlich and his best friend tried their hands at constructing a home-made air raid shelter. In the next raid a bomb landed close by. Wunderlich was not in the shelter, but his friend was, and it was Wunderlich who found the body. At fourteen he was impressed into ancillary military duties, digging trenches and the like; it was a time when old men and schoolboys were being forced into uniform, and though Frau Wunderlich pleaded that her son was required at home to help keep the family, her pleas fell on deaf ears. For the rest of his own short life Wunderlich took care to disguise from one and all the legacy of pain left by these early sufferings.

When the war was over Wunderlich devoted more and more of his energy to dance music. With a group of friends he started up his own band – for some obscure reason they called themselves 'Die Hutmacher' ('The Hatmakers') – and besides playing his various instruments he started to provide the vocals as well, making it his business to keep up with all the latest hits from the United States. In 1947 his name appeared for the first time in a theatre programme – he was entrusted with a role designated as 'Der Hofarzt' ('The Court Doctor'), in an amateur production of RUMPELSTILTSKIN, and gradually it became evident that he possessed the makings of a voice. He was advised to try his luck with a singing teacher named Käthe Bittel-Valckenberg in Kaiserslautern, and for the next year he pedalled over there once a week for lessons – it was more than twenty miles each way, and he only had an ancient bicycle with solid rubber tyres. When he was nineteen, a distinguished music teacher named Professor Joseph Müller-Blattau, who had come to live in Kusel, sent him off with a most perceptively worded recommendation to audition for the Music High School in Freiburg. 'It is most urgently desirable,' the Professor wrote, 'that a grant should be awarded, to give him a chance of regular training, without the permanent necessity of performing dance music; because one can already say that Fritz Wunderlich, given a thorough training, has a great future as a singer.' The world should contain more people like Professor Müller-Blattau.

The day of Wunderlich's audition was an eventful one. Unused to rail travel, he settled himself nice and early in what he thought was the rear coach of the train to Freiburg, only to discover half an hour later that the rest of the train had moved off without him. He eventually hitched a ride on a milk float to the nearest mainline station and presented himself at the Music High School in the nick of time. As one of his audition pieces he sang Schubert's song 'Der Wegweiser', and when he had finished he said he was afraid it had been 'ziemlich schmalzig' ('pretty corny'). The chief examiner, Frau Professor Margarethe von Winterfeldt, replied that yes, it had been pretty corny. 'Well,' said Wunderlich, with a disarming grin, 'that's what I'm here for – to learn to do it better.' Frau von Winterfeldt, who clearly knew a good thing when she heard one, took him on as her personal pupil, and by the end of four years in Freiburg he had indeed learnt to do it better.* In July 1954 in a student production given in the Paulussaal, which held no less than two thousand people, Wunderlich appeared for the first

---

* Until the end of his life Frau von Winterfeldt remained Wunderlich's only voice teacher, and he lost no opportunity of expressing his debt of gratitude and affection.

time in what was to be his 'Schicksalsrolle', his 'role of destiny', Tamino in DIE ZAUBERFLÖTE. The extent of his personal success and the ecstatic reception which he was accorded by the public overwhelmed him and when he described the occasion in a letter to his mother, he ended with the words 'Ich bin in tiefster Seele glücklich und auch ein bischen stolz' ('In my deepest soul I am happy, and also a little bit proud').

Wunderlich's Tamino happily exists in its entirety on CD, in a definitive performance with the Berlin Philharmonic Orchestra under Karl Böhm (*DGG 429 877–2 – three discs*). To appreciate Wunderlich's quality as an operatic artist one only needs to listen to a few bars – the vividness and immediacy of his vocal and musical personality are handed to the listener like a visiting card with every phrase that he sings. To give but one example – when Tamino learns from the off-stage voices of Sarastro's priests that Pamina is still alive, he expresses his gratitude in eight bars of recitative, opening with the words 'Sie lebt? Sie lebt? Ich danke euch dafür!' ('She lives? She lives? My thanks to you for that!'). If you listened to nothing but Wunderlich's handling of these eight bars you would know that this is no run-of-the-mill Tamino. The voice is one of exceptional clarity, lyrical but virile, and with a highly individual timbre. The articulation is incisive and commanding, the delivery passionate and committed. The intensity of personal involvement in the words 'mit jedem Tone meinen Dank zu schildern' ('with every tone to express my thanks') makes this Tamino a flesh and blood creature – a man to arouse one's sympathies, not just a tenor to be admired for his skill; and the final phrase 'wie er hier, hier entsprang', with the second 'hier' on a high A of sovereign ease and authority, establish him not simply as Prince Charming, but as a young hero, somebody who can take on whatever the forces of darkness may choose to throw at him.

I scarcely suppose that the Tamino which Wunderlich served up at the age of twenty-three to the citizens of Freiburg quite measured up to the Tamino on the Böhm recording, but it

was enough to ensure that during his fifth and last year of
study his grant was supplemented by a number of handy fees
for such things as local concerts and oratorios. He had his
first taste of life in a professional opera company, too, when
the Stadttheater in Freiburg called on him to take over a role
in Millöcker's operetta DER BETTELSTUDENT. One of his
performances was attended by the agent Felix Ballhausen who
recommended him to Ferdinand Leitner, Music Director of the
Würtemberg State Opera in Stuttgart. Wunderlich auditioned for
Leitner, and in classic style he cracked on his high notes – to
go as a total nobody and audition in one of the large German
opera houses *is* one of life's more terrifying experiences – but
Leitner was too shrewd and too experienced to be put off by
that. Wunderlich was given a five year contract on the clear
understanding that it would be quite a while before he could
expect anything other than the smallest of roles; but in fact his big
chance came much sooner than anyone expected. For six months
he had contented himself with the least prominent of the Masters
in DIE MEISTERSINGER, the Messenger in AIDA, and various
other odds and ends, when he heard that the management were in
a fix because Josef Traxel, Stuttgart's resident Tamino, had had to
pull out of a ZAUBERFLÖTE that same evening. On the strength
of his student performance eighteen months before, Wunderlich
declared himself capable of taking over. The management had no
alternative but to risk it, and in the event not only did Wunderlich
sail through without a mistake, but the sheer determination and
physical energy with which he flung himself into the role fairly
took his more experienced colleagues' breath away. For his very
first entrance, in order to make Tamino's flight from the deadly
serpent as convincing as he could, he took a run of about ten
metres out of the wings, and in that vein he continued until the
final curtain fell.

This approach to the task in hand, as all around him came to
recognize, was 'echt-Wunderlich', typical of him in every aspect
of his life. He was an all-or-nothing man, and whatever he did,

whether it was cooking, carpentry, photography, or any of his other numerous hobbies, had to be done with total involvement. There was no knowing what he was going to get up to next. The first time he sang in Edinburgh, a young man on a tight budget, he was nearly slung out of his hotel for concocting an Irish stew in his bedroom, and on the same trip he brought with him from Germany a spongebag full of live worms – not as an ingredient for the stew, but because he knew that Scotland was famous for its fishing, and he did not want to be caught unprepared. His engaging boy-next-door personality, and the extreme youthfulness of his appearance, rapidly endeared him to the Stuttgart public, and his infectious friendliness made him equally popular with his colleagues. As his fame grew, and with it his bank balance, he remained unaffectedly amiable to one and all. Although I was lucky enough to hear him many times, I only met him personally on one occasion, when we were both singing in the June Festival of 1965 in Zurich, he in one of his most famous roles, Don Ottavio in DON GIOVANNI. When he heard that I too had sung Don Ottavio he immediately began to ask me how I coped with a certain phrase which he found technically awkward. I replied, somewhat obviously, that I thought it would be more to the point if *I* picked up hints from *him*.

During Wunderlich's Stuttgart years he built up a nationwide reputation as an oratorio singer, and he was still only twenty-six when he was first asked to take part in the prestigious biennial Bach Festival in Ansbach. Several of Wunderlich's finest oratorio performances are preserved on CD, and it is fascinating to hear how he tempers the theatricality of his operatic singing to suit the less extrovert nature of religious music without sacrificing one jot of the intensity and the personal involvement which were among his most precious attributes. The great German baritone Dietrich Fischer-Dieskau was later to describe his reaction when he first heard Wunderlich open his mouth at an Ansbach rehearsal – 'It gave me a sort of shock, because the voice had a meltingly lovely quality, but at the same time that essential grain of metal in the sound, such as had not been heard from any German tenor for a long time.' From two superlative Bach full sets one can tell exactly what Fischer-Dieskau meant. They are the CHRISTMAS ORATORIO (DGG Archiv Produktion *413 625–2 – three discs*), with Janowitz, Ludwig, Crass, and the Munich Bach Choir and Bach Orchestra under Karl Richter, and the MATTHEW PASSION (DECCA *41 4057–2 – three discs*) with Ameling, Höffgen, Pears, Prey, the sumptuous-voiced Finnish baritone Tom Krause (younger even than Wunderlich), and the choral and orchestral forces of Stuttgart under Karl Münchinger. Wunderlich's singing of Bach recitatives has the same arrestingly communicative quality as his Tamino without ever taking the sentiment or the drama of his message further than is fitting to the devoutness of its context. In the arias, the long and searching passages of coloratura are punctiliously articulated, but the delivery never runs the risk of becoming academic or impersonal. In Beethoven's MISSA SOLEMNIS (*DGG 423 913–2 – two discs*), technically a less immaculate recording than either of the Bach sets, having been a combined recording and live broadcast, Wunderlich does not have the opportunity to emerge with such prominence. He does succeed, however, in tackling the cruelly high tessitura without ever sacrificing his customary suaveness of tone and, together with Janowitz, Ludwig, Berry and the Vienna Singverein, he manages to sustain that peculiar blend of reverence and energy on which this mighty work depends. Herbert von Karajan conducts the Berlin Philharmonic Orchestra, and it was with these same forces that Wunderlich made one of the finest of all his recordings, Haydn's CREATION (*DGG 435 077-2*). He did not in fact live to complete it, and one or two brief passages had to be sung in by another tenor. Mercifully, however, the bulk of the role is pure Wunderlich, and it is singing of a quality beyond praise. To call it perfect would be to denigrate it, because mere perfection excludes individuality, and it was Wunderlich's habit to place his personal stamp on every bar that he sang.

Wunderlich's musicianship soon became something of a legend. On one famous occasion, when he was only twenty-eight, he undertook to rescue a concert performance, complete with simultaneous broadcast, of Handel's opera ALCINA by singing the leading tenor role opposite Joan Sutherland, with one brief preliminary run-through. He had some half dozen highly complex arias to sing, and he had never seen or heard the music before, but I remember being told by the British baritone Thomas Hemsley, who was also in the cast, that Wunderlich not only read the part faultlessly but also sang it with the utmost finesse of phrasing and interpretation. Blessed with such a facility as this, it would have been only too easy for him, as the deluge of offers came pouring in, to make the fatal mistake of forgetting how to say No, especially as his basic salary from the Stuttgart Opera was not a princely one. He was indeed happy to take on what most singers would call a daunting workload, but despite his breezy exterior he approached every aspect of his career with the utmost seriousness, and he was resolute in his determination not to take on roles which he considered too heavy for him. Two of his maxims were that 'vocal cords are not fists', and that 'up till the age of thirty-five a voice needs nursing' – an utterance which, in retrospect, was to have a particularly tragic ring to it.

This professional good sense did not mean, however, that Wunderlich was turning his back on his gusty youthful joie de vivre – at the Stuttgart Opera Ball he was always ready to black his face, brandish his trumpet, and oblige with his Louis Armstrong take-off, or dress up in a sailor-suit and sing saucy sea-shanties to his own accompaniment on the accordion – it was just that a firm line was drawn between work and play. After his first couple of years in Stuttgart he began to make occasional appearances abroad – in the Festivals of Aix, Edinburgh and Florence, for instance – and in 1959 came his real international breakthrough, when he sang the role of Henry Morosus in Richard Strauss's DIE SCHWEIGSAME FRAU in the Salzburg Festival. The recognition which this brought him, both from press and public, assured his reputation as the outstanding

German lyric tenor of the new generation, and the major opera houses of the world began to compete for his services. In 1960 he and his wife Eva, who had been a harpist in the Stuttgart Orchestra, moved house to Munich, where he had signed a three-year contract with the Bavarian State Opera, and from then onwards, even after he was contracted to the Vienna State Opera, Munich was to remain their home.

Wunderlich's Munich contract committed him to seventy performances a year, and in Stuttgart he still had a guest contract for a further forty to fifty. Add to that the Salzburg Festival and numerous concerts, recordings and broadcasts, plus an agent who claimed that ninety-five per cent of the work which he did on Wunderlich's behalf consisted of turning down other offers, and you have a story which could be summed up by the single word – Success. Up in the sky, however, there was one small cloud, and it greatly irked Fritz Wunderlich. From the age of thirty-one he began to devote more and more of his thoughts to the interpretation of Lieder, the classical German songs. This is a notoriously difficult repertoire for an opera singer to master – it is the finer points which count, with no chance of hiding any tricky little spots behind the sweeping gesture or the passionate sob. Wunderlich jumped in at the deep end, by giving his very first Lieder recital in Vienna, and it was good enough for the frequently acid-penned Karl Löbl of the *Express* to write 'if one can speak of such a thing as German *bel canto*, Wunderlich is its ideal exponent.' After Wunderlich's first recital in Munich, however, a critic named Walter Panofsky, a man whose opinion Wunderlich respected, wrote an adverse review under the headline **An Opera Tenor as Lieder Singer**. Wunderlich, who was immensely self-critical, took the article to heart and consulted his great friend, the baritone Hermann Prey. Prey's advice was that he should betake himself to Professor Hubert Giesen, an elderly and widely experienced accompanist and Lieder expert in Stuttgart. Giesen asked Wunderlich to sing him the opening of Schumann's 'Dichterliebe', but after the first page he stopped playing. 'What do you think of it?' asked Wunderlich. Hesitantly, because Wunderlich after all was a very big star, Giesen said 'I don't think it's much good'; whereupon Wunderlich, with a smile on his face more suitable to someone who has just been paid an extravagant compliment, replied 'Just what *I* thought!' This congenial encounter led to many hours of intensive study, to a series of triumphant Lieder recitals and, in the nick of time, to two superb recordings. The first recital was given, as a kind of dress rehearsal, on 30 April 1963, in Wunderlich's home town of Kusel, and next on the list came the acid test – the Theater an der Wien, as part of Vienna's Summer Festival. The Viennese critics, who are not famous for being easily pleased, especially when Lieder-singing is the subject under discussion, were ecstatic. Wunderlich sent off a set of their reviews to Walter Panofsky accompanied by a sincere and courteous letter of thanks for having spurred him on to this fresh field of conquest.

The second half of Wunderlich's Vienna recital consisted of the 'Dichterliebe' cycle, and in the Autumn of 1965 he and Giesen recorded it. It is now available, together with four songs by Beethoven and nine by Schubert, on DGG *429 933-2*, and it is hard to imagine any lover of Lieder not wanting to have this disc. It brings to mind two of Wunderlich's own remarks about this particular branch of the singer's art – first, that it is the singer's business to interpret the music rather than the words, because that has already been done by the composer; and secondly, that it is not possible to sing Lieder until one has totally eliminated any suspicion of problems with vocal technique. To take this second point first, on the DGG disc that is precisely the impression that Wunderlich gives; indeed by the ripe old age of thirty-five he had reached that enviable stage at which technique does not appear to be on the agenda – he simply sings, and every imaginable nuance is available to him. Oddly enough, a phrase which many singers find the trickiest of the whole cycle occurs on the very first page – the high G on the penultimate syllable of the phrase 'die Liebe aufgegangen'. With Wunderlich it is as carefree a tone as any other, and precedes an utterly organic tapering away of the sound on the final unstressed syllable – a tiny touch, the merest detail, but it is on such things that Lieder singing depends. To revert to Wunderlich's first point, he did not of course mean that the words are not important – indeed nobody ever articulated text with greater care than he. By paying cardinal attention, though, to the manner in which the composer has set those words, he ensures that the expression achieved by words and music together is never something artificial or arbitrary, imposed on them by the singer in order to achieve some momentary effect. The mood of each song in the 'Dichterliebe' cycle, several of them miniatures of less than a minute in length, produces in Wunderlich an instinctive colouring of the voice – from a tinge of nostalgia in 'Im wunderschönen Monat Mai', to the darker hue of introspective melancholy in 'Hör' ich das Liedchen klingen', and an edge of nervous anger in the surprisingly rapid 'Ich grolle nicht' – but never does one have that feeling, which can be so alienating in the case of some Lieder singers, of 'Ladies and gentlemen, just listen to the cleverness with which I am about to sing this song!' *Ars est celare artem.*

The four Beethoven songs on this same disc include a rapt account of 'Adelaide', and it is fascinating to compare it with the version recorded by the young Jussi Björling back in 1939. It would be hard to find people more different in personality than these two, and yet in this one song the attributes which they possessed in common – innate musicianship and voices of surpassing beauty – do bring them surprisingly close together. In 'Resignation' Wunderlich makes the singing of Beethoven's uncomfortable vocal line seem like the most natural function in the world; in 'Zärtliche Liebe' he sounds like the sort of young man any sensible girl would fall for on the spot; and in 'Der Kuss' he displays something which certain other Lieder singers sadly lack – a natural and unforced sense of humour. Several of the Schubert songs, too, gain immeasurably from his fresh and spontaneous approach. There is such a dash of unpremeditated charm in 'Liebhaber in allen Gestalten' ('Lover in All Shapes'), in 'Der

Einsame' such a touching sense of companionship in the solitary dweller's chat with the crickets who chirp to him of an evening, and in 'An die Musik' such transparent honesty in Wunderlich's expressions of gratitude to the art of music. Lieder singing is very much a matter of being private in public. The thoughts and emotions expressed are often intimate ones, and it is a great help if the listener can take to the singer as well as the song.

Wunderlich's fresh and apparently instinctive approach to the singing of Lieder makes him an interpreter par excellence of Schubert's 'Die Schöne Müllerin' (DGG *423 956-2*). These songs were written for a high voice, and though I know that they have been memorably recorded by several outstanding baritones, downward transposition can have a somewhat muddying effect on certain of the piano accompaniments. A baritone voice, too, can often sound a little more mature than a tenor, and as the protagonist of this cycle is a young man starting out in life, to hear it sung by that rare being, a tenor whose voice still glistens with the sheen of youth while his insights into the work are already those of a mature musician, is, to my mind, ideal. In any case, the cheery optimism of the opening songs, the naive tenderness of 'Morgengruss', and the lightly underplayed tragedy of the dénouement all receive from Wunderlich as persuasive and sensitive an interpretation as I ever hope to hear. For good measure the record company has tacked on three individual songs, 'Die Forelle', 'Frühlingsglaube' and 'Heidenröslein'; and when this disc reaped a harvest of awards within the recording industry it was no more than it deserved.

Wunderlich's singing of Lieder is characterized by an engagingly uncomplicated emission of tone – you are never aware of him in any way fabricating the sound – and the same naturalness of delivery, albeit at a greatly heightened scale of intensity, made him easier on the ear than many another tenor in the operas of Richard Strauss. I well remember how Narraboth's opening phrase used to soar above the sinister carpet of orchestral sound when the curtain went up on SALOME; and when Queen Elizabeth II paid a State Visit to Germany, and attended a gala performance of DER ROSENKAVALIER in Munich, witnesses avowed that the first time she raised her opera-glasses to her eyes was when Wunderlich launched into the Italian tenor's aria. Strauss's other little bit of self-indulgence at the expense of Italian tenors, the 'duettino' in CAPRICCIO, was another echt-Wunderlich vignette; he and the soprano Lucia Popp used to chase each other up and down Strauss's flights of zany coloratura, to the studied boredom of Elisabeth Schwarzkopf's Countess, and the great delight of the audiences in the Vienna Opera. Yet another of Wunderlich's outstanding Straussian roles happily exists 'in toto' on CD. This is his Leukippos, the passionate shepherd in the opera DAPHNE, who dares to challenge Apollo and duly pays the price. The recording (DGG *423 579-2*) was taken from live performances of a resplendently cast production in the Theater an der Wien, during a Strauss Festival in 1964. Wunderlich's ardour is admirably matched by the radiance of Hilde Güden in the title-role, and the refulgent Apollo of the young James King; and as the opera is conducted by its dedicatee, Karl Böhm, Strauss devotees could scarcely ask for anything more.

A role such as Leukippos, lyrical but intense and taxing, marks the direction which Wunderlich was bound to have taken, had he lived beyond that fateful age of thirty-five. The tone is so perfectly focussed and projected that the so-called 'jugendliches Heldenfach', the middle-weight roles such as Max in DER FREISCHÜTZ, would soon have been his for the taking, and Wieland Wagner was constantly trying to steer him towards Bayreuth. The heaviest music which he recorded was in fact Mahler's 'Das lied von der Erde', (EMI *CDC 7 47231 2*), and it is a superb piece of work. The tenor solos are usually entrusted to a dramatic singer, not a lyric one, but Wunderlich first undertook them in a concert in Vienna, shortly before his thirtieth birthday, at the suggestion of Herbert von Karajan. The following year he sang them again in the Royal Festival Hall, and three and a half years later he was back in London to record them. On both the latter occasions the conductor was the venerable Klemperer, and it was an experience which Wunderlich referred to as 'learning to sing Mahler first hand'. Apart from the lungpower which is needed, particularly in the first solo, this is psychologically more sombre territory than a lyric tenor is usually called upon to explore. Wunderlich, however, sounds as much at home with the autumnal pessimism of the 'Trinklied' as he does with the vernal optimism of the most carefree of Schubert songs, and the repeated phrase 'Dunkel ist das Leben, ist der Tod' ('Dark is life, dark is death') produces an unusually haunting effect when the voice that sings it combines such maturity of *Weltschmerz* with the passionate energy of youth.

For a man whose career lasted barely ten years, Wunderlich, happily for us, made an astonishing number of recordings covering a wide musical field. One package which does justice to his versatility is a three-disc set entitled 'Fritz Wunderlich, the Great German Tenor' (EMI *CZS 7 62993 2*). The first two discs are devoted to operatic excerpts, some being solos, and others ensemble scenes involving several outstanding artists – Anneliese Rothenberger, Pilar Lorengar, Gottlob Frick and Hermann Prey to name but a few. With the exception of 'Ombra mai fu', from Handel's SERSE, every track in the set is sung in German, which may sound off-putting for a selection in which Donizetti, Verdi, Puccini, Tchaikovsky, Massenet, Thomas and Smetana easily outnumber Lortzing, Flotow, and Nicolai; but again and again it is that Viennese critic's remark about 'German *bel canto*' which is brought to mind. Admittedly, having spent the first few years of my own career singing this same repertoire in German, it may seem less strange to me than to most British listeners when the BOHEME duet becomes 'O du süssestes Mädchen' instead of 'O soave fanciulla', or Pinkerton's 'Addio fiorito asil' becomes 'Leb' wohl mein Blütenreich'. It is remarkable, though, with what mastery Wunderlich sustains a mellifluous Italianate legato while at the same time articulating mouthfuls of German consonants with such meticulous clarity that any competent secretary would be able to take dictation from him. His singing of Nemorino's 'Quant' è bella, quant' è cara' from L'ELISIR D'AMORE, despite emerging as 'Welche Huld und welche Reize', arouses memories of Benimino Gigli, so golden is the tone and so effortless the delivery; and the liveliness of the vocal acting in the BOHEME excerpts gives a tantalizing glimpse of what a spirited and seductive Rodolfo he would have been – after waiting until he felt ready for the role, he was due to sing it on stage for the first time in 1967.

This EMI selection also contains one or two interesting rarities, such as Nureddin's aria from Act I of Cornelius's DER BARBIER VON BAGDAD, and that alarmingly demanding virtuoso number 'Viens, gentille dame' from Boïldieu's LA DAME BLANCHE. (It always strikes me as distinctly bathetic that the character who indulges in this floridly romantic outburst should go by the name of George Brown.) Mozart, of course, is represented. We have Belmonte's first aria from DIE ENTFÜHRUNG – this was the role which Wunderlich sang in his last Salzburg Festival, confirming, in the view of virtually every critic present, his right to be regarded as the finest Mozart tenor of his day – and two excerpts from DON GIOVANNI, the aria 'Il mio tesoro' (or 'Folget der heissgeliebten'), and the Act I duet, with the Donna Anna of Elisabeth Grümmer. This was the first role in which I ever saw Fritz Wunderlich. It was in the June Festival of 1963 in Vienna, under the baton of Herbert von Karajan. The cast was a starry one – Leontyne Price, Hilde Güden, Graziella Sciutti, Eberhard Wächter, Walter Berry and Rolando Panerai – but the lion's share of the applause went to Fritz Wunderlich as Don Ottavio. Two years later he made his Covent Garden debut in the same role, but it was a lacklustre production, and Wunderlich himself was not in his best voice. *The Times* treated him to what must have been the most dismissive review he ever received – 'Mr Fritz Wunderlich looked scruffy in Ottavio's costume, and needed some Italian coaching.' Philip Hope-Wallace, however, in the *Guardian*, was less dyspeptic – 'His singing of "Il mio tesoro" was important, stylish and beautifully managed: the house did not fail to notice this.' Don Ottavio should also have been the role for Wunderlich's debut in New York, during the opening week of the new Metropolitan Opera, but that was a debut which never took place.

On the third disc of the EMI set Wunderlich turns to the lighter muse – we are offered sixteen operetta tracks and two romantic ballads, and they are pearls of great price. Apart from those first appearances in the Freiburg BETTELSTUDENT, and some open-air performances in his early Stuttgart days as Caramello in EINE NACHT IN VENEDIG, Wunderlich never actually appeared on stage in operetta, but it was a style of music which he loved to sing. Indeed, he went so far as to say that every opera singer should sing this repertoire, a view with which I certainly concur. 'When you sing operetta,' he used to say, 'you don't have to bother about being clever, you can just let go with the voice,' and he practised gloriously what he preached. He did not mean that operetta is easy – you only have to tackle some of the Emmerich Kálmán roles to disabuse yourself of that notion – but simply that it must be done with élan and not with artifice. When you sing operetta you must be seen and heard to be enjoying yourself, and that is what Wunderlich achieves to an exhilarating degree. In Caramello's 'Komm in die Gondel', with its long, arching phrases and immaculately poised high As, you can hear him revel in the sheer joy of singing, while the same character's 'Lagunenwalzer', with its wry comments on the fickleness of women, is an object lesson in how to communicate with an audience. Whether he is letting fly with the infectious bonhomie of Octavio's entrance song from Lehár's GIUDITTA (and how many tenor roles in Grand Opera *open* on a high A?), or bathing in the nostalgia of Tassilo's 'Grüss mir mein Wien' from Kálmán's GRÄFIN MARIZA, this is Wunderlich singing straight from the heart, with the floodgates open. There isn't a song on this disc which I would not unhesitatingly recommend to any lover of great singing but, even so, I think that the six tracks devoted to that delightful and inexplicably undervalued composer, Leo Fall, would be my pick of the bunch. Wunderlich's performance of 'O frag' mich nicht' from DER FIDELE BAUER is one of the finest pieces of operetta singing to be recorded since the heyday of Richard Tauber, and it is matched by a generous selection of five excerpts from the role of Achmed Bey, in DIE ROSE VON STAMBUL. Achmed is a gentleman who never opens his mouth without a gorgeous tune emerging from it – the title-song and that most buoyant of waltz duets, 'Ein Walzer muss es sein', are but two examples – and in these recordings the smile on Wunderlich's voice, his mastery of Viennese *rubato*, his elegance of phrasing, and the clarity of his diction combine to make this my idea of the *ne plus ultra* of operetta singing. Moreover, as if all this were not enough, in the aria 'Zwei Augen, die wollen mir nicht aus dem Sinn', a masterpiece of wistful charm, Wunderlich gives his listeners' hearts a little extra tug with his prowess as a whistler – or a *siffleur*, as I believe one is supposed to say at this exalted level.

There is another mixed bag to be found on a single Eurodisc CD, *GD 69018*, but this time I cannot be quite so unrestrainedly enthusiastic. There is plenty to be admired – a poetic version of Tamino's 'Bildnisarie', for instance, and a tellingly simple delivery of Knappe Veit's 'Couplets' from Lortzing's UNDINE. Liszt's 'Es muss ein Wunderbares sein' is one of the most private recordings I know – the song is directed at you, and you alone – and Tchaikovsky's 'Nur wer die Sehnsucht kennt' (they are both sung with orchestral accompaniment) trembles tantalizingly on the brink of the 'ziemlich schmalzig', without ever quite toppling over. When we reach the operetta section, however, we are subjected to several classic examples of what happens when German commercial musicians decide that it is time for the orchestrations of Johann Strauss, Carl Zeller and others to be 'brought up to date'. Several of these tracks started life as radio transmissions, and it is maddening to hear such stylish and forthright singing hamstrung by versions of such paltry vulgarity. When it comes to 'O sole mio' and 'Granada' complete with echo chamber it becomes a case of *caveat emptor*.

Not surprisingly, Deutsche Grammophon offer a worthier summing-up of Wunderlich's career with their mammoth five-disc set, *DGG 435 145-2*. Two of the discs are simply the Lieder recitals which I have discussed above. Another two are devoted to opera and, although they consist predominantly of further recordings made for various radio stations, they also include the 'Bildnisarie' from the Karl Böhm ZAUBERFLÖTE, and two ENTFÜHRUNG excerpts under Eugen Jochum, which present Wunderlich at the peak of his artistry. This cannot quite be claimed for every one of the remaining operatic excerpts. Radio tapes tend notoriously to be made under pressure of time, and the technical quality of certain of these tracks is variable, particularly in the balance of voice and orchestra. There are a number of duets with Hermann Prey, a colleague who shared many happy times with Wunderlich, both on and off the stage; and there are extended excerpts from two Handel operas, SERSE and GIULIO CESARE, the former conducted by Kubelik and the latter by Leitner, in which Wunderlich displays a formidable capacity for singing dramatic coloratura without apparently feeling the need to breathe. Once again there are some interesting rarities – notably 'Ne parle pas, Rose, je t'en supplie', from LES DRAGONS DE VILLARS, by an obscure French composer named Aimé Maillart,* which finds Wunderlich at his most touchingly lyrical, and the trio from Act II of Constantin Kreutzer's opera DAS NACHTLAGER VON GRANADA. Though Kreutzer was a German, this trio, with its extended and dreamy *cantilena*, could almost have come from the pen of Vincenzo Bellini, and Wunderlich treats the tenor line accordingly. Another of the most attractive tracks is indeed by Bellini himself – the duet 'Prendi, l'anel ti dono' from LA SONNAMBULA (written two years before DAS NACHTLAGER), in which Wunderlich and

---

* This opera still crops up occasionally in Germany under the title DAS GLÖCKCHEN DES EREMITEN.

Erika Köth very creditably don the mantles of Schipa and Galli-Curci. As in the EMI set, though, German is sung throughout, which must I fancy limit the attraction of the Italian numbers to the international public. There is nothing however to spoil the enjoyment of two Lortzing tracks – Georg's Act I aria from DER WAFFENSCHMIED and Chateauneuf's Act II aria from ZAR UND ZIMMERMANN – unless in the former it be the irony of hearing Wunderlich expound the philosophy 'don't waste a moment of your life, because you never know when you may lose it'; or the knowledge that the latter was his final recording, made ten days before he died.

The last disc in the DGG set is devoted to Wunderlich letting his hair down. This time 'O sole mio' and 'Granada' are mercifully preserved from the horrors of the echo chamber, and though one has to admit that this is not natural Wunderlich territory (on the subject of his Italian, let alone his Neapolitan, that *Times* critic had a point), one would have to be in a very sour mood not to respond to the sheer exhilaration of his 'Funiculi-Funicula'. He then moves on to safer ground with ten songs, some German, some Viennese, accompanied by the orchestra of the Vienna Volksoper under the baton of the Grand Old Man of Viennese music, Robert Stolz. With the zest of 'Ob blond, ob braun', originally written by Stolz in his Berlin days for a Jan Kiepura film, and with the brilliant attack of 'Ein Lied geht um die Welt', once a vehicle for the top notes of the ill-fated Joseph Schmidt, Wunderlich has no difficulty in standing shoulder to shoulder with those legends of the past. When he tackled the Viennese songs, however, as opposed to the German ones, he knew that he would be standing in the most daunting of shadows, that of Richard Tauber. Comparisons between the two of them are inevitable. They were both the greatest Mozart tenors of their time, they both excelled as singers of Lieder and of operetta, they were both chameleon-like musicians, who could sing virtually anything and still go straight to the heart of whatever style they sang in, and they were both irresistibly cheery people to have around. The great difference between them (apart from totally dissimilar vocal colouring) was that Wunderlich was German and Tauber Austrian. For Tauber, a song like Benatzky's 'Ich muss wieder einmal in Grinzing sein' was part of his birthright. For Wunderlich it was a style that had to be learnt – so learn it he did. For this one number he is accompanied by a Schrammel group, familiar to many a tourist from evenings at the *Heuriger*, and the recording manager appointed himself honorary coach in matters of Viennese dialect. Wunderlich may not have ended up sounding quite such a dyed-in-the-wool 'Wienerkind' as a Tauber, a Patzak or a Kunz, but the singing is exquisite, and the sum total should be enough to charm most birds from the trees.

The Vienna State Opera became Wunderlich's favourite house to sing in, and he celebrated his thirty-fifth birthday by singing DIE ZAUBERFLÖTE there twice in the one day; in the evening there was an ordinary scheduled performance, and in the afternoon an unpaid charity gala in aid of the victims of some recent flooding. When he arrived in his dressing room, the wardrobe ladies had decked it out in festive style, with a huge figure 35 in gold above his mirror, and his make-up table covered with cakes, bottles of wine and so on. The cast turned the occasion into an impromptu party, and the Director of the Opera, Dr Egon Hilbert, who had put on his best suit as he was to open the charity performance with a speech to the audience, sat on a cream bun and had to go on stage in borrowed trousers!

By this point in his career, Wunderlich seemed truly to be the singer who had it all. Though not perhaps a classically handsome man he was a highly sympathetic figure on stage and, thanks in no small measure to the work which he did in his early Stuttgart years with the great director Günther Rennert, he had overcome his initial stiffness as an actor. (The first time Rennert was offered the young Wunderlich as a member of one of his casts he tried to turn him down on the grounds that he was a clumsy actor and his nose was crooked.) Added to that were the voice, the musicianship, the temperament, the physical strength and, almost the most valuable to Wunderlich, a happy family life with a beautiful, talented wife and three young children whom he adored. He had reached that self-appointed age of thirty-five at which he considered himself vocally mature. The world was at his feet.

At the end of August 1966, Wunderlich flew to Edinburgh, where he gave a Lieder recital with Hubert Giesen, and sang three performances of DIE ZAUBERFLÖTE as a guest with his old company, the Stuttgart Opera. After the last of these performances he sought out the conductor, his old mentor Ferdinand Leitner, and arranged to go and see him when they were back in Germany to discuss one or two points in the role, which both of them felt had grown a bit stale. First though, there were recordings to be made in Munich (some TRAVIATA excerpts, and the ZAR UND ZIMMERMANN aria, all on the DGG set), and then he was off to a friend's house in the countryside near Pforzheim for a few days' shooting, which was one of his new enthusiasms. His wife was to join him at the weekend, and late on the Thursday night he decided to ring her up. He tripped on the stone staircase (possibly over a loose shoelace) and reached out to grab the rope banister. The rope came away from the wall, and he fell, hitting the back of his head on the steps and fracturing his skull. One of the other guests in the house was a doctor, and everything possible was done, but Wunderlich never regained consciousness, and early on the morning of Saturday 17 September, in the University Clinic of Heidelberg, he died.

Wunderlich's death took place, just as Mozart's had, shortly before his thirty-sixth birthday, and it was a strange coincidence that DIE ZAUBERFLÖTE, which had launched his career, should also have brought it to its close. Countless tributes to his artistry appeared in newspapers all over the world, but Dietrich Fischer-Dieskau probably summed him up as neatly as anyone when he described him simply as having been 'in a class of his own'. The word most frequently used in the obituaries was 'irreplaceable'. This can often turn out to have been an ill-chosen description, but in the case of Fritz Wunderlich it was justified. As I write, he has been dead for exactly twenty-five years, and no one has taken his place.

RECOMMENDED CDs: INDIVIDUAL SINGERS

A list of suggestions for readers who would like to sample the voices of any of the singers in this book, by listening to one introductory disc:

Jussi Björling – *RCA Victor GD87799* (Duets and Scenes by Bizet, Puccini and Verdi)

Enrico Caruso – *Nimbus Prima Voce NI 7803* (Twenty operatic arias)

Giuseppe de Luca – *Nimbus Prima Voce NI 7815* (Selection of arias, duets and songs)

Kirsten Flagstad – *Decca 425 986-2* (Wagner – DIE WALKÜRE, Act III, Sir Georg Solti and the Vienna Philharmonic Orchestra)

Tito Gobbi – *EMI CDM 7 63109 2* (Twenty-one operatic arias)

Alexander Kipnis – *Lebendige Vergangenheit 89019* (Sixteen operatic tracks and two Russian folk songs)

Lotte Lehmann – *EMI CDH 7 61020 2* (Wagner – DIE WALKÜRE, Act I, with Lauritz Melchior, Bruno Walter and the Vienna Philharmonic Orchestra)

Alfred Piccaver – *Lebendige Vergangenheit 89060* (Eighteen operatic arias)

Ezio Pinza – *Pearl GEMM CD 9306* (Twenty-one operatic arias)

Rosa Ponselle – *Nimbus Prima Voce NI 7805* (Eleven operatic tracks and five songs)

Tito Schipa – *Nimbus Prima Voce NI 7813* (Seventeen operatic arias and two duets)

Luisa Tetrazzini – *Nimbus Prima Voce NI 7808* (Fourteen operatic arias and five songs)

Eva Turner – *EMI CDH 7 69791 2* (Introductory talk, twelve operatic arias and six songs)

Fritz Wunderlich – *DGG 429 933-2* (Schumann 'Dichterliebe', four Beethoven songs, nine Schubert songs; accompanist Hubert Giesen)

RECOMMENDED CDs: COMPILATIONS

Several companies have issued compilation CDs, several of which include one track or more by singers in this book:

'Wagner Singing on Record' *EMI CMS 7 64008 2 – four discs* (Flagstad, Lehmann, Kipnis)

'50 Years of Mozart Singing' *EMI CMS 7 63750 2 – four discs* (Gobbi, Pinza, Kipnis)

'Immortal Voices of the Vienna Opera' *Lebendige Vergangenheit 89999* (Kipnis, Lehmann, Piccaver)

'Great Singers, 1909–1938' *Nimbus Prima Voce NI 7801* (Tetrazzini, Caruso, Ponselle, Turner, Schipa)

'Divas, 1906–1935' *Nimbus Prima Voce NI 7802* (Tetrazzini, Ponselle, Lehmann, Turner)

'Great Singers Vol. 2, 1903–1939' *Nimbus Prima Voce NI 7812* (de Luca, Pinza, Flagstad, Björling)

'Divas, Vol. 2, 1909–1940' *Nimbus Prima Voce NI 7818* (Ponselle, Flagstad)

'Covent Garden, 1909–1940' *Nimbus Prima Voce NI 7819* (Caruso, Tetrazzini, Turner, Lehmann, Flagstad)

'Covent Garden on Record, Vol. II' *Pearl GEMM CDS 9924 – two discs* (de Luca, Tetrazzini, Caruso)

'Covent Garden on Record, Vol. III' *Pearl GEMM CDS 9925 – two discs* (Lehmann, Piccaver, Turner)

'Covent Garden on Record, Vol. IV' *Pearl GEMM CDS 9926 – two discs* (Flagstad, Kipnis, Pinza, Ponselle)

SELECT BIBLIOGRAPHY

Not many of the singers in this book have been the subjects of really dependable biographies, though the following can be recommended:

The Great Caruso by Michael Scott (Hamish Hamilton, London, 1988)

Caruso by Howard Greenfield (G.P. Putnam's Sons, New York, 1983)

Flagstad by Howard Vogt (Secker & Warburg, London, 1987)

My Life by Tito Gobbi (Macdonald and Jane's, London, 1979)

Lotte Lehmann, A Life in Opera and Song by Beaumont Glass (Capra Press, Santa Barbara, 1988)

INDEX

INDEX OF INDIVIDUAL NUMBERS

ABOUT THE AUTHOR

After leaving Oxford, Nigel Douglas studied in the Opera School of the Vienna Music Academy. He has sung over eighty leading tenor roles with major companies throughout Britain and Europe, directed productions for Sadler's Wells and for the Australian Opera, and written and presented over two hundred programmes on opera and operetta for the BBC, including the Radio 4 series 'Singer's Choice'. He lives in Kent with his wife, two daughters and a son.